'Making It Happen' In Public Service

Devolution in Wales as a Case Study

Michael Connolly, Stephen Prosser,
Rod Hough and Kathryn Potter

imprint-academic.com

Published in the UK by
Imprint Academic, PO Box 200, Exeter EX5 5YX, UK

Published in the USA by
Imprint Academic, Philosophy Documentation Center
PO Box 7147, Charlottesville, VA 22906-7147, USA

ISBN   1 84540 060 7
ISBN-13   9781845400606

A CIP catalogue record for this book is available from the
British Library and US Library of Congress

Contents

Preface

In 2004 as Stephen Prosser left a meeting in the Assembly there was an opportunity for a short conversation with Sir Jon Shortridge, the Permanent Secretary: 'What would your reaction be if I suggested writing a book on how the civil service made devolution happen in Wales?' Astonishingly, he said 'yes' almost immediately, said he thought it was a good idea, asked for a short paper setting out the idea, and added that whilst he'd need to check it out with the First Minister he didn't envisage any problems.

A one-page paper setting out the ideas was prepared and sent to Jon Shortridge within a day or two and then nothing happened for about two months. Convinced that he had changed his mind the very idea of writing the book was shelved. And then they met again at another conference and he said: 'How's the book coming on?' At first, Stephen thought he was talking about another book and when it became clear that Jon was referring to the devolution book rather tentatively Stephen explained that he was waiting for a green light from him. Two days later a letter landed on Stephen's desk: 'I have spoken to the First Minister about the possibility of your producing a book on how the change to devolution was managed in Wales. He is very supportive of the enterprise.'

A research team needed to be put together. The core would be two University of Glamorgan professors (although the team was changed half-way through the project owing to the chronic illness of one professor) and two civil servants seconded to the project by the Assembly for two days per week: one from the Welsh Assembly Government and one from the Assembly Parliamentary Service.

As a research team we would have unprecedented access to Assembly files, politicians and civil servants. The entire set of devolution files were made available to us, all but two of the politicians we asked for an interview agreed to our request (we interviewed all

Party leaders), and a focus group and interviews were held with nearly 50 staff. It was agreed that the writers would have full editorial control over the content of the book although we agreed to submit a draft copy to allow any factual errors to be corrected and as a check that we had respected any personal staff information. We emphasised that we were committed to telling the civil servants' story (and not the politicians' role in devolution), and that we would exercise mature judgement in revealing our sources where that might lead to a breach of confidence. However it was agreed that WE would tell the story and that we would have complete independence to call it as we saw it.

What followed was unprecedented access to the files (including the comments of a range of UK politicians on the original devolution White Paper), working documents and people, and we have done our best to use every scrap of relevant information to tell our story. The vast majority of interviews were taped and politicians and civil servants alike trusted us to respect what they told us 'on' or 'off-the-record' and as attributable or non-attributable. The Assembly did not fund the project and no member of the team received any payment from the Assembly for this work (other than the normal salary received by the part-time researchers).

On many occasions we've asked ourselves why the First Minister and the Permanent Secretary agreed to the project so readily. We believe there are three reasons for this:

- They are genuinely proud of what was achieved, particularly during the 1997-99 period, and want their story to be told.

- There is a belief in the notion of organisational learning and a view that the story will help the Assembly in its development and also that it will help other organisations in the public sector.

- They trusted us to be fair: fair to our need to demonstrate academic freedom and credibility, fair to the Assembly and fair to our various sources of information. We also believe that the decision to grant full editorial control to us so readily allows the civil service to distance itself from any 'unhelpful comments' (to use civil service parlance).

As we met the various civil servants the thing that surprised us most of all was their eagerness to tell anecdotes about the events leading up to devolution and about the early days of the Assembly. It was very much the same with politicians who had been involved in the early days. Why were they so keen to tell us their stories? It seems that the stories revealed their pride in pulling off a major coup: devolution in two years and from a standing start; that the two years were exciting times for them and the stories remained vivid and an useful shorthand for telling their tale; that the anecdotes or vignettes were an effective way of painting the picture; and that, as in most places, storytelling is a popular means of defining the very nature of the organisation. Far less theoretically, it might also have been that they and we enjoyed a good old-fashioned gossip over large quantities of tea and coffee.   As we conducted the interviews, and heard more and more stories to place alongside our organisational theories and diagnostic approaches, it struck us that an intriguing strategy would be to take a *Canterbury Tales* approach to the book, in that we would be able to tell everyone's story and allow readers to make up their own minds. That meant we would trust the reader's intelligence and so find it unnecessary to interpret every point or indeed every contradiction: an intelligent reader can do that for themselves (and will find many examples where the deeply and sincerely held views of the person interviewed were proven incorrect – and, tactfully, we did not point that out to the interviewee at the time). Such an approach appealed greatly to us and concurs with our belief that storytelling is a legitimate academic device in organisational analysis. Of course we have made our judgements and interpreted evidence as appropriate. Hence, we decided that to take a *Canterbury Tales* approach in each and every chapter would encourage unnecessary repetition of points made previously and hinder, if not break up, the development of themes that should be pursued in an orderly manner. And we felt some responsibility to the reader to offer our (reasoned) comments and observations as well.

Therefore, the book has thematic chapters examining certain dimensions of change but it also has its *Canterbury Tales* approach where we tell the story through the voice of someone else. Part A of the book is principally theoretical; Part B highlights the change management agenda thematically; Part C follows *The Canterbury Tales* approach; and Part D draws conclusions and is reflective.

So what you have before you is the result of an interesting year where we have read countless files — files that have never before been made available to researchers — where we have held a focus group, guided interviews, spoken to various people 'on' and 'off-the-record', and generally lived the project as we believe it has a valuable contribution to make to understanding change in the public sector, especially when it involves the role of Government.

We would like to record our thanks to Sir Jon Shortridge for his vision and enthusiasm, and to the First Minister and the Presiding Officer for supporting and approving this project. Without them nothing would have happened. In addition the civil service seconded Rod Hough and Kathryn Potter to the project, greatly assisting it in many ways. We referred earlier to the fact that there was a change of the research team partway through the project. Unfortunately Siobhan McClelland had to drop out due to illness, but we thank her for her contribution and wish her well. The University of Glamorgan approved the secondment of Michael Connolly to the project at a crucial time and again that was extremely helpful. A huge vote of thanks goes to the people who gave of their time willingly to be interviewed. They shall remain nameless, as convention demands, but they are not forgotten. Nonetheless two parts of the Assembly need to be named: Debra Carter's Information Department who made the files available and led us through the gargantuan indexing system and Iona Thomas-Evans and her team of text processors who expertly turned the interview tapes into the typed word. Although the text processors were first class we still smile at one typed version of an interview with a politician where his reference to 'asylum entity' puzzled us until our notes showed that he had referred repeatedly to 'a silo mentality'. Such is life.

Finally we thank members of our family for their forbearance as we struggled with this project. We recognise that they often pay the costs of such projects in part because we are sensitive souls and in part because they told us.

Chapter 1

Introduction

Setting the Scene

The advent of devolution in Wales, Scotland and, more hesitantly, Northern Ireland has stimulated debate in many areas including the law, constitutional affairs and policy formulation and implementation. A number of authors (for example, Cole et al 2003, Laffin and Thomas 2001, Laffin 2002, Osmond 2005, Rawlings 2003) have discussed aspects of the management, leadership and organisation development dimensions of the various devolution arrangements. This book adds to that literature by focusing on the change and its management in the move from Welsh Office to emergent National Assembly for Wales through the first and second Assembly terms. This was — and remains — a major change management initiative on the part of the civil service. As the Permanent Secretary to the National Assembly for Wales Sir Jon Shortridge has said,

> From the perspective of the Civil Service, it is hard to overestimate the scale of the change that the transition from Welsh Office to National Assembly represents (Shortridge 2002).

From the perspective of officials the absence of any significant policy making capacity in Wales meant that the change was even more substantial. There is a risk that this understates the Welsh Office's policy capability, as policy making in areas such as education did take place, though there is no doubt that the policy making capacity was limited. Further — and something that is often not appreciated fully — the unique features of devolution in Wales, especially the creation of the corporate body, added to the impact of the scale of the change. Not surprisingly we believe the resultant story will be of interest to academics as well as managers including those among the civil service, and perhaps the non-managers in that community as well.

The now famous notion of devolution as process rather than event has particular resonance in the significant management of change agenda undertaken by those who were tasked with making devolution happen — the civil servants. From the narrow referendum 'yes' result of 18 September 1997 to the 1 July 1999, when the Welsh Office ceased to exist and virtually all the powers vested in the Secretary of State for Wales were transferred to the National Assembly and delegated to the First Minister, there was less than two years in which to prepare for devolution.

The Assembly was starting from a very low base and hence the challenge to ensure successful implementation was enormous. Although Wales had a history of administrative devolution from 1964 to 1999 and a certain level of administrative autonomy, as we have stated above and despite our caveat, the Welsh Office had little experience of policy making and was highly dependent on Whitehall, culturally as well as administratively.

In 1999, the Welsh Office was one of the smallest government departments supported by nearly two and a half thousand civil servants (see the last section in Appendix 3) and headed by a Secretary of State and two Ministers who operated largely out of Whitehall. The main task of this territorial offshoot of Whitehall was to implement the policies of the UK government within Wales rather than to develop and implement policy initiatives of its own (Deacon 2002). In essence the Welsh Office relied on the lead Whitehall department to do the bulk of the policy legwork before it was fine-tuned to reflect a Welsh perspective.

Once devolution was up and running, the role and nature of the civil service in Wales underwent a sea change. The Assembly's civil servants were now expected to relate to nine ministers and special advisors based in Cardiff, as well as to the Assembly committees, before whom they might be publicly questioned. Civil servants were expected to devise and deliver an increasingly Wales-driven agenda rather than a largely Whitehall one.

Jon Shortridge (2002) made it clear that, at the time the Assembly was established and with so much change taking place, he was determined not to undertake a major restructuring of the office and considered it of great importance to maintain as much stability as possible. His guiding principle, therefore, was to maintain as much consistency and continuity as he could at the very top of the organisation. The twin themes of 'continuity and change' became the watchwords for devolution and constitutional reform, and indeed have become something of a guiding principle for the civil service in Wales. For Welsh Office civil servants, the ongoing business and systems of what was — as we need to remind everyone — a small government department had to be kept going at the same time as making devolution happen. 'Continuity and change' is a useful phrase as it suggests a degree of tension that reflects the reality of the situation and it is one of the themes that emerge in our narrative. But it is a theme that is multi-faceted. For some it implied the nature of organizational life undergoing major change: others, mistakenly, expressed the view that the imperative to maintain business as usual was predicated on the old Welsh Office continuing to function in much the same way, despite the fact that it now had to be accountable to 60 elected members.

Other tensions existed. In contrast to the seeming stability at the very top (though that can be over-stated), there was substantial turbulence below. Welsh civil servants experienced difficulties generated in part by the fusion in the Government of Wales Act of the executive within the Assembly into a single corporate body where responsibility for discharging both legislative and executive functions rested within one organisation. Officials reported confusion, real ambiguities in role and potential conflicts of interest.

There were changes affecting those civil servants who had been employed in the old Welsh Office and those civil servants who arrived as new Assembly employees. Loughlin and Sykes (2004) have reported that many civil servants found it difficult to cope with the new world that had been thrust upon them. Some of them did not cope well with the changes and much greater expectations, the greater transparency — life in a goldfish bowl — and the demands of nine Cabinet Ministers. There was also the slim referendum vote in 1997, which meant that the Assembly as a whole was under considerable pressure to demonstrate that it was able to add value to what had administratively gone before.

There have been tensions between civil servants in Whitehall, the Assembly Government civil servants on the one hand and the parliamentary civil servants working in the Bay on the other. The emergence of the Presiding Office, now known as the Assembly Parliamentary Service (APS), in the Bay has seen a very different civil servant emerge though formally at the time of writing it remains part of a single civil service, responsible legally to the Permanent Secretary. Civil servants in the Bay are the nearest Welsh equivalents to the staff employed by the Scottish Parliamentary

Corporate Body, who provide support for the Scottish Parliament. With the absorption into the Assembly of a number of quangos, including the Welsh Development Agency and ELWa, the pool of pre-1999 civil servants will be diluted further. There has been what has been described as a new job specification for civil servants – 'generic skills weighed towards the building of effective relationships with politicians and the managerial ability to achieve better performance in a service delivery context' (Parry 2004).

The Pace of Change

Change is synonymous with devolution and the rate of change has been rapid. The National Assembly has been operating for six years and there have been two full sets of elections. From the very early days of devolution, questions have been raised about the nature and adequacy of the settlement and the institutional design involving an untried and untested single corporate body model with a single legal personality and with no formal division between executive and legislature. As early as 2001, an internal Review of Procedure had been carried out by an Assembly Committee which recognised the need for sharper separation of powers. In 2001 came the putative split between the legislative branch of the Presiding Office (now renamed the Assembly Parliamentary Service) and the executive branch of the newly self-styled Welsh Assembly Government. In 2002, came the setting up of a Commission on the Powers and Electoral Arrangements of the National Assembly for Wales chaired by Lord Richard, the former Leader of the House of Lords. The 'Richard Commission' published its report in 2004 setting out a series of recommendations for reform of the National Assembly for Wales.

The most recent and significant changes were announced in June 2005 by the Secretary of State for Wales when he presented the long awaited White Paper, *Better Governance for Wales,* to Parliament. The White Paper contained proposals to amend the *Government of Wales Act 1998* in order to 'develop the devolution settlement to make it work more effectively and so deliver better governance for Wales'. The Secretary of State identified change under three main themes to develop the devolution settlement and to make it work more effectively for Wales: the formal separation of the executive and legislative branches, to avoid confusion and to improve effective scrutiny; enhanced legislative powers; and changes to existing electoral arrangements. The *Government of Wales Bill* has been published as we finalise the book, and the proposed changes will enter the statute book presumably in time for the elections to the National Assembly for Wales in 2007.

Peter Hain, Secretary of State, spelt out his commitment to change in the White Paper's first pages:

> After the experience of six years of the Assembly in operation, and two full sets of elections, it is appropriate now to review and improve the working of the Assembly. This is not to make change for change's sake, but to ensure that it continues to meet people's needs in Wales and remains accessible and accountable to them.

But life in the civil service does not stand still, even for a major project such as the one under consideration. The Home Civil Service itself has been subject to many attempts to reform it, with terms such as change, reform, and modernisation commonly used. There has been debate about the impact of the New Public Management (Ferlie et al 1996, Massey and Pyper 2005; Ingraham and Lynn 2004; and Osborne and Brown 2005), debureaucratisation (Dowding, 1995) and the necessary continuance of bureaucracy (du Gay), the end of the civil service as a distinct entity (Chapman, 1997) and the possible death of the 'Whitehall paradigm' (Campbell and Wilson, 1995). Understanding the changes brought about by devolution requires being aware that they occurred in real time, with much else going on.

Wales has seen devolution unfold at an extraordinary pace and with increasing confidence and we believe that the time is ripe to reflect on the lessons that devolution has offered and to utilise this learning to inform existing and future devolution arrangements. There can be no better time to examine the key management issues associated with the advent and consolidation of devolution, to identify the managerial mechanisms utilised in managing the devolution change and the impact of leadership within the emergent and consolidated National Assembly for Wales. In doing so, we identify the strengths and weaknesses of management of change approaches and lessons to be learned both for the National Assembly, other devolved governments and newly devolved organisations. By providing opportunities for organisation development and learning, we also make a contribution to an evidence-based approach in management, leadership and policy-making.

The Research Project

The book is based on a research project which examined the civil service's role in bringing devolution to Wales. It was supported by the Assembly's Permanent Secretary, Sir Jon Shortridge, with the approval of the Presiding Officer, Lord Dafydd Elis-Thomas, and the First Minister, Rhodri Morgan. This then is the story of the impact of devolution on the civil service told to us by the civil servants and the politicians who made it happen.

The term 'the story' is quite deliberate and reflects our view — supported by much recent academic writing — that narrating the organisation (Czarniawska1997) offers useful insights into understanding organisational life. Perhaps 'stories' may have been a more appropriate term. In seeking to understand the organisational process of change, we also seek to uncover what Gabriel has described as 'the living folklore' which all organisations are said to possess, though this is not equally dense or equally vibrant in all of them. Gabriel contends that 'this folklore, its vitality, breadth, and character, can give us valuable insights into the nature of organisations, the power relations within them, and the experiences of their members' (2000: 22). Gabriel (2000) for instance, has argued that stories open valuable windows into the emotional, political, and symbolic lives of organisations, offering researchers a powerful instrument for carrying out research. In addition Rosabeth Moss Kanter (2004: 388) argues for the value of letting people tell their stories:

> I think that people learn best through stories ... believe that the most useful ideas are grounded in a deep understanding of how the world actually works. That is why I value getting out in the field, talking with people in their own settings.

In sum we believe that stories enable us to examine organisational politics, culture and change, revealing how wider organisational issues are viewed, commented upon, and worked upon by their members.

Thus we talked to a wide range of civil servants. In addition, whilst the book's primary focus is not to examine politics, policy or constitutional issues, these are intricately bound up in the narrative. We therefore listened to the stories and perspectives of politicians past and present from all parties in the Assembly and heard their views on how the change was managed. A number of these stories are so insightful and interesting that we have produced a number of chapters in which their voices are heard with limited comments from us, though of course we have included their insights, with others, in reporting our findings.

In addition this was augmented by unprecedented access to National Assembly documents and to civil servants of all grades. The result we hope is a book of interest to a wide audience.

The Book

The next chapter locates our empirical work in a theoretical framework and hence outlines our approach to understanding organisational change and its management. Chapter three examines the story of devolution. The first section discusses the overall process. However there was a specific and interesting debate which is important to understand and which is examined in more detail. This involves the decision to designate the Assembly as a corporate body. Many — but not all — now argue that this was a mistake, but how it was arrived at is of interest to those studying change. The next two chapters report our findings on two key related themes, people and culture. Chapter six examines a recent and important structural change, namely the Executive Board. We then move onto the 'tales' from a number of key players, which if not offering the raciness of some of the Canterbury Tales, provide reflective and interesting perspectives. Chapter seven reports on five such tales: The Architect's Tale (Ron Davies), The Chief Servants' Tales (Rachel Lomax and Jon Shortridge), the Junior and Middle Servants' Tales, a Tale from the Merged Bodies and finally a Tale from the Bay. A number of interviewees were willing to discuss how they saw aspects of the future of the public service in Wales and the role of the civil service and we report on these in chapter eight. Finally we turn to some concluding reflections in chapter nine. We have included a number of appendices, the first of which reports on our research approach, the second provides some details on the annual staff Attitude Surveys and finally we provide some specific information on a number of features such as cabinet members, election results as well as providing details of the Assembly officials.

Chapter 2

Reflections on Managing Change

Introduction

The main purpose of this chapter is to outline our framework for thinking about organisational change in general and the impact of devolution upon the civil service in particular. The intention is that this will help you, the reader, to understand our selection and organisation of material. The literature on organisational change is substantial, especially if we include the literatures on innovation, project management, implementation and so forth. Furthermore, this literature has been written for a range of reasons, from guide-books on how to do it, to weighty intellectual tomes, via memoirs of managers and textbooks. In all of these categories there are the good, the bad and the ugly. Hence a guide to our approach seems essential.

The Process Framework

Recent models of change emphasise three features, namely first, the dynamic nature of change — changing (a continuous process) rather than change (a one-off event); second, the context of change; and finally the complexity of organisational life. A major contribution in taking forward this perception has been the work of Andrew Pettigrew and his colleagues (e.g. Ferlie et al 1996, Pettigrew 1985, 1987, Pettigrew et al 1988 — for a critical commentary on Pettigrew see Caldwell 2005, Collins 1998). Pettigrew formulated the issue of research into change as follows:

> Theoretically sound and practically useful research on strategic change should involve the continuous interplay between ideas about the context of change, the process of change and the con-

tent of change, together with skill in regulating the relations between the three (Pettigrew 1985:19).

Pettigrew's work was conceived as a direct challenge to 'ahistorical, aprocessal and acontextual' approaches to organisational change; especially planned change approaches, instrumental ideals of managerial agency, and the variable-centred paradigms of organisational contingency theories (Pettigrew 2003). Caldwell (2005: 93) argues that there are four core elements to Pettigrew's work, namely:

a) the iterative, non-linear or processual nature of change over time;

b) the multiplicity of internal and external 'levels of analysis', including those within organisations and their environments;

c) the central influence of micro-politics and conflicts between organisational actors over the direction, rationality and outcomes of change; and

d) the unintended consequences, unpredictability and paradoxical nature of all rational action, management planning and strategic decision making.

This perspective relates to our methodological approach, which emphasises storytelling. It recognises that 'Organisational life is ... pluralistic, multi-faceted and multi-layered, inhabited by people who have differing perceptions of 'reality' and where there are inevitably complex patterns of cause and effect. It also accepts the dynamics of changing, as planned changes confront time delays, unintended consequences and successive redesign of interventions' (Wilkinson 1997: 509).

In addition it is worth pointing out that Pettigrew was interested, as are we, in theoretically sound and practically useful research on change. It is fair to note that the efficacy of this dimension of Pettigrew's work has been questioned by some critics (see Collins 1998), but we remain interested in reflecting on any lessons to be learned. We have structured the remainder of this chapter by using Pettigrew's schema of context, change and process.

Context

Most of the early literature on change was acontextual, ignoring the nature of the organisation and the environment within which it operated. However more recent studies stress the importance of context. Dawson (1994: 42) for example distinguishes between an external and an internal context. We recognise that the distinction depends on drawing boundaries and accept that in some senses such boundaries are arbitrary. Nonetheless the distinction seems a useful starting point. The former relates to a range of environmental factors, including legislation, social mores, technological innovations as well as political and economic developments. The latter focuses on the nature of the organisation: its culture, history and operating structure.

Outer Context

The organisational environment has long been recognised as the key contingency which generated the need for organisational change. The case of devolution is yet another example. The challenges for managing change which devolution has thrown up arose as a result of political and legal decisions. This point resonates with an observation made by Ferlie et al (2003) who stress the importance of the political and policy context. 'Political and policy considerations are significant and pervade the leadership, strategy and management of public service organisations' (Ferlie et al 2003: S9).

Change occurs in real time. A number of writers have presented a metaphor of managing chaos (Tom Peters for example) but in our view this metaphor is exaggerated and ultimately unhelpful as there remain high degrees of stability in the environment (see Sturdy and Grey 2003, and Grey 2005 for a critique of the uniquely chaotic context argument). However, as we have argued, introducing planned change does not take place in a laboratory in which everything else is put on hold until the change is fully implemented. Other changes occur. Thus devolution occurred within a context of the UK Labour Government's efforts to improve service delivery (Massey and Pyper 2005), and with that came a collection of specific initiatives to which the Welsh Office and subsequently the Welsh Assembly Government civil servants had to respond. Parry utilises the concept of modernisation which he describes as being at the heart of recent organisational change in the British civil service, coming together in the creation of devolved governments in Scotland, Wales and Northern Ireland in 1999 (Parry 2003: 1). Modernisation is defined by Parry in this context as 'the obsolescence of past forms and the availability of a new alternative'. A focus on one specific, albeit major, change, as in this book, should not blind us to the fact that responses to other initiatives were required, taking up the time and energy of staff at all levels. This fits into the idea of 'continuity and change', a phrase often used by the civil service in Wales—and referring to the on-going business and systems which had to be kept going at the same time as making devolution happen. Richard Rawlings describes the interplay between these twin elements as lying at the heart of all basic constitutional development, including, we would say, the organisational and management implications (Rawlings 2003:17).

The position is further complicated by the fact that government reforms are not always implemented as fully as the aims and objectives indicate. Pollitt and his colleagues (1999) point out that, despite the rhetoric surrounding results orientated evaluations of public services, in fact most audit and evaluation remains processional and compliance driven. Hood and Peters (2004) stress the complications of the unintended effects of any change—'surprises' as they term them—arguing that New Public Management reform has been beset by (an inevitable) set of paradoxes (see also Talbot 2005, Quinn and Cameron 1988). In addition the rhetoric surrounding any specific reform is not always matched by the reality. Indeed there has been a substantial debate in the literature around the extent to which New Public Management represents a significant departure from administrative traditions. Does NPM for example constitute a discontinuous change or an incremental development (see for example p. 2005, Lynn 2001)?

This in turn leads on to the question, how do we understand the context? At one level, this can be seen as a simple management problem - if there are a range of changes someone has to determine priorities, to determine which changes the organisation responds to and how. But at another level, a host of theoretical and methodological issues arise around the question of how we make sense of the organisational environment. There is evidence that managers tend to interpret the environment through what Argyis and Schon (1978) describe as their theories in use, based on a reflection of their experiences. The problem is that these are resistant to change, even when demonstrably wrong (Johnson 1990). Further these theories are frequently reinforced by the organisational paradigm, or interpretative schemes (Bartunek 1984), so that the individual's prejudices are reinforced. In some recent work, Christenson (1997, 2003) has distinguished between sustaining and disruptive innovations. While these ideas have arisen in the context of the private sector, they have some relevance for the public sector (see Connolly et al forthcoming). One element emerging from Christensen's ideas is the notion that radically new ideas may not be fitted into a well-established organisation, simply because they are not seen for what they are. The full implications of using new technologies are not utilised because the theories in use of managers limit their understanding.

An interesting dimension of this is that an event, indeed an environment, is not in itself disruptive; the issue is how it is interpreted. In essence, there is a process of what Greenwood et al (2002) term theorisation, which they define as the development and specification of abstract categories and the elaboration of cause and effect (p. 61, see also Munir 2005). Devolution and its impact on the civil service in other words was not just an event, but was understood by actors in particular ways. A number of chapters in the book, especially chapters three and six, articulate a number of these and how they emerged and changed.

At root, 'sense making' is undertaken by people at every level in the organisation. The street level bureaucrat (Lipsky 1980) offers her/his interpretation of organisational rules as s/he acts out her/his role and this may be at odds with the official rhetoric of the organisation. At a different level, the chief executive and other relevant managers or officers have a particular concern with key stakeholders. Public managers are constrained by the fact that they work within a set of legal, regulatory and policy rules and demands, and are required to be accountable for their and their organisation's actions (Ferlie et al 2003: S9). This means that their concern with institutional legitimacy (Meyer and Rowan 1979) may well reflect their understanding of the central ideas of these stakeholders. We say more about some of these matters when we raise the issue of leadership and culture later in this chapter.

In turn, this further emphasises the fact that it is sometimes difficult to determine the organisational boundary, especially within public sector organisations. Grey (2005) argues that where one draws the boundary of the organisation is arbitrary (see also the special edition of Human Relations 2004 No. 1). Of course legally it may be clear but from a viewpoint of understanding and managing change the law may not be the only — or most — relevant perspective.

Inner Context

The contextual approach argues that the intra-organisational context is important to understanding and managing change. The challenges of understanding and managing change in a large bureaucratic public sector organisation are not the same as a small private sector organisation. Even within the public sector managing change in Her Majesty's Revenue Commissioners presents different challenges to managing change in a hospital or a primary school. Organisations in fiscal crises may respond differently to change compared to fiscally secure organisations.

These statements are obvious once stated, but much of the literature doesn't seem to take these differences into account. The question arises as to the impact of a range of intra-organisational factors (size, culture etc) on managing change. There is some limited evidence which can help us. Thus large organisations are more complex than small ones. The argument runs that the more complex an organisation the more difficult it will be to achieve deep and pervasive change. In addition to size organisations may be more complex because of the range of tasks they undertake or their geographical disparity, increasing the number of sub-units and functions with which the organisation is concerned. This in turn may increase the challenge of successful change management.

Large organisations are often conceptualised as coalitions of coalitions (Quinn 1996: 91). They are understood as being dominated by highly pluralist and incremental forms of decision-making (Ashburner et al 1996: 1). Changes in such organisations are, as a result, often incremental or first order changes, an issue we return to shortly.

The institution with which we are concerned — the Assembly - is a relatively large (4000+ staff) and growing public sector organisation (see Appendix three last section). It is likely to be perceived as a bureaucracy, but like many civil service departments in the UK, it has a substantial policy element and a wide range of functions to manage. As chapter three will describe, the Welsh Office had been in existence as a separate body for over forty years, and while it had changed, essentially accruing more powers, forty years is a considerable time scale within which to establish traditions and practices. Further it is part of the British civil service, a body substantially longer in existence. While many staff were local and remained with the Office for some time, a number, especially senior staff, moved around the civil service and brought these different experiences with them. Post devolution the Assembly has gained in size, partly as a result of mergers, with more to come, so people new to the civil service have recently joined. In addition the range of services for which the Office was responsible meant that it was a reasonably differentiated organisation, creating problems of co-ordination and the need to overcome silos. So, in this research project, we are dealing with a well-established, reasonably large, differentiated, and growing organisation, facing a set of new and reasonably new challenges.

An important dimension of internal context is the role of culture and its relationship with change management. Culture has become popular as a concept in understanding organisations, certainly since Peters and Waterman's book 'In Search of Excellence' (Alvesson 2002, Bate 1994). A key dimension of this is the supposed relationship between culture, change and performance. Strong cultures, it is argued, support strong performance, but may inhibit change. Thus Metcalfe and Richards (1984) argued that strong cultures filter new ways of looking at the world through the old ways, often generating a disbelief system (see also Metcalfe and Richards 1987). Mahler (1997) explores the relationship between culture and learning, arguing that culture provides a reservoir of meanings against which organisational learning is shaped.

While culture remains a popular term, there are however a range of issues which have arisen. The term has in recent years come under some attack, not least because a number of the exemplar companies in the Peters and Waterman book ran into serious difficulties. Further the very slipperiness of the concept has led academics to be wary of using it and there is evidence that managerial efforts to bring about desired culture change have not been very successful (see for example Weeks 2002).

Nonetheless the notion of culture and its importance remains. Thus Alvesson (2002) in a major review of the concept writes that culture is 'highly significant for how … organisations function: from strategic change, to everyday leadership and how managers and employees relate to and interact with customers as well as how knowledge is created, shared, maintained and utilised' (p. 2). The use of the cultural metaphor enables us to interpret many traditional management concepts in interesting ways. For example it enables us to recognise the role that managers/leaders play in the social construction of reality. Leadership in this sense is the management of meaning: organisational members turn to leaders to help make sense of the organisation-environment links. Finally, managers themselves see value in the concept, using the term to explain and explore management issues. Given this — and not surprisingly — academics continue to explore the nature and implications of the concept of culture.

The term is borrowed from anthrop
ment as to its meaning (Alvesson 2004: 3)
inent anthropologists have drawn att
vagueness about the term. As a result Smirci
'organisational analysts held varying conceptions
Allaire and Firsirotu in their review of the organisat
erature draw attention to a study which identifies 164 d
the term. Generally however — and following Frost et al (19
ture refers to the meanings, values, beliefs, myths, stories, as v
the rites, rituals and ceremonies that abound in organisations. Fr
et al add that it also refers to the interpretation of events, ideas and
experiences that are influenced and shaped by the groups within
which people live. Alvesson (2002: 3) goes even further including
values and assumptions about social reality, though he qualifies that
by indicating that values are less central and useful than meanings
and symbolism in cultural analysis. Recognising the range of perspectives on the subject, Alvesson, nevertheless, suggests that 'view-
ing culture broadly as a shared and learned world of experiences,
meanings, values and understandings which inform people and
which are expressed, reproduced, and communicated partly in symbolic form is consistent with a variety of approaches to the conduct
of concrete studies'. In talking about culture, we are talking about a
process of creating — and re-creating — organisational reality that
allows people to see and understand particular events, actions,
utterances, or situations in particular ways.

Commentators have sought to define a number of approaches to
culture (see for example Meyerson and Martin 1987, Bate 1994, Martin and Alvesson 2002). One major fault line is Smircich's distinction
between culture as a variable and as a root metaphor, or as Bate
(1994) puts it between culture as something an organisation has and
something an organisation is.

On the first of each of these perspectives culture may be seen as
'the social or normative glue that holds an organisation together'
(Smircich 1983: 344). Culture 'expresses the values or social ideals
that organisation members come to share ... These values or patterns
of belief are manifested by symbolic devices such as myths ..., stories
..., legends ..., and specialised language' (Smircich 1983: 344). Culture provides 'the shared rules governing cognitive and affective
aspects of membership in an organisation and the means whereby
they are shaped and expressed' (Kunda 1992: 8, quoted by Alvesson:
3). Alvesson (p.4) goes on to argue that culture on this view is not

ology, where there is no agree-
Indeed a number of prom-
ntion to an essential
h (1983) argues that:
of culture' (p. 339).
on/culture lit-
finitions of
5) – cul-
ell as
ost

en' the heads of a group
publicly expressed. Cul-
inisations must get right
nal to the organisation,
e a sense of loyalty and
naving an integrated cul-
de, internally consistent
87, Newman 1996). Paul
ork as an example of this
centre of a network link-
skills, staff, style and sys-
s in a high performing
book is in large part a
culture potentially inte-
grates the organisation and ... formance.

This view of organisational culture is important, not least because managers are themselves interested in it. Organisation culture 'may be another critical lever or key by which strategic managers can influence and direct the course of their organisations ... The belief is that firms that have internal cultures supportive of their strategies are more likely to be successful' (Smircich 1983: 346). This fits the integrationist paradigm identified by Meyerson and Martin (1987) in which culture is unique to an organisation and is an integrating mechanism.

The alternative view sees culture as a way of understanding organisations. Strategy therefore is seen through a cultural prism: it is culture. Bate, for example, quotes Weick who plays with definitions of strategy and culture to demonstrate their identity. This relationship is again raised by writers who view organisations as paradigms, i.e. 'organised patterns of thought with accompanying understanding of what constitutes adequate knowledge and legitimate activity' (Smircich 1983: 350). Authors in this tradition see organisations as 'cognitive enterprises' (Argyis and Schon 1978). In talking about culture we are really talking about a process of organisational reality that allows people to see and understand particular events, actions, utterances, or situations in distinctive ways. Thus Karl Weick (1979) talks about a process on enactment, of people unconsciously creating their own world.

While the distinctions are clear, in practice most academics employ both aspects. Alvesson (2002) accepting this point, takes forward the notion that the base metaphor itself requires metaphors to understand it, that when the idea of culture as a metaphor is taken seriously we must understand that underpinning it are other metaphors. 'When people talk about culture in organisation studies, for example, what do they think of? What are their gestalts? Is culture seen as 'personality' writ large, 'an overall control mechanism', a 'community' or what?' (Alvesson 2002: 29). His point is that the concept of culture is a heavily burdened one and we need to be careful about how we use it and what we want from it.

If we start off asking about the origins of organisational culture, the first view (culture as a variable) tends to suggest that management creates the culture — what is sometimes referred to as cultural engineering. The literature gives a prominent role to leaders, especially the organisational creator. In turn that implies that there is a coherent, unifying culture. While it can be accepted that the leader, especially where s/he is the creator of the organisation, is a crucial element in determining its culture, there is more to organisational culture than leadership style. Williams et al (1989) argue that: 'some consultancy based authors have drawn conclusions far beyond the available evidence. It is really extraordinary that, for example, Deal and Kennedy and Peters and Waterman have made statements about the nature of organisational culture based in the main on the statements of CEOs and senior executives of multi-nationals; these interesting, but largely second-hand, executive stories are probably truly the myths of culture' (p. 10). In organisations there are often many different and competing value systems that create a mosaic of organisational realities rather than a uniform corporate culture. As Riley (1983) puts it 'increasingly people are warned that organisations are not the rational monoliths they appear, but complex mixtures of game-playing, rule-following, self-promotion, competition, and hidden agendas'. One view by a management guru expresses it as follows:

> Even in massive multinationals bestriding the globe and having more annual turnover than ten countries' combined Gross Domestic Product, it is impossible to say that there is only one corporate culture ... Most multinationals I know ... need uniformity to hold the organisation together, but also need sufficient diversity to stop it from dying (Garratt 2003).

In many public sector organisations for example different professional groups may create their own culture and guide their activities with reference to common and integrated sets of norms and priorities generated by each profession. However professions are themselves different in developing a cultural sense. Thus, for example, the distinction between locals and cosmopolitans indicates that some professionals are more likely to adhere to professional standards and values than others. But to the extent that they do, sub-cultures may well develop in the organisation. Meyerson and Martin (1987) speak of a differentiated cultural paradigm, characterised by differentiation and diversity. This in turn raises questions about the nature of the relationship between power and the creation of corporate culture, and returns to the point about large (public sector) organisations as coalitions. Organisation culture will reflect the political relationships between differing groups, including professions.

Meyerson and Martin (1987) add a third paradigm, one characterised by ambiguity. In some senses this helps us with the Welsh Office, an organisation which held together integrationist and differentiated cultures, and represented an organisational culture to which various groups reacted. Change, especially major change, offers a way of exploring these issues.

In addition to leaders and various groups, at least two other factors are important. One is the history and traditions of the organisation. If culture is a socially constructed phenomenon its development takes place within a social environment, one interpreted for example by long serving staff members. This suggests that culture is created and recreated by members of staff as they undertake their work. Hence geographically separate parts of the same organisation working to the same rules and strategies may develop cultures which differ to some degree simply because staff work at different locations.

Equally, the organisation is part of a broader community, or set of communities. Indeed a great deal of the managerialist literature is devoted to changing the ways customers are viewed by organisational members, something which (despite the limitations of the marketing perspective on public sector organisations) occupies the time of many senior members in the public sector. The nature of these (two-way) interactions will inform the culture of the organisation.

All of this suggests that many cultures are not amenable to management inspired change — organisational cultures are not designed (Quinn 1996, p. 99) — and that there are competing cultures in organisations, with the formal rhetoric at odds with other voices. Professional groups for example tend to generate their own culture(s) and the public sector is often the location of differentiated or fragmented cultures. This suggests that senior managers will have problems in manipulating cultures, though Johnson (1980) for example argues that leaders can manage symbolic actions. But as Weeks (2004) argues attempts by senior managers to secure a normative culture are not always successful.

A related issue is the impact of the culture of the organisation on performance. The managerialist literature tends to emphasise that strong cultures (that is unitary, deeply held cultures) impact positively in performance and, as already argued, are a factor in encouraging the growth of interest in culture. There are a number of points to be made. First, if the shape of the organisational culture is not in the gift of senior mangers, seeking to engineer the culture may be a waste of resources (though that does not invalidate the argument that strong cultures impact positively in performance). Second, it is possible that culture helps to influence performance evaluations. Whether a university judges research output of a particular sort as the core activity may well reflect in part its culture. Thus the core task may well be defined by the organisation's culture.

Third, there is an argument within the literature that the causation runs from performance to culture. Success is determined by factors other then culture, and that success shapes the culture. Fourth, equally it is possible that strong cultures can inhibit success. New chief executives can find themselves faced by a complacent culture hostile to their notions of what the organisation is about and how success should be determined. Finally, in turn this leads to the argument made by Alvesson namely that 'there are no recipes for success that just can be copied and applied without consideration of time and space' (Alvesson 2002: 69).

Change

The nature of the change under consideration is also significant. The change we are considering here is a large-scale, institutional level change. It is, in the language of Robert Quinn (1996), a deep rather than an incremental change, and such changes involve extensive learning processes (p. 84). Within the context of the public sector, these are changes in which issues of governance and the formal and legislatively driven relations between government and the public organisations become important (Lynn 2001 see also Osborne and Brown 2005: 59–60). In this case this is the heart of the change. Geva-May (2002) argues that institutions need to be considered as part of an 'inter-relational triangle' that comprises policy formulation and political cultures together with institutional configurations. And such changes are liable to be long term. As Rachel Lomax, the Permanent Secretary during the planning stages of devolution and now Deputy Governor of the Bank of England, told us: 'Devolution was a watershed moment, but the changes it unleashed may go on unfolding for many years to come.' Indeed!. Chou En-lai was once asked about the impact of the French Revolution and declared that it was too soon to say: the working out of major and radical change is complex and can take a long time. The developing nature of devolution will generate changes well into the future.

There are a number of points that arise. First, how a change is defined by different actors in the organisation may vary enormously. Within the public sector, arguments for a specific innovation are often speculative and normative. In essence innovation involves mortgaging the present, secure if imperfect, for the risky future. We often do not know the relationship between resources, activities, outputs and outcomes. As economists put it, the production function of many public services is unspecified. In such circumstances, any specific change may well be interpreted not as seeking to improve public services but as undermining individuals and resisted accordingly. And of necessity politics matters — politics in the sense of public policy-making and the struggles associated with normative definitions of good policy. The views of politicians and other key stakeholders matter.

Second, notions of change vary over time. Wilson (1992) argues that the very notion of strategic change involves assumptions about the linearity of change that are questionable. Instead change and change management strategies are frequently rationalised, with the prospects of being able to learn and to interpret events from the perspectives of the participants (losers and winners). And to complicate matters further, change usually generates unintended consequences. As a result, Kimberly and Quinn (1984) argue that we frequently swap one set of paradoxes for another (see also Quinn 1988, Talbot 2005).

Third, a major change of the sort in which we are interested will in essence be made up of lots of differing changes. There is not one decision in which someone — a Welsh God — declares: 'Let the Assembly be made and England defeated', but a stream of decisions, which take place simultaneously and sequentially. And as we have pointed out earlier, other initiatives take place. Hence those who are managing major change may not be in control of the change process.

'Events, dear boy', as Harold Macmillan famously declared, arise and impact on the dynamics of change management.

Finally, we are examining a multi-dimensional change with different dimensions, each of which may throw up differing issues. Thus IT changes provide different challenges to changes in management structures: both seem to generate their own set of problems. Hinnings et al (1991: 378) argue that the more the proposed change is concerned with 'management structure and process issues, the greater the difficulties in introducing change because of their heterogeneous and unspecified nature'; and maybe because many staff are suspicious of management change. As a result of all these factors, major change at times is incoherent, complex and chaotic, with shifting rationales and challenges.

Process

Three aspects of process seem to be important from the literature. First, increasingly, power and politics are judged important. Andrew Pettigrew puts the argument:

> The possibilities and limitations of change in any organisation are influenced by the history of attitudes and relationships between interest groups ... and by the mobilisation of support for a change within the power structure at any point in time. Changes are a product of processes which recognise historical and continuing struggles for power and status as motive forces, and consider which interest groups and individuals may gain and lose as proposed changes surface, receive attention, are consolidated and implemented, or fall from grace before they ever get off the ground (Pettigrew 1985: 27).

This perspective sees organisations as political systems and hence managing change involves accommodating the micro political interactions of individuals and groups—sustaining the coalitions we spoke about earlier.

If power and politics are important processes in managing change, then we need to understand the implications of differing power structures. Organisations where power is highly diffuse require different processes compared with those where this is not the case. Power is not an unambiguous term, and has generated a considerable literature (Lukes 2005, Walsh et al 1981). It describes the nature of relationships and involves not only overt exercise of power, but also what has been described as non-decision making, as well as the deeply embedded structures and cultures of organisations. Culture(s) of course reflect, in part at least, the political process, as it (or they) will have arisen from the outcomes of past political struggles. In such circumstances certain groups may not even challenge on certain issues, even when they appear to be disadvantaged.

This sort of analysis indicates why senior managers in general don't like political perspectives on organisations. Politics is too easily characterised as about self-interest, something which inhibits the success of the organisation. It is, however, worth remembering the moral foundations of politics, to quote the title of Ian Shapiro's book (2003). John Dunn offers four arguments for the existence of politics, from original sin or moral error (it is always useful when the opposition is evil), through conflicts of interest, partiality of interest and what he calls the logic of collective action (Dunn 2000: 9-30). Politics clearly is about self-interest, but it is about more then that: it may be about the deeply held moral views by professional and other groups. And of course these groups' interests and moral views may coincide, adding to the confusion of organisational life. In any case, politics (whatever it is (see Dunn 2000)) is a reality in organisational life.

Leadership

The nature of politics in organisations impacts on the susceptibility of the organisation to change and should influence the management approach. This leads on to the issue of leadership in change management. As Hinnings et al (1991) express it:

> Emphasis is placed upon the importance of leadership in developing vision, building coalitions of committed people and ensuring that the necessary capacity for handling change is built up (Hinnings et al 199 380).

The role of leadership in change is clearly one that excites much interest. A recent government report observed that:

> We are conscious that good leadership is as vital to the success of the public sector as it is elsewhere. We are committed to much better delivery of our public services. This cannot happen without significant improvements in the quality of public sector managers and leaders (Department for Education and Skills and the Department of Trade and Industry 2002: 3).

The same report (p.11) argues that the leadership problem in the public sector is much worse than in the private sector. Hence, and not surprisingly, across the public sector significant efforts have been made to increase the quality and calibre of leadership, through for example the National College for School Leadership, the NHS inspired but short-lived Leadership Centre and the PIU's leadership activities. In part this is linked to debates about recent distinctions between transformational and transactional leadership, with the former having the ability to generate deep and meaningful change due to their charismatic qualities. The demands on public sector leaders grow — entrepreneurial leaders, leaders who can ensure that public sector organisations are ready for changes in mission and structure are among the desirables (Osborne and Brown 2005: 93–94).

Despite this, as Pye (2005) puts it 'understanding leadership is problematic' (p. 32). Yukl (1989) in his survey of the field concludes that there is precious little consensus on precisely what leadership is, how or whether it can be installed into individuals, or even how important it is (see also Yukl 2006). He argues that 'most of the theories are beset with conceptual weaknesses and lack strong empirical support. Several thousand empirical studies have been conducted on leadership effectiveness, but most of the results are contradictory and inclusive' (1989: 252). 'What is clear is that there appears to be no reliable predictive theories of leadership; leaders are recognised after certain actions have taken place, but even this recognition is insufficient to provide a solid guide to leadership skills, let alone how to distinguish management from leadership' (Grint 1995: 125). To quote Fernandez (2004: 197) 'The leadership literature is plagued by weak, inconsistent and contradictory findings ... (it) remains balkanised in to several competing clusters of theories and approaches, each emphasising different aspects of leadership. In addition, much of the leadership literature makes no allowance for context, either organisational or national. And John Story (2005) argues that only a very small proportion of it focuses on senior executive leadership issues.

Perhaps noticing a tendency among leaders to take credit for organisational successes but to blame external factors for failures, an alternative perspective on leadership has developed in which scepticism has been expressed over the voluntarist and heroic nature of much of the literature on strategy, reform, change and leadership (Brunsson and Olsen 1993). Thus Leahy and Wilson (1994) seek to locate leadership in a context, describing leaders as 'tenants of time and context'. This perspective seeks to locate the role of leaders not just in terms of their persona but also in terms of their interaction with the context. There is evidence of the organisation reacting positively or negatively to the leader's style, anointing the leader as acceptable. A style or approach per se is successful (or not) in the social context of the organisation.

Part of this debate also focuses on distinctions between leaders and managers. Kotter (1996) for example posits a series of opposites between managers and leaders — managers bring order, while leaders cope with change. As Milner and Joyce (2005) point out such distinctions are in practice difficult to sustain and such distinctions are definitional rather then real.

There also has grown up a literature on the distributed view of leadership, drawing on Story's (2005: 90) distinction between leadership *in* an organisation and leadership *of* an organisation (emphasis in original). Leadership is not just about senior management, but is distributed across the organisation. Indeed chief executives may have a deliberate policy of empowering people across the organisation. Thus Connolly et al (2000) have argued that successful head teachers deliberately encourage heads of department to exercise leadership roles and skills. Part of the relevance of this perspective is that different approaches to change management may be required in different parts of the organisation as different parts of the organisation may face different challenges. Indeed the organic organisation is structured on this basis. But allowing what is referred to as distributed leadership poses problems, not least for a bureaucratic organisation such as the civil service. This has been described as:

> ... a classical Weberian one in the sense that the presumption would be that it would faithfully carry out the preferred policies of the Government of the day irrespective of that Government's political complexion. It is also a Civil Service which would have an independence based on the continuity that resulted from a career commitment on the part of the overwhelming majority of civil servants (Fry, 1997).

There are three points which emerge and which are worth discussing. One is that much of the literature on the charismatic leader assumes a relatively small group of people who interact with the leader and hence can be influenced by her/him. In a relatively large organisation, especially a bureaucratic one, this group may be a comparatively small percentage of the whole. Even if it is argued that her/his followers holding middle management roles spread the leader's vision, they may be less charismatic and messages may be reinterpreted as they go down the chain.

The second issue is the relation between the political and the civil service leadership. Ferlie et al (2003) make the point that 'we need to understand much more about how political leadership influences public organisations, how political leadership can be exercised in different ways from managerial leadership and how managerial leaders have to develop political nous and act politically on occasions' (p. S9). Milner and Joyce (2005) support this view and make the interesting point that in the public sector managers are expected to lead when politicians hold key power dimensions. Milner and Joyce (2005) go on to emphasise the importance of political skills of managers, of their ability to interact successfully with politicians.

Linked with this is an interesting discussion around defining the exact impact of public managers on the outcomes of the organisation (see O'Toole et al 2005). Public management clearly matters, but as O'Toole et al point out, 'the systematic validation of the management-matters hypothesis has been limited and sporadic' (O'Toole et al 2005: 46). They construct a model using Mark Moore's framework (1995) of public management, involving a tripartite distinction of managing upwards, downwards and outwards and test it in the context of education districts in Texas. Clearly, more empirical work will be needed, and, although they demonstrate that management does matter, the range of management techniques and styles and their impact on outcomes requires much more exploration. Milner and Joyce (2005) in their review of the literature identify credibility as a key factor in employees' perception of leaders' effectiveness, but it is not clear how this is connected with outcome. Interestingly they also suggest that the qualities of effective managers across the public and private sectors are the same, though of course perceptions of credibility may vary in different organisations and sectors.

Finally, the third point is the role of middle managers in providing leadership especially during change. While there has been a considerable debate about middle managers and their contribution to change (see Page and Jenkins 2005 for an important recent view of middle managers as policy makers in the civil service), Balogun (2003) argues that middle managers are best characterised as change intermediaries fulfilling four interlinked roles during change implementation — undertaking personal change, helping others through change, implementing change in their section, and keeping the business going. This latter aspect is often neglected, yet organisations while changing, have to continue delivering services. This takes resources, especially energy, and adds pressure to staff. Balogun

(2003: 80) argues that much of the alleged resistance to change associated with middle managers may stem more from organisational
constraints, such as a lack of support and time which prevent them
carrying out the changes rather than deliberate obstruction. Manag-
ers/leaders need to be aware of this and act accordingly.

It is clear that leadership matters, especially during major change,
but we need to be careful about being overly prescriptive and to
examine evidence carefully.

Communication

Finally in terms of key processes, we need to reflect on the deliberate
managerial processes for managing change. Among these processes
formal communication strategies, including participative strategies,
are crucial. There is evidence that increased participation can
improve the implementation of planned change, but the effectiveness of participation and communication strategies depends to some
extent on the culture of the organisation as well as the techniques
used. To put it bluntly, organisations with participative cultures are
likely to have successful change management participation strategies: staff feel in these circumstances that there is a history of being
taken seriously. Organisations without such a history run the risk
that participation strategies will be viewed cynically.

Conclusion

Managing change, as can be seen, is a complex business. Herbert
Kaufman in 1985 argued that chance and not skill was the main reason for organisational survival. More recently Ormerod (2005)
argued that organisational failure is more common than success, a
view shared by Grey (2005) in his combative little book. Managing
change successfully then may require luck as well as judgement but
managers have to adopt strategies and tactics and the impact of
those adopted by the organisation is important to understand.

In our research, following this review of the literature, we have
been concerned to explore key elements of the context, including
how it shifted, throwing up various new issues, including new structures, cultural changes, and the managerial processes, including
leadership. If there is a central theme it is how the wide range of people involved — politicians, as well as senior, middle and junior civil
servants — understood the processes of which they were a part and
how they see the future of the civil service in Wales as a result of
devolution.

Chapter 3

Devolution in Wales

Introduction

The purpose of this chapter is to outline the process by which the National Assembly for Wales was created and within that to indicate the nature of the changes that we consider in the remainder of this book. The intention is not to reproduce another interpretative narrative as excellent ones already exist—see especially House of Lords 2002, Laffin and Thomas 2000, Rawlings 2003, Barry Jones and Osmond 2002 and Osmond 2005—our intention is to examine aspects of the process relevant to our change management theme. The broad outline of the birth process is well known, though the pace of events still leaves many a little breathless and recalling the (moments of) pain.

We have already indicated in chapter one the main stages along the devolution highway, but they are worth recalling and elaborating. In May 1997, the New Labour government entered office with a mandate to introduce a package of constitutional reforms. In July 1997, a White Paper, *A Voice for Wales*, was published setting out the proposals for devolution. The Welsh people, by a very narrow margin, approved these in a Referendum in September 1997 and in July 1998 the Government of Wales Act entered the statute books, establishing the statutory framework of the new devolutionary arrangements. In May 1999, elections to the new Assembly took place using a set of voting rules new to Wales.

And the pace of change has not slackened. One First Minister has been driven from office, in dramatic fashion, and Labour in Wales has experienced a period of coalition government and two periods of minority administration (the second since Peter Law became an Independent in April 2005). Additionally, a major internal review of the workings of the Assembly reported in February 2002 producing, in March 2002, the putative separation of the Assembly's executive and legislative branches with the Welsh Assembly Government (WAG) coming into existence. In July 2002, the Richard Commission was established to review the Assembly's powers and electoral arrangements, and it reported in March 2004 recommending further changes. As Richard Rawlings aptly put it, 'from basic reform to fundamental review in this time frame is some constitutional record' (Rawlings 2003 p. 1). If nothing else this sequence justifies Ron Davies's famous remarks about devolution being a 'process and not an event'.

For the purpose of this book there are three important implications. First, and as Rawlings (2003 p. 18) says, there was a strong dose of contingency and a lack of route maps and this, combined with the speed of change, often gave the impression that they were 'making it up as they went along'. This reinforces the point made in the previous chapter concerning the unpredictable and multi-dimensional nature of change. Despite the unpredictability it is also true to say that there was also a strong element of continuity in that the blueprint for the 'new world' order had a close relationship with the old blueprints, noticeably the 1979 devolution proposals. Continuity was also defined as 'keeping the show on the road', whilst at the same time managing fundamental change to allow devolution to take place. Second, institutional changes of this type indubitably ensure that politics and administration are closely intertwined. The interplay between politicians and the civil service is inevitable, expected and intriguing (as can be seen from the various Tales in chapter seven). Finally, and again to quote Rawlings (2003 p. 18), there is a dual character to Welsh devolution — it is both a small step and a giant leap, it is limited devolution when seen in the wider UK context, but transformational given Welsh constitutional history. Our interviewees confirmed these three important implications.

We start however with the Welsh Office, whose character and structure was the base for the National Assembly.

The Welsh Office

Established in October 1964 and opened in April 1965, the Welsh Office marked an important milestone in Welsh politics (Deacon 2002). It followed a century of religious, cultural and political developments which had contributed to strengthening a Welsh national identity, including the rise of Nonconformity in the 19th century, the establishment of institutions such as the National Museum of Wales, National Library of Wales and University of Wales, the recognition of Cardiff as the Capital City of Wales, and the establishment of Parliamentary committees such as the Welsh Grand Committee (see McAllister 1999).

With offices in Whitehall and Cardiff, the first Secretary of State for Wales, and his two junior Ministers, had a staff of 225 and limited responsibilities for such things as Local Government, Housing, Highways, Water and Sewerage, Regional Economic Planning, Town and Country Planning, New Towns, Welsh Language, Forestry, National Parks, National Museum, National Library, Ancient Monuments and Historic Buildings. Compared with the Scottish Office, the Welsh Office was clearly low in the Whitehall pecking order and the next 15 years saw further responsibilities being transferred to it such as Health, Tourism, Industry and Export, Primary and Secondary Education, Child Care, Agriculture (most functions), Higher and Further Education (excluding Universities) Teaching and Manpower Planning. As a result of these additional responsibilities staffing increased to over 2,000 but, nonetheless, the essential role of the Welsh Office was to implement in Wales policies devised in Whitehall and that limited function did not alter significantly until the arrival of devolution.

Political pressure for devolution had been developing (see for example Bogdanor 1999, Trindale 1996) and in 1979 the then Labour Government held — or more precisely was forced to hold — a referendum on devolution, according to many a venture designed to limit the growth of Welsh nationalism. The Labour Government's proposals to establish a National Assembly were comprehensively defeated — the 'Yes' (pro-devolution) vote was 243,048 (20.3%) compared with a 'No' vote of 950,330 votes (79.7%). Devolution in Wales appeared to be dead.

Nonetheless, as Barry Jones (1997: 55) points out, 'despite the overwhelming failure of the devolution referendum ... the territorial management of Wales continued to pose problems for the British State'. In part, this owed something to concerns about the effectiveness of the Welsh Office as well as issues about the political legitimacy of Conservative governments in Wales during the 1980s and early 1990s, and this included talk of a growing 'democratic deficit'. The civil service workforce increased from 2,324 in 1980 to 2,562 in 1990, before being cut back to 2,035 in 1997.

A New Government

On 1 May 1997, a Labour Government was returned to office, with a
mandate to hold a Referendum on an Assembly for Wales. As the
Party's Manifesto put it:

> As soon as possible after the election, we will enact legislation to
> allow the people of Scotland and Wales to vote in separate refer-
> endums on our proposals, which will be set out in white papers.
> These referendums will take place not later than the autumn of
> 1997. A simple majority of those voting in each referendum will
> be the majority required. Popular endorsement will strengthen
> the legitimacy of our proposals and speed their passage through
> Parliament ...
> ... The Welsh Assembly will provide democratic control of the
> existing Welsh Office functions. It will have secondary legisla-
> tive powers and will be specifically empowered to reform and
> democratise the quango state. It will be elected by an additional
> member system.

Notwithstanding this commitment, there were two key issues
outstanding: first, the long process of building consensus around a
model of devolution, something that had existed in Scotland, was
missing in Wales, where there was no equivalent to the Scottish Constitutional Conference: and second—in part reflecting this—the
Labour Party's proposals for Wales were not as well thought out as
those in Scotland. As one interviewee put it:

> I think that's a little harsh but thinking about devolution for
> Wales had not been as fully developed as it had been in Scotland.
> There had been a constitutional convention in Scotland, whereas
> in Wales it was pretty much the 1970s' model of devolution. I
> don't think it was ever regarded as likely to be wholly satisfac-
> tory. But it was a case of taking what we were given and making
> the best of it—as Ron used to say: 'devolution is a process not an
> event'. So the challenge was to make the devolution model which
> was on offer as workable as possible, in the time available; and
> not to let it get picked apart, as happened in the 1979.

This is a view supported by many of our interviewees. The devolution policy had not been thought through in practical terms—it was
described, by some, as a policy originally written on the back of a fag
packet or, more generously, something that was in Ron Davies's
head. It fell therefore to the civil service—with some senior politicians—to take the notion of devolution, turn it into legislation, create
a new approach to government, develop new sets of policies, and
different ways of working—and ensure it was politically feasible. It
was translating the sketchy skeleton of policy produced by politi-

cians many of whom had a limited understanding of government and, in the view of many, had produced a compromise based on a political rather than a constitutional assessment.

Practical issues became crucial. Where will the Assembly be? What will it require? Could everything be got ready? What will it cost? The Government of Wales Act had to be drafted, and although some claimed that there was no precedent the old Act became a useful guide and whilst there are important differences many point to the similarities between the two documents. To quote one senior politician, 'Basically the 1978 Bill was taken off the shelf and dusted down'.

The process of the detailed shaping of devolution was focused within Wales. There is no doubt that the civil service played a key role in developing the nuts and bolts of the devolution policy. And central to the civil service contribution was the role of the Devolution Unit — 'the elite Devolution Unit of the Welsh Office' as Rawlings (2003: p. 42) describes it. This was formally established shortly after Labour came to power and was in operation until after the Assembly elections in May 1999. Rawlings argues that this Unit was the driving force in the middle, responsible for drafting the White Paper, including negotiating it through Whitehall, organising the referendum and the Assembly elections and negotiating the bill through Parliament. In short the unit's responsibility was to make Devolution happen.

The Devolution Unit worked closely with the Devolution Implementation Group consisting of Ministers (the Secretary of State and his two junior ministers), two political advisers, the Permanent Secretary and a number of other civil servants. The evidence suggests that this group worked closely with formal roles blurred. There is little doubt about the sheer excitement of the involvement of both politicians and civil servants in the devolution project.

> What I really remember is those weekly policy meetings with the three new Ministers, where they would literally roll up their sleeves and say 'right [clapping hands], what can we do?' and the sheer sense of excitement: energising stuff, they were great meetings, wonderful. The meetings, to test and probe, were held once a week in the Secretary of State's room in CP1, and involved Ron Davies, Win Griffiths, Peter Hain, Rachel Lomax, Jon Shortridge and Martin Evans and/or Hugh Rawlings: others would come along depending on the topic. At the very start of the process, Jon Shortridge met the whole Devolution Unit team and said 'this is history in the making, these are public records, every-thing-

but-everything is to be minuted, is to be recorded properly. It is
very important that we leave a thorough, comprehensive record
of this process'.

This work was crucial but the ground rules of the debate had been
agreed and limited, resulting in a narrowing of the key issues. As
one interviewee commented:

> A couple of important things were secured [before the election].
> The first was agreement that the major work on devolution
> would be done in Wales rather than by some gigantic team at the
> centre (i.e. in Whitehall) which is what happened in the 1970s.
> That gave us more control over our own legislation. The purpose
> of the machinery, which was set up at the centre of government
> was to facilitate and co-ordinate devolution preparations in Scot-
> land and Wales (and Northern Ireland). It was relatively light-
> weight at official level, with a Cabinet Committee to oversee
> things at Ministerial level. This agreement was secured by nego-
> tiation with Sir Robin Butler (then Cabinet Secretary) and the
> Scots and the Irish. I had little plotting meetings with the Scots
> and Northern Irish Permanent Secretaries before the election and
> then regularly during the devolution debates, so that we were all
> working together as closely as possible
>
> The other key agreement – this time with incoming Welsh
> Office Ministers – was that we would not attempt to get more
> powers devolved to Wales than the Secretary of State already
> had. So devolution was essentially about changing the political
> arrangements for exercising the powers that had already already
> been devolved to Wales. I think that limited the scope for bound-
> ary disputes and 'argy-bargy' with Whitehall Departments and it
> made it feasible for us to draft the legislation and pass a Bill in
> double-quick time.
>
> There was a third big issue which wasn't addressed before the
> election but became clear during the first year, the decision not to
> re-open the Barnett formula.[1]
>
> Those three agreements meant there was so much less to argue
> about. Our aim was not to get bogged down. To be successful we
> needed to move fast and stick to the same timescale as the Scots.
> To have reopened the Barnett formula or argued for more pow-
> ers to be devolved to Wales would have opened a can of worms
> and risked sparking disagreements that could have become
> incredibly bitter and maybe even scuppered devolution.

This was crucial, not least because a number of the civil servants
had been part of the previous devolution failure and had not enjoyed

---

[1]   The Barnett Formula refers to mechanism through which government
funds are distributed to Wales, Scotland and Northern Ireland.

the experience, to put it mildly. It had been one in which there had been a substantial amount of public criticism.

The pivotal factor in the development of this project was the role of Ron Davies. Davies, the new Secretary of State for Wales, was deeply committed to devolution and provided political leadership, as well as enthusiasm and energy for the project. To quote another interviewee:

> We didn't know what Welsh devolution was about: the Conservative Government's policy was not to have devolution. We obtained all the relevant Labour Party material on devolution, and there wasn't very much there, but we had to take this material and from it try to build a sufficiently robust policy that was true to the key strands in the manifesto and other published documents ... Obviously when Ron arrived, the whole process for developing thinking changed, and we had a board chaired by him which met every Monday and he drove the work programme. This was a pretty intensive period, the election was on 1 May, the White Paper was published in the third week of July, having gone through the Cabinet's Devolution and Legislation Committee as well as the Cabinet itself and been printed. We didn't have a great deal of time to do this and we certainly weren't able to do the sort of detailed constitutional research which ideally we might have wanted to do. These were ideas which were being developed, tested and challenged in real time.

Adding to the uncertainty was the sense that success in the Referendum was not inevitable and everyone was aware of the implications of the absence of a consensus view in Wales.

> It was not clear precisely what the new institution would look like, nor of course was it clear that the referendum, if it were held, would come out with a yes vote. So people were, as usual, having to plan, to feel their way forward on a suite of presumptions without actually being committed wholly or completely to any of them. And political management in that context and handling the measure of incoherence and grave uncertainty was perhaps the most testing issue for the [civil] service.

Again this interviewee stressed the importance of political leadership. And this was repeated by a number of other interviewees, some of whom were only too aware of the tensions within the Welsh Labour party over devolution. Substantial numbers of Labour MPs had, after all, resisted successfully the previous attempt to secure devolution and some were still around and had not changed their minds. Political leadership was necessary to secure the Labour Party's commitment to devolution and everyone we spoke to recognised the significance of the role played by Ron Davies in creating devolution for Wales. One story illustrated the respect in which he was held:

> ... the image of the man when the Government of Wales (GOW) Bill was going through the Lords. No other Secretary of State had ever done this: Ron Davies went and sat on the cushions at the foot of the throne behind the wool-sack of the House of Lords, where only members of the Commons are allowed, and watched the late Lord Gareth Williams bring the Bill through the final stage of debate. This showed his respect for Gareth Williams and was certainly counter to the culture of the republican Ron Davies!

Another civil servant said:

> Through all of the stages Ron Davies was watching the politics. Ron's vision was for Devolution in Wales, first and foremost, and the most important thing for him was that Devolution be achieved. He didn't want failure and so he had a vision of something that could be sold to the Parties. He would take no hostages. He'd compromise and bend to secure his aims. His vision was pragmatic not idealistic. He had informal meetings with all of the Parties (except the Tories) as it was vital to have their support to win the Referendum. The arms up picture[2] after the Referendum result was how it was in reality – a real partnership.

And political support was more than helpful in civil service negotiations with other Whitehall departments:

> I realised that if I started a debate with the Ministry of Agriculture about the extent to which animal health powers should be devolved to the National Assembly, we'd probably still be discussing it and I realised that I was arguing from a position, relatively speaking, of weakness. Where I had the strength was in the manifesto commitment and policy documents. That was in the bank and that was based on Secretary of State powers. So I could say to MAFF, or to the Department of Education or DTI, these are our powers anyway so it's no skin off your nose. I realised if I started saying that we wouldn't mind other powers being transferred, it would have opened up the whole process for evaluation: it would have weakened my political position and offered up for discussion something which I had already had in the bank. That might have resulted in two things: first of all, it would have lengthened the whole process – and I really wanted to use the General Election buzz for the referendum – but also it might

---

[2]   This famous photograph showed Ron Davies with a number of other senior politicians from a range of political parties, arms aloft celebrating victory in the referendum.

have meant a re-examination of those things which had already been devolved. At that stage I was quite clear in my mind that devolution was a process and, once begun, it would go further: what I needed to do was win the referendum, get the legislation onto the statute book and create circumstances for further change, and hey presto off it goes. During that initial period, when we were framing the White Paper which underpinned the subsequent legislation, it was winning the referendum that was the key thing. Time and unity were the two big issues — time in terms of the September deadline we'd set ourselves and unity in terms of keeping the Labour Party on board and not giving too many hostages to opponents.

Another interviewee added another dimension to these negotiations:

There were also issues concerning the degree of Devolution in particular areas. Planning policy was easy to devolve as most of the 'stuff' was in guidance documents rather than in legislation. But water legislation and animal health was very complex legislation with different Acts for different things. Those areas also had nightmare officials in London. A number of times they worried about what they thought might be 'barmy actions' by the National Assembly. By dealing with them you got to understand what colonial attitudes must have been like: some Whitehall officials thought we were higher executive officers and ex-Valleys councillors. Others did it properly, as Government policy, and to a large extent officials followed the lead given by their ministers. The Treasury was very helpful.

The White Paper and the Referendum

The new Labour Government moved rapidly to implement its devolution proposals and the First Reading of the *Referendums (Scotland and Wales) Act 1997* was held a fortnight after the General Election, and publication of the White Paper *'A Voice for Wales'* followed on 22 July 1997.

The main features of the White Paper were:

- An Assembly of sixty members. Forty members would be elected by the usual 'first past the post' method (in constituencies mirroring those of Westminster MPs) and twenty would be elected by the Additional Member Voting System to represent five regions of Wales (reflecting the then five European Parliamentary constituencies, each comprising between seven and nine Assembly Constituencies). The allocation of regional seats would be calculated according to the total vote for each

Party in that region, reduced according to the number of Constituency seats that it had already won in that region.

- The vast majority of the responsibilities of the Secretary of State for Wales would pass to the Assembly.

- Almost all officials working to the Secretary of State would transfer to work for the Assembly; however they would remain members of the UK Civil Service.

- The post of Secretary of State for Wales would continue, serving to channel to the Assembly the money voted by Parliament, to represent the interests of Wales during the preparation of new primary legislation by the UK Government and to make representations on behalf of the Assembly on non-devolved matters (for example taxation and social security).

Royal Assent for the *Referendums (Scotland and Wales) Act 1997* was given on 31 July, and on 18 September 1997, the creation of a National Assembly was narrowly endorsed in a referendum, a referendum which took place one week after the Scottish one as a tactic intended to take advantage of the momentum from the expected Scottish success. The referendum was managed in Wales with some support from the Home Office.

The Home Office has a permanent election team, they have to cover things like disability issues, postal balloting, etc, so we relied on them quite a bit. We appointed a Counting Officer for Wales and decided to keep to local authority boundaries and local election voting rules.

The Referendum result, as we have stated, was very close:

'I agree that there should be a Welsh Assembly'		559,419 votes

'I do not agree that there should be a Welsh Assembly'		552,698 votes

It has been argued that the result, narrow as it was, depended on the inter-party campaign—the 'Yes For Wales' Campaign—and that a key factor in this was the commitment to proportional representation (Laffin and Thomas 2000, Osmond 2005). Without this commitment Plaid Cymru and the Liberal Democrats would have not supported the referendum, and it is clear that many in the Labour Party were at best lukewarm about PR.

The Government of Wales Act

The Government of Wales Bill received its First Reading in the House of Commons on 26 November 1997. The Committee Stages,

Readings, Reports, Amendments and consideration of Amendments continued until 29 July and Royal Assent was granted to the Government of Wales Act (GOWA) 1998 on 31 July 1998. This gave an Assembly of sixty members, nine of whom would form an executive committee or cabinet with the First Secretary being elected, by the whole of the Assembly, and then appointing the remaining eight Ministers. The Assembly itself became organised around six main committees – subject committees reflecting the Assembly ministers' portfolios. The other key committee, the Business Committee, was established to allow the Cabinet and minority party representatives to formally organise the work of the Assembly. The Deputy Presiding Officer also attends this Committee.

National Assembly Advisory Group

In parallel with the passage of the Government of Wales Bill, the Secretary of State established the National Assembly Advisory Group (NAAG), a non-statutory group charged with considering how the Assembly might operate in practice. As a civil servant told us:

> Pretty well straight after the referendum result, Ron Davies announced the setting-up of the National Assembly Advisory Group: this came as a surprise to us but there may have been work going on behind the scenes. NAAG was up and running by December 1997, and operated until August 1998. Its purpose was to help build consensus and raise public awareness and debate after the tight referendum result

Rawlings (2003: 43) argues that NAAG played two key roles in the devolutionary process. First, it reflected and reinforced the new kind of inclusive politics. Comprising representatives of all four main political parties in Wales, the NAAG helped ensure cross-party support for changes made to the Bill during its passage, in particular the adoption of a more Cabinet-style approach. To quote Laffin and Thomas (2000) NAAG 'had an important symbolic role in consolidating a post-referendum consensus across the main political parties ... and the Welsh cultural elite' (Laffin and Thomas 2000: 561). It is fair to say that NAAG members were carefully chosen – 'carefully balanced' is Rawlings' term. As civil servants told us:

> There wasn't a competition to join NAAG, the members were carefully selected to be balanced and representative. John Elfed Jones was invited to be the Chair (I can't remember who suggested him) and the four parties nominated members. I think two of the parties claimed that the person they had originally pro-

posed was not intended to represent their party — they just
thought that they would be a useful member of the group — so
they nominated a second person.

It was very intense work, with no downtime, but the adrenaline kept you going and it was very rewarding — a career highlight. With its sub-groups, NAAG was sometimes meeting twice
a week. We took it a task at a time, first drafting policy papers for
NAAG's consideration, then a consultation document and then
organising the roadshows. NAAG and its subgroups generated a
lot of papers and work — for example I found myself proof-read-
ing the consultation document to the printers on Good Friday.
The consultation period continued into May and then we had to
pull together the responses for publication in August. The great
thing about the Devolution Unit work was that we were not 'top-
ping and tailing' Whitehall's work: we were starting from
scratch. Also we were ahead of Scotland in that our White Paper
was published first and our Bill was passed first. The Scots often
claim that their model is not like Westminster but in my view
they are very similar in practice and it was in Wales where we
were breaking the mould.

NAAG discussed the Local Government and Cabinet models.
Some parties expressed concern that the Local Government
model would undermine the Assembly, and business representatives were concerned that it wouldn't be able to act quickly
enough to make urgent decisions. There was also pressure from
Welsh MPs in Westminster. NAAG voted in favour of going for
more of a Cabinet model and the Bill was changed.

NAAG was deliberately meant to symbolise a more inclusive style of
government. It was an approach which was not always popular:

> There were people who expressed scepticism about the more
> inclusive approach to politics and some politicians clearly
> wanted a different approach, which at times put the civil ser-
> vice — whose role it was to implement the Government of Wales
> Act — in a difficult position. Once the Assembly had declared a
> clear preference for moving away from the GoWA model it was
> easier, but it was a problem whilst the moves to change the settle-
> ment were still covert.

In addition, Rawlings argues that in making recommendations on
Assembly procedures and committee structures etc, NAAG provided useful cover to Ministers and officials in moving towards
what he calls a more dynamic model of public administration.
NAAG was necessary as Ron Davies had no statutory authority at
the time to create a Standing Orders Commission.

The general view is that NAAG played an important and constructive role. It came together effectively, drew up a programme of

work and produced a report. The Group met for the first time on 12 December 1997 and continued to meet regularly until July 1998, working closely with the Devolution Unit. The NAAG Report was published on 24 August 1998. However Laffin and Thomas (2000) report that several members of NAAG reported some difficulties between them and civil servants initially, though our interviewees did not confirm or agree with this.

Standing Orders Commission

The Standing Orders Commission was appointed under the Government of Wales Act 1998 to draft Standing Orders for the Assembly, for submission to the Secretary of State.

> A decision was taken that there would be a Standing Orders Commission to set up the SOs. We got advice from the clerks in Parliament and it was clear that we needed SOs even more than the legislation. The problem was how to get the SOs as we didn't have a National Assembly or the equivalent of a Scottish Convention. Therefore we needed a Standing Orders Commission with cross party representatives and it was set up after the Royal Assent to the Devolution Bill.

The Secretary of State provided guidance to the Commission, which largely reflected the recommendations of the NAAG.

The Commission met for the first time on 9 September 1998 and submitted its report to the Secretary of State in January 1999. On 12 April 1999, the Secretary of State made the National Assembly's first Standing Orders, adopting most of the Commission's proposals.

> The Standing Orders Commission wasn't set up as quickly as NAAG, and there was a gap following publication of the NAAG report, during which Ron Davies left and Alun Michael arrived. The Commission was chaired by Gareth Wardell and comprised mainly lawyers. It met monthly, which was much more efficient as it gave us time to prepare the papers properly and the members' time to read them. Also there wasn't the temptation to put off a decision until the next meeting, in a few days time.
>
> It was good to have a different group of people looking at the NAAG recommendations: Peter Price, for example, had European political experience, and there were some sceptics in the group. We also had informal advice from parliamentary clerks — for example, Paul Silk advised us on election procedures for office-holders in a way which ensured that clerks could not be accused of influencing the outcome.

Corporate Structure and Its Implications

The National Assembly for Wales was created as a single corporate body — the unique character or 'strange autonomy' (Rawlings 2003: 86) of Welsh devolution. This meant that one organisation was responsible for discharging both legislative and executive functions, rather than separate organisations being responsible for each of these as in the traditional Westminster/Whitehall model. We discussed with a range of interviewees why this model was chosen and some of the consequences of the decision and the story is one of the interesting dimensions of devolution in Wales. How the corporate body model arose and how it has developed are issues relevant to our central concerns and set out in detail in the final section of this chapter.

Location, Location, Location

There were a number of other key issues. The decision as to where to locate the Assembly building concerned Ron Davies greatly. He wanted City Hall in Cardiff and assumed that it was available. However when this proved not to be the case he looked for alternative sites, including Swansea. Eventually in April 1998, the Secretary of State announced that the Assembly would be located in Cardiff Bay. In addition to Crickhowell House, there would be a new purpose-built debating chamber adjoining it and an international Design Competition was held and a Design Panel, under the Chairmanship of Lord Callaghan, considered the short listed plans of six architects, before unanimously agreeing to recommend to the Secretary of State the design concept from the Richard Rogers Partnership. On 20 October 1998, the Secretary of State for Wales announced that he had accepted the Design Panel's recommendation in favour of the Richard Rogers Partnership.

There were a number of senior people who felt that the Secretary of State was overly concerned with the building, an issue and decision that might be better left to the Assembly when it was set up. In March 2000, following a meeting of the New Assembly Building project steering group, the First Secretary decided to put the building project on hold while the National Audit Office completed its study into the Assembly's accommodation arrangements. In June 2000, the Assembly reaffirmed its decision and a 'turf cutting' ceremony was held on the site of the new Assembly building on St. David's Day 2001.

A Change of Secretary of State

On 26th October 1998, Ron Davies resigned as Secretary of State for Wales after his 'moment of madness' on Clapham Common. The following day, Alun Michael was appointed to be the new Secretary of State for Wales. There was little doubt however that Ron Davies's departure was greeted with considerable disappointment as he was seen as deeply committed to devolution, something widely recognised across Wales. It was feared also that a change of Secretary of State might hinder progress:

> The fact that Ron went the way he did was a huge spanner in the works. We couldn't get on with preparing for the Assembly, getting the carpets down, getting the Assembly room ready. ... So time that, in other circumstances, would have been devoted to preparing the staff, and certainly the more senior members of staff, was spent basically looking at our navels.

There was, as Laffin and Thomas (2000: 563) highlight, a change of gear: Davies was immersed in devolution and saw his career in Wales, while Michael clearly had a Westminster focus. But by that stage much had been put in place. NAAG had reported and the Standing Orders Commission had started work. Hence Alun Michael had little choice but to accept the bulk of the Assembly design, to use Laffin and Thomas's (2000) terminology. The final Standing Orders stuck closely to the recommendations, the draft went to Alun Michael in early 1999 and the draft Standing Orders were published in March 1999.

The Assembly Election 1999

The Representation of the People Order, setting out the arrangements for the Assembly elections, was made on 10 March 1999. Full Assembly elections would take place on the first Thursday in May at four yearly intervals, unless the Secretary of State decided, in consultation with the Assembly, to move the date back or forward by up to one month. The first election took place on 6 May 1999 and the outcome was:

Labour	28 seats
Plaid Cymru	17 seats
Conservative	9 seats
Liberal Democrat	6 seats

It is interesting to note that John Osmond reports that: 'in an unguarded moment Rhodri Morgan confessed that the Welsh system had been devised to ensure that Labour would achieve a majority of seats in at least three elections out of four. Experience so far has signally failed to fulfil these expectations.' (Osmond 2005: 7). While it is clear to us from our interviews with Ron Davies that this was not his view (coalition/consensual government may well have appealed to him), it does however add an extra — and possibly unexpected — dimension which the civil service had to deal with, namely coalition and/or minority government.

First Steps

The Assembly met in plenary for the first time on 12 May 1999, electing the Presiding Officer (Lord Dafydd Elis-Thomas AM), the Deputy Presiding Officer (Jane Davidson AM) and the First Secretary (Rt. Hon Alun Michael AM MP).

The first Cabinet members (see Appendix 2) were appointed on 12 May. The first Panel of Subject Committee Chairs was elected on 19 May (see Appendix 2) and, on 23 June 1999, the Assembly passed a Motion to elect Chairs to the Audit, Legislation, Standards of Conduct, European Affairs, and Equal Opportunities Committees in a plenary session. The Opening Ceremony of the National Assembly for Wales was attended by HM the Queen, HRH the Duke of Edinburgh and HRH the Prince of Wales on 26 May 1999, an event into which considerable thought went:

> My job at the Assembly was to organise the opening event. I started with an almost blank paper. The Secretary of State had decided an outline for the day but there were no details, so I had huge freedom to draw it all together. I had to think of everything. Unlike Scotland there was no Order of the Thistle to accommodate. We deliberately tried to catch the mood of the people: it had to be something that people would react to positively. The Permanent Secretary said that he wanted the newspaper headlines to say what a great thing the National Assembly was. It was the longest royal visit for ages, and the first time the 'three royals' had travelled together to and in Wales since the investiture, and there was also the Prime Minister. The hardest decision was what to do to mark the opening: how to convey the transfer of power from Westminster to Cardiff. My first idea was to get the Government of Wales Act from the House of Lords but this proved extremely difficult, so we made our own. The Gregynog Press made a facsimile of the Government of Wales Act. It is the only document that has been signed in both languages by the

Queen—she signed it at the top as on Acts of Parliament. The Queen gave the Scottish Parliament a mace, but this is a symbol of royal authority, so we made our own Tlws, which was carried in by two 18 year old first time voters. The headline in the Telegraph the following morning was 'Wales takes the future into its own hands' and the Echo said simply 'Proud to be Welsh'.

On 16 June 1999, the Assembly delegated its functions to the First Secretary. *The National Assembly for Wales (Transfer of Functions) Order 1999*, which had been made on 10 March 1999, came into effect on 1 July 1999, transferring the powers of the Secretary of State for Wales to the National Assembly for Wales. At the same time, the vast majority of the Welsh Office staff transferred to the Assembly, with the remainder forming the new Wales Office supporting the Secretary of State for Wales. The former Welsh Office ceased to exist.

The reaction of the civil service was interesting:

> We put a lot of effort into putting Crickhowell House right. It's very important that people feel that they are welcome. I wasn't there but I suspect the AMs needed to assert themselves over the civil service—it happened in Northern Ireland and I think it happened in Scotland.
>
> I felt the Assembly needed to take ownership of the whole project and if they felt it was too fitted-up in advance they would rebel against it, but of course a lot of what we were doing was predicated on the notion that Ron would be the First Minister [Secretary], and if he had been, it would have made a lot more sense.

A Change of First Secretary

On 2 November 1999, the Assembly rejected a motion of no confidence in the First Secretary, tabled by the Conservatives. However, two months later, a motion proposed jointly by Plaid Cymru, the Conservatives and the Liberal Democrats that 'the National Assembly for Wales has no confidence in the First Secretary' led to the resignation of Alun Michael, an event described by Thomas and Laffin (2001) as the first Welsh constitutional crisis. They argue that it reflected the Assembly's determination to act as a polity. In particular they argue that the Labour group saw their role as more than just supporting the leader. The Cabinet immediately elected Rhodri Morgan as Acting First Secretary and, on 15 February 2000, the Assembly elected him First Secretary.

Partnership Government

On 5 October 2000, a new coalition partnership between Labour and
the Liberal Democrats was announced. The Partnership Agreement
'Putting Wales First: A Partnership for the People of Wales' was pub-
lished on 6 October 2000. The new Partnership Cabinet was
announced on 16 October, with the First Minister the Rt. Hon Rhodri
Morgan AM MP and new Deputy First Minister Michael German
AM, Leader of the Liberal Democrats, signing the Partnership
Agreement on 17 October.

On 16 October, it was announced that the Cabinet, 'in order to distinguish clearly between members of the Cabinet and members of
the civil service where the term 'Secretary' is a common title', had
adopted the term 'Minister'.

Other developments undermined the very idea of the corporate
model. On 10 October 2000, the Assembly voted to establish the
House Committee and to create a separate budget for the Office of
the Presiding Officer, enabling it to assume an element of independence from the rest of the Assembly and the Office of the Presiding
Officer was renamed the Presiding Office on 10 November 2000. On
12 July 2000, the First Minister announced the agreement on an
all-party review of the Assembly's procedures, working within the
framework of the Government of Wales Act 1998. 'The Assembly
Review of Procedure Group' met for the first time on 6 December
2000.

On 14 February 2002, the recommendations of the Assembly
Review of Procedure were adopted by the National Assembly, voting unanimously in Plenary that 'there should be the clearest possible separation between the Government and the Assembly which is
achievable under current legislation'.

Welsh Assembly Government

In November 2001, the First Minister announced that the term
'Welsh Assembly Government' or 'Llywodraeth Cynulliad Cymru'
would be used in future to describe the policies and actions of the
government, as distinct from the legislative parts of the Assembly.
From the moment of this announcement there were, in effect, two
parts to the Assembly — the Welsh Assembly Government and what
became known as the Assembly Parliamentary Service — and no-one
should underestimate the key problems faced by senior civil servants (who indicated to us their strong support for this initiative) in
establishing governance arrangements to ensure that a single corpo-

rate body, acting as if it were two separate bodies, acted lawfully. This challenge is glossed over by some but clearly has been of great importance in ensuring the probity of Assembly actions.

Political Changes

Following the second Assembly Election (1 May 2003), the Labour Party formed the Welsh Assembly Government. Lord Elis-Thomas was re-elected as Presiding Officer and Dr John Marek AM was re-elected as Deputy Presiding Officer (he had succeeded Jane Davidson AM when she had been appointed to the Partnership Cabinet in October 2000). This gave the Labour Party a majority and Rhodri Morgan AM was re-elected as First Minister.

On 18 April 2005 Peter Law, the Assembly Member for Blaenau Gwent, resigned from the Labour Party in response to his Party's decision to impose an all-female shortlist on the Blaenau Gwent Parliamentary constituency for the forthcoming UK General Election. The loss of this Assembly seat to the Labour Party brought another period of minority Government.

The Richard Commission

The Commission was established on 18 April 2002 under the Chairmanship of Lord Richard, fulfilling a commitment in the Partnership Agreement *Putting Wales First* to

> Establish an independent Commission into the powers and electoral arrangements of the National Assembly in order to ensure that it is able to operate in the best interests of the people of Wales.

Terms of Reference: Assembly Powers

The Commission should consider the sufficiency of the Assembly's current powers, and in particular:

- whether the Assembly's powers are sufficiently clear to allow optimum efficiency in policy-making;

- whether both the breadth (i.e. the range of issues over which it has control) and the depth (i.e. the capacity to effect change within those issues) of the Assembly's powers are adequate to permit integrated and consistent policy-making on issues where there is a clear and separate Welsh agenda;

- whether the mechanisms for UK Government policy-making as regards Wales, and the arrangements for influence by the

Assembly on these, are clear and effective, and in particular whether they correct any apparent shortcoming from the previous item;

- whether the division of responsibility between the Assembly and the UK Government places inappropriate constraints on Whitehall policy-making, both on matters over which the Assembly has control and otherwise.

The Commission should consider any possible financial implications arising from the implementation of its proposals.

Terms of Reference: Electoral Arrangements

The Commission should consider the adequacy of the Assembly's electoral arrangements and in particular whether:

the size of the Assembly is adequate to allow it to operate effectively within a normal working week, and without placing undue pressure on Members;

the means of electing the Assembly, including the degree of proportionality, adequately and accurately represents all significant interests in Wales; and

any changes which may be recommended to the Assembly's powers make either necessary or desirable changes to the size of the Assembly or the means of electing it.

Outcome

The Commission held 115 open evidence sessions, 3 seminars and 9 public meetings across Wales and received over 300 written submissions in response to its two consultation papers. The Commission's Report was published on 31 March 2004. Its main recommendations included a legislative Assembly for Wales with powers to pass primary legislation in the policy areas devolved to it in 1999. In the interim, the framework delegated powers approach should be expanded as far as possible with the agreement of the UK Government and Parliament. To exercise primary powers, the Assembly would need an increase in membership from 60 to 80, elected by the Single Transferable Vote system of voting.

The changes would be incorporated into an Act put through Westminster and the new Parliamentary style Assembly could be elected by May 2011.

Following a debate in Plenary on the Report (6 Oct 2004), a motion was passed that the Assembly, having considered the report of the Richard Commission,

> calls on the First Minister to urge the Secretary of State for Wales to bring forward proposals to amend the Government of Wales Act 1998 for the following purposes:
>
> (a) to effect a formal separation between the executive and legislative branches of the Assembly;
>
> (b) to reform existing electoral arrangements in order to eliminate anomalies;
>
> (c) to enhance the legislative powers of the Assembly.

The report generated debate in Wales and beyond. Described as the best report in this area since Kilbrandon, many commentators have characterised it as radical (see for example a number of the papers in Osmond 2005). In some ways nonetheless it takes forward the 'continuity and change' theme, as it builds on what already existed and used devolutionary arrangements in Scotland as its model.

However, the Richard Report met with political flak which concentrated on both the development of political powers and the electoral proposals and the outcome of which is reflected in the White Paper.

Better Governance for Wales: The White Paper

On 15 June 2005, Secretary of State for Wales Peter Hain launched the White Paper 'Better Governance for Wales' declaring that 'After the experience of six years of the Assembly in operation, and two full sets of elections, it is appropriate now to review and improve the working of the Assembly. This is not to make change for change's sake, but to ensure that it continues to meet people's needs in Wales and remains accessible and accountable to them.'

The Secretary of State identified change under three main themes that the Government believed needed to be tackled to develop the devolution settlement and to make it work more effectively for Wales.

First, the Assembly has called for a formal separation between its executive and legislative branches, so that it is clear to the public who is actually responsible for decisions.

Second, there is considerable support for finding ways of enabling the Assembly Government to secure its legislative priorities more quickly and more easily, within its current areas of responsibility.

Finally, it is claimed that voters are confused and concerned by the way the Assembly's electoral system permits candidates who lose in a first past the post constituency ballot still to become Assembly members representing the same area through the regional list system.

The White Paper rejected the Richard Commission recommendation of STV, a step too far for many in the Labour Party.

The White Paper envisaged that a Government of Wales (Amendment) Bill would be published in autumn 2005, though it now seems that this matter is deemed too important for an Amendment Bill and a Bill for the Government of Wales was published in December 2005.

Staffing the Assembly

A final and key issue of interest here is the role of the civil service. Two important decisions were taken initially, the first being that Welsh civil servants would remain part of the Home Civil Service and the second that the civil service would support the Assembly. The first decision was seen as central to maintaining the Union and as important in reassuring civil servants. However, as the House of Lords Select Committee report (2002) pointed out, in practice things work somewhat differently (p. 42 para 151). In common with UK departments, the National Assembly has considerable autonomy in staffing matters, extending to levels of staffing, promotions and grading and pay settlements. Thus the devolved administration has 'considerable room for manoeuvre in developing staffing policies and arrangements that are appropriate to their needs, within the framework of the Home Civil Service' (para 151). The House of Lords' report argues that officials presented a number of considerations in favour of the existing arrangements. These include:

- acting as a guarantor of impartiality against politicians who might seek to interfere with it;
- being part of the Home Civil Service was seen as being part of a known brand, facilitating exchange of staff (though in the case of Wales this up to now has not been significant);
- it links officials into a broader context; and
- finally it enables close working across government.

With the exception of the penultimate point, the House of Lords Committee did not seem to place much credence on these arguments, arguing, for example, that the Northern Ireland Civil Service did not demonstrate a lack of impartiality. Further Richard Parry's point, in evidence to the committee, that membership of the Home Civil Service is not needed to guarantee civil service standards, because there were already multiple crown services in the UK, was well made. Parry did however argue that retaining a Home Civil Service prevented the Welsh Assembly from needing to write codes and personnel procedures. The report, in any case, did accept the point about the sense of detachment and concluded that retaining a single Home Civil Service remained sensible. In addition, it was put to us that if the Welsh civil service had ceased to be UK civil servants, there .was no guarantee that they would have been 'Welsh Civil Servants': instead they feared that the Assembly might have opted for Assembly officials becoming the equivalent of local authority officials — appointed by members. As we discuss in chapter eight some of these debates have been resurrected in the debates on the future of a Welsh public service.

As a result of the corporate nature of the Assembly, the civil service was expected to support the Assembly: serving both the Ministers discharging executive functions and also the legislative branch of the Assembly, which holds Ministers to account. This could be managed on a pragmatic basis for most civil servants most of the time but it could place officials, particularly at the higher levels of the civil service, in difficult positions of apparently conflicting loyalties.

A protocol was issued at the start of the life of the Assembly:

> The Assembly's staff serve the Assembly as a whole. However different staff have different day to day responsibilities. Some staff work directly to the generality of Assembly Members in the Office of the Presiding Officer and under the Presiding Officer's direction. Their role will be to support the work of the Assembly in its plenary sessions and committees, and to provide other services to Members to support them in carrying out their roles fully and effectively…
>
> The majority of the Assembly's staff … will work for the Assembly Secretaries and the Assembly Cabinet as a whole.

It might be thought that the distinctions might not be entirely clear in all circumstances and, as Rawlings (2003: 163) points out, in one situation there was a dispute as to whether the Assembly had the right to determine certain structural features of the civil service. It demonstrated tensions in the corporate model in a dynamic situation and there was a recognition of this with the Assembly looking to separate those civil servants who worked for the Government (executive) and those who worked for the Assembly (Parliament).

The Hain White Paper recognised that the various changes would have further implications for the civil service. Civil servants would in future act exclusively in support of the Welsh Assembly Government Ministers. This would affect most obviously the position of those staff currently working in the Assembly Parliamentary Service. They are the nearest Welsh equivalents to the staff employed by the Scottish Parliamentary Corporate Body, who provide support for the Scottish Parliament as distinct from the Scottish Executive.

Staff serving the Welsh Assembly Ministers would continue to be civil servants. Staff supporting the Assembly Parliamentary Service would, like servants of both the UK and Scottish Parliaments, not be part of the civil service. The Assembly as a legislature and scrutinising body would employ its own staff, although it would be expected to maintain terms and conditions for staff broadly comparable to those applying to Assembly Government civil servants.

However in these early years, civil servants working for ministers were not paired with an official departmental head, as in Whitehall (and indeed Stormont). Instead the expectation was that the ministers would work with a range of officials, reflecting, as Jon Shortridge puts it, 'the Assembly was .. established to break down the compartmentalised mentality' (quoted in Rawlings 2003: 163). It is interesting to note that as the Welsh Assembly Government organisation matured the Permanent Secretary moved to establish Ministerial Departments, wherever possible.

The civil service has grown since devolution, especially in a number of policy areas, including economic policy, agriculture and rural affairs and social policy. Remembering that Ron Davies had made much of keeping costs down and promised that no more than 100 additional civil servants would be necessary, the growth has been substantial — over 50% — and has impacted on the old Welsh Office culture (see Appendix three). No one in 1999 could have predicted this growth, nor the numbers of 'outsiders' coming into the civil service.

In addition a number of quangos have been drawn into the Assembly and in July 2004, Rhodri Morgan announced the merger of the Welsh Assembly Government with three Assembly Sponsored Public Bodies or quangos:

- Education and Learning Wales (ELWa);
- the Welsh Development Agency; and
- the Wales Tourist Board.

On 30 November 2004 further changes were announced by the First Minister:

> Our policy is that where executive Assembly sponsored public bodies undertake functions which are governmental either on policy or delivery, they should be brought in-house. You can justify the existence of arm's-length bodies in government, but there is no such thing as arm's-length public money. Ministers are always responsible for its allocation and the Assembly is always responsible for its scrutiny. There is no dodging that responsibility.

As a result, the functions of the Welsh Language Board were to be merged into the Welsh Assembly Government from April 2007 and changes were also made to the Arts Council of Wales and the Sports Council for Wales, which would continue in existence. In addition the Qualifications, Curriculum and Assessment Authority for Wales would be merged with the Assembly Government by April 2006.

There is little doubt that the civil service faced a range of challenges with devolution; commentators speak of a culture shock, as the civil service came to terms with the demanding environment of the Assembly. In particular, the ability of the civil service to come to terms with its new policy making role has been deemed its hardest challenge (Rawlings 2003: 168-170) but the service has also sought to develop in its own way the public management agenda of Whitehall: the 'Delivering Better Government' initiative, (the Welsh variation of Modernising Government) as well as e-government and EFQM quality management. The point we made in the previous chapter that the changes of devolution did not come singly but in conjunction with other changes is borne out. There has been a Human Resources and Diversity project team, a Leadership and Teamworking group, a Better Policy project team, and new IT changes are being introduced, with all the issues they bring. And, of course, there is encouragement to spread the use of the Welsh language. Rawlings was right in saying: 'the somewhat sleepy Welsh Office, this is not ... the constitutional development that is national devolution locks up with these broader trends in public administration, and allows the local administration greater scope for experimentation and innovation in the tools and techniques of (small country) governance' (Rawlings 2003: 172).

A number of key changes have been introduced to meet these challenges. The administration's policy unit has been 'shook up', at the request of the First Minister, an old critic of the lack of policy expertise in the Welsh Office, and the unit, called the Strategic Policy Unit, has expanded and incorporates the Cabinet's special advisers and is responsible to the First Minister. In addition, an Executive Board has been created, amongst other things, to provide advice to the Permanent Secretary on input to Cabinet, and managing the priorities and targets of the Welsh Assembly Government. It includes a number of key civil servants, a political adviser, and two external or non-executive directors. We will say much more about the Executive Board, a key and interesting feature, in a later chapter.

Continuing changes are likely to occur, as devolution itself develops. Thus far we have not talked of a separate Welsh civil service, similar to the Northern Ireland Civil Service, being created. As we have indicated, and everyone agrees, the conditions of service and broad traditions of the Home Civil Service offer reassurances, important given the range and number of changes. However it is likely that some developments will occur over time. Nonetheless — and central to our concerns — there is no doubt that the civil servants and the civil service have been greatly affected by devolution. To quote Rhodri Morgan:

> The main focus of the Assembly civil servants has moved to Wales itself and to relations with the wider world. Officials have had to quickly develop new skills and competencies, in particular those concerning policy development, engagement with the Assembly's partners and sensitivity to Ministers' political agenda. (Rhodri Morgan quoted in Rawlings 200: 158)

Passing the Mantle

In addition, and supporting the importance of our Macmillan remarks about *events*, the head of the Welsh Office, Rachel Lomax, moved on, to be replaced by Jon Shortridge. The unexpected departure of Rachel Lomax in 1999, to the role of Permanent Secretary at the Department for Work and Pensions, placed additional pressures on the remaining senior civil servants in Cardiff. The two leading figures of devolution — at least in terms of 'making it happen' — the politician Ron Davies and the civil servant Rachel Lomax, were no longer to play a leading role in making devolution a reality in Wales.

The civil service mantle passed to Jon Shortridge, who had been overseeing the devolution processes through his individual responsibilities and through his oversight of the Devolution Unit, and although this transition was relatively easy for someone experienced in devolution policy and planning, the impact on the organization of managing yet another unexpected change should not be underestimated. Not only did it mean a change of leadership at the top of the organization but it also led, domino-like, to changes in other senior posts. It also meant the loss of Rachel Lomax's knowledge and commitment to the devolution process.

Jon Shortridge's appointment certainly represented *continuity*, as he knew the workings of the Welsh Office intimately, but it also represented significant *change* at the highest level of the civil service. As we show elsewhere in this book (see chapters 4 and 7c), Jon Shortridge's leadership style was (and presumably remains) different from that of Rachel Lomax and this change had to be 'taken in their stride' by senior civil servants. The change was helped by the fact that whilst there was a genuine feeling of loss, following Rachel Lomax's departure, this was more than compensated for by Jon Shortridge's appointment: senior civil servants were pleased that one of their own had been chosen to lead them into a new world, with its uncharted waters. Most of the senior people we spoke with concurred that it was Jon Shortridge's leadership that made a substantial contribution to the Assembly civil service's ability to, in their words, 'keep the business going' and 'avoid reputational damage' during a period of tumultuous change.

Conclusion

As we indicated at the beginning the story of Welsh Devolution has been complex, has thrown up interesting constitutional innovations and is constantly in flux. And it is clear that the story is not yet over: changes will occur. In some ways the initial model is one that has satisfied few and it is not surprising that this is now being tested and expanded to something more solid. The story of the rise and fall of the corporate nature of the Assembly illustrates this and it is to this that we now turn.

THE SINGLE CORPORATE BODY
AND THE CIVIL SERVICE

Introduction

The National Assembly for Wales was created as a single corporate body. This means that one organisation is responsible for discharging both legislative and executive functions, rather than separate organisations being responsible for each of these as in the traditional Westminster/Whitehall model.

One of the reasons why a corporate structure was favoured when the original legislation was drafted was that it drew upon existing practice in local government at that time. But over the past few years, Welsh local authorities have moved to a Cabinet style of government with executive members taking decisions and being held to account by overview and scrutiny committees.

Under the Assembly's existing arrangements, executive functions are not conferred on Ministers as happens in the traditional model. Instead they are conferred on the Assembly as a whole. The Assembly Members then delegate these functions to the First Minister by a vote in a plenary session -delegations which can be withdrawn at any time by another plenary resolution (White Paper 2005).

We have already referred to the corporate body model; and the corporate nature of the Assembly, how that evolved, and the role of the civil service in its introduction, as being a key part of the story of devolution in Wales. The National Assembly for Wales was created as a single corporate body — what Rawlings (2003) referred to as the unique character or 'strange autonomy' of Welsh devolution — and this meant that one organisation became responsible for discharging both legislative and executive functions, rather than separate organisations being responsible for each of these as in the traditional Westminster model.

We discussed with a range of interviewees why this model was chosen and were surprised by the different explanations given to us. Although it was difficult, but not impossible, to find people who defended the impeccable logic behind the original decision, it was far easier to find those who, from the start, believed that the concept of a single corporate body would never work. These two statements, from the most influential of politicians, illustrate this early concern over the efficacy of the constitutional arrangement:

> The first line [of the Government of Wales Act] goes something like: 'there shall be a corporate body to be known as the National

Assembly for Wales' and the equivalent first line of the Scotland Act is 'there shall be in Scotland a Scottish Parliament'. If you can keep it nice and simple in Scotland, why can't you just say there shall be a National Assembly for Wales full stop? Why do we have to add a definition? The only explanation I was given was 'Everybody knows what a Parliament is and nobody knows what an Assembly is (Rt. Hon. Rhodri Morgan, First Minister).

During the passage of the Devolution Bill, a number of us were brought alongside by Ron Davies to support him and the development of the concept. From the beginning, although it's easy for me to say now with hindsight, I had serious doubts about the nature of the structure — and I was in good company. I had serious doubts about the possibility of civil servants being able to function as parliamentary officials: those doubts have been proved right and we are now in the middle of a difficult separation (Lord Dafydd Elis-Thomas Presiding Officer).

Various Explanations for the Creation of a Single Corporate Body

For the first three months of the research period we were intrigued by the number of different explanations given to us for the introduction of a single corporate body. Each time we were given an explanation most speakers set out to convey to us that their view was definitive: it was the real reason for a decision that most people now considered problematic. Other people, some of whom are senior politicians and civil servants, merely shrugged their shoulders and explained that the whole issue was shrouded in mystery.

Those people who took a view, and there were many such people, held their views strongly and it was clear to us that within the ranks of politicians and senior civil servants many diametrically opposed views existed and we became determined to discover the 'truth' of that initial decision (something which we recognised may be odds with our methodological approach but to which we were inexorably drawn). We were not prepared to take the diplomatic route of the White Paper and conclude that:

> One of the reasons why a corporate structure was favoured when the original legislation was drafted was that it drew upon existing practice in local government at that time'. 'One of the reasons' was not good enough.

These are the six most popular reasons — some of which have become the stuff of urban myth — held by politicians and senior civil servants. They are not of course mutually exclusive, but they have different emphases.

Reason 1: Vision or Idealism

A single corporate body was a visionary, imaginative, innovative new form of government for Wales driven by Ron Davies and his passionate belief in partnership. His view was that, in Wales, most politicians were centre-left, and even the Tories had similar objectives for Wales: so he saw no problem in having a cabinet that was comprised of a Labour health minister, a Tory agriculture minister, a Plaid education minister and a Liberal environment minister (for example). There was a widely held view that had he stayed, Ron Davies, with the support of Dafydd Wigley and others might just have pulled it off. Others think it was naivety in the extreme but agree that 'vision or idealism' was the reason.

> Some things haven't worked well but that's down to politics. We created a certain framework and the British people, and politicians, are not used to such a framework. The French could understand it: power rests with the people; it's transferred to elected representatives; they select a president or ministers. That's the model here in Wales with the National Assembly, led by the principle of delegation and so the National Assembly can do it all themselves (i.e. they can run all services) if they wish. It was only when Alun Michael was faced with a lack of confidence that the National Assembly decided to withdraw the delegated powers given to him (Senior civil servant).

> I think there were two main assumptions in the Bill, that Ron Davies would be First Minister (Secretary) and that there would be a Labour majority, and neither of these assumptions came to pass. I think everything was predicated on that. Whatever his motives, Ron Davies felt that he was strong on what he called 'inclusive politics': he had a very close personal relationship with Dafydd Wigley and I think he felt that could transcend all sorts of political difficulties. That's why I hold to the view that you can't design structures on the basis of personality, you have to design them to withstand any eventuality. Maybe it was a just sign of the times, maybe it was undue optimism – a new style of politics that would go against nearly every other political system in the world (Current Cabinet Minister).

> In those early NAAG days the conception of the then Secretary of State Ron Davies and others was that there would be an all-party group: a 'Rainbow Alliance' (as it was later called) running Wales, and I think that was reflected in early drafts of the Government of Wales Bill that, what are now the Chairs of the Assembly Committees would have been members of the Government, so they would have been drawn proportionately from the four parties (Politician and NAAG member).

Reason 2: Pragmatism

Ron Davies was a pragmatist and he knew that Number 10, and many senior Labour Party politicians, were unlikely to concede too much to Wales. The support for devolution was not widespread. So Ron Davies, using his belief in devolution being a 'process rather than an event', took what he could get as he didn't want to 'frighten the horses' and he knew that he would be able to get more at some other time.

As one senior politician told us:

> You'll have to speak to Ron Davies but he's previously told me, though perhaps not in these words, that it was the best deal he could get out of the Labour Cabinet at the time. Remember Ron wanted speed, and all his deals were done two years before 1997. He got the political parties on board prior to the 1997 election. Local Government re-organisation[3] was all part of that same deal. The Tories opposed it but all the other parties agreed it because it was applying the right model for devolution.

A senior civil servant elaborated on this view:

> My take on it, for what it's worth, is that it wasn't so much a question of what Ron could get out of No 10, it was what Ron could sell to the divided Labour Party, the Wales Labour Party, and at the same time he had got to try and reach out to some extent to opinion in other parties who just felt that the Assembly would be South Wales Labour.

This latter quote illustrates how vision and pragmatism may well have come together. It might have been that Ron Davies had a vision of an inclusive polity, but given the fragility of devolution policy in Wales and the history of fears about the consequences of the exercise of power in a devolved Wales, creating a coalition in favour of devolution made political sense. Many politicians and civil servants nonetheless would concur with the following comment:

> It was a wild pipe dream. Why would the Conservatives and Plaid want to help Labour? The game of politics doesn't work like that. It meant a confused electorate and it resulted in no overall control in the first term. Then there was the confusion of who's in charge of what. Democratic chaos. Rhodri Morgan was right to say 'enough is enough' and to separate WAG and the rest. People don't understand a gooey, grey mass of legislative and executive Assembly: who's responsible, who's accountable?

---

[3]   This of course had been Conservative policy.

Reason 3: Myopia or Tunnel Vision

The Labour Party had been out of power for 17 years and the only type of government they were familiar with was local government. Therefore, and especially as they saw Wales as little more than a region (or a 'super district council', in the words of their critics), they applied the local government model to Wales even though, and somewhat inexplicably, they were developing plans to change local government to a cabinet style of government.

These are the views of two senior civil servants:

> The Labour Party came in after a long time without being in power in central government and the democratic model they were used to running was the one they had in Local Government.
> The Labour Party was wrong. What happened, was that the Labour Party in opposition, not having any experience of government for 20 years or 18 years or whatever it was, reached the conclusion on the form of the Assembly based on the only thing that they knew, which was local authorities. And the Assembly was set up effectively as a large local authority.

This view may even have been supported by an assumption that many AMs would come from local government and be comfortable with a world they knew.

Reason 4: Error

It was a mistake: a mistake that occurred as a result of the 'terrible time and work pressures' to make devolution happen against tight deadlines and the legal necessity to create a legal personality — a single corporate body — for the Assembly. Whilst they spotted the need to create executive committees (a cabinet with ministers), rather than advisory committees, they failed to spot the repercussions of this decision.

Two senior civil servant quotes pointed to such an error:

> I still feel sadly it was a big mistake and we've lost a bit of time as a result of the brave efforts to come up with a world first, a multi-party approach to governing a country.
> The turning point was the Alun Michael debacle, where AMs started to assert themselves. AMs had been cosy from 1999 for about 6 months, they were glad to be members of the Assembly, and then the Alun Michael issues arose. Then we saw a big flaw in the constitutional arrangement of the Assembly and the Assembly Government. We thought it could work but it didn't. This was the beginning of the separation of the APS and WAG.

The following quote is typical of what a number of politicians and civil servants told us:

> One corporate body was just not on and it was a political and civil service error. It was rather naïve to think we could make it work: a single corporate body and a belief in 'let's all work together', in non-confrontational politics, in all Party committees developing policy, in not using the title minister, and in not being clear about the status of the Cabinet and Executive as opposed to the Assembly corporately. The novelty and impracticality of it became apparent and AMs said they wanted a traditional Parliament and Executive and scrutiny via committees. Early on there was a vote by AMs who said that what they wanted was not one corporate body but as much separation as the statute would allow. Everyone tried to make it work but the new structures didn't gel with reality and so the civil servants were wrong footed and were serving ministers, committees, and the AMs thought everyone could have access to the civil servants, but Ministers said that only they could have access to civil servants. Also the PO and others thought that as the civil servants were all working to the Permanent Secretary, who was working for the First Minister, and that they were secretly collaborating with the PS and the FM against the interests of the PO.

One civil servant, with brutal honesty, reflected on the process:

> We had to draw up a project plan and at an early stage (and this is one of the weaknesses of project management) we had to decide on a critical path and once we were on it we had to follow it. We didn't have time to look at different models and we should have been more thoughtful—evidence based—to see what Parliaments across the world were doing.

In an earlier interview one civil servant told us that in the early days of planning devolution 'Ron Davies saw himself as Gordon Gecko (Michael Douglas) in the film *Wall Street*: there were lots of people going into his room, there was tight project management in place, decisions were made quickly on everything. You went in and came out with a decision even though he challenged you. This was essential and we wouldn't have achieved it if there had been micro management.'

When we related this story to the civil servant who had commented on the possible deficiencies in project management he added, somewhat poignantly:

> Perhaps that was the down side of Ron's 'snappiness' over decisions.

Reason 5: Conspiracy Theory

The suspicion between some politicians and certain civil servants, and even the civil service at large, existing in the early days of devolution (and still existing for some even today) is reflected in the following quote, a view that was repeated in a number of interviews:

> Many of the politicians felt that the view of the civil service was to have as little change as possible and there was a view that committees of the Assembly would be staffed by AMs who would be given papers on time but nothing else. The Welsh Office wanted to run the show as before and the principle of holding the government to account was suppressed as far as it could be. The attitude was: 'Why make a rod for one's back?' The Assembly started, so claim some AMs, with evidence of that behaviour and someone said that in the early days the agenda for the Assembly committee meetings had to be OK'd by the First Minister. That's unthinkable now, just as in Parliament the Prime Minister wouldn't approve the work of the committees. But it was not absurd at the beginning of the Assembly and there is a view that the civil servants wanted to control the Assembly and that the intention of the Welsh Office was to carry on as before devolution, with the 60 AMs acting as a super-consultative body who could be ignored or patronised.

Reason 6: Bewilderment

The mystification or bewilderment theory is best explained by the words of First Minister Rhodri Morgan speaking of his experience as a Westminster MP at the time of the devolution White Paper and the Government of Wales Bill and Act:

> Certainly, the mental picture I had, until seeing the first line of the Government of Wales Act, was that everybody accepted that the system we were going to set up to govern Wales was going to be a weaker, more attenuated version of the system that was going to be set up to govern Scotland but was not going to be different in the basic model — namely that people would be elected and if one of the parties had a majority they would form an administration. There would be committees which would probably be far more important than at Westminster. Then we found that it was a totally different model, based on local government law and at the same time that everybody was wanting to move local government law away from a corporate body towards cabinet/back bench/front bench/separate scrutiny. There are no doubt reasons, which constitutional lawyers could probably explain to you, why it had to be done that way. It was certainly a surprise to me.

Discovering 'The Truth'

Was the introduction of the single corporate body a masterful con-spiratorial civil service plan? Or, more boringly, was it a mere error? Was Ron Davies exercising a careful pragmatism or was he fenced-in by Number 10's limited aspirations for Wales? Or was the entire ven-ture a part of the new Secretary of State's idealistic notion of a new form of inclusive politics for Wales, one based on meaningful part-nership?

In our interviews we raised these different explanations with a number of people and partly owing to the structure of our interview plan, and partly owing to the diaries of the people to be interviewed, we had the opportunity of asking Rachel Lomax, Jon Shortridge and Ron Davies last of all.

Lord Elis-Thomas, the Presiding Officer, told us that there were officials who agreed with him and who struggled to get more flexi-bility for the body. He also claimed to have worked 'fairly closely' with the officials who were on the Bill team, along with a number of others, when they were trying to create a Cabinet system and super-impose it on the single body. However, he did not think that there was an understanding of 'the qualitative difference between the vesting of powers in the Secretary of State and then those powers being vested in the corporate body'. He believed that there was a cul-tural issue which confirmed 'my prejudiced view' that what was being created was a 'business as usual' model that would ensure that the old Welsh Office systems would continue to function, despite the fact that it now had to be accountable to elected members.

Professor Nick Bourne, apart from being a Party leader was a member of NAAG and interestingly, for the purpose of our research, was an academic lawyer. His views were given partly as politician and partly as former academic:

> I never thought that it was going to work and that was a view shared on NAAG. We thought we would be much better served by a Westminster-type model, which people understand and allows for differences in political approach that wouldn't be so easy in a Cabinet made-up of all four political parties. Ron Davies accepted that and the Bill was changed, although there remained an overhang of some of the thinking that had gone into the origi-nal idea of a united body. In consequence of that, some features remained in the Bill, like the corporate status feature which led to friction (probably not too strong a word), certainly stresses and strains, once you have a system where you have a governing party and the opposition parties and, initially at least, a civil ser-

vice that is really just serving the government, without the division that they have in Westminster.

We asked Professor Bourne that if NAAG had felt that the single corporate body wouldn't work — and many backbench MPs agreed with NAAG's view — then why did it go ahead? He replied:

To be fair, I don't think we articulated our objection quite that clearly. We said we thought we needed a traditional model of Government and Opposition but we didn't, perhaps, put our constitutional hats on and take it a stage further and say 'therefore we need a split between Executive and Legislature and therefore we can't have a corporate body status'. I think the thing that was really driving us was the idea that we did need to have a Government party, or parties, and Opposition parties, and once that went through I think many of us heaved a sigh of relief and said: 'Well at least we're going to have a system where people would know that they were voting for a clear manifesto, and we wouldn't have a mish-mash of everybody in the Government together'. Probably what we should have articulated is that there are consequential changes but we didn't really take it forward to that next stage. So I don't think it would be fair to lay the blame at anyone's door: things were moving on apace and there were strict deadlines, so I think one would have to go back and look at the pressures that existed. With the benefit of hindsight we should have seen much earlier the need to separate the Executive from the Legislature.

We asked him whether, as an academic lawyer, he thought this separation could have been achieved whilst retaining the single corporate body legal identity.

In a *de facto* sense but never wholly satisfactorily, I don't think. We're almost there now but it hasn't been carried through to its logical conclusion. We've muddled through it in a very British way but still, in the minds of the public, the Assembly gets blamed for things, or occasionally gets the credit for things, when it's really down to the Welsh Assembly Government.

Three senior civil servants shed further light on the reason for the constitutional arrangements:

It was confusing. There were a lot of people not really thinking about what it was going to be like, it was difficult to know what it was going to be like, and to some extent it was unknowable. I think, in effect, the Civil Service had assisted at the birth of this creature and to a large extent made the birth in the timescale possible. Once it was born it necessarily took on a life of its own and started developing, to some extent, in ways that couldn't reasonably have been foreseen. Nobody would have foreseen the toppling of the First Secretary— as he was still then called— so quickly, and that sort of thing, and nobody would have foreseen accurately at the outset that Assembly politicians would grow such a strong consensus, so quickly, that some way needed to be found to delineate the division more sharply between the administration of the day and the Assembly as the democratic body of the 60. So, as we moved towards that clearer demarcation it became clearer and clearer that the bulk of the Civil Servants were going to be working for ministers, rather as in a conventional way to the Department, and that there would be a group of officials who would work also for the Assembly as a body corporate but really as the House of Commons Clerks' Service. I think we actually all grew rather more comfortable because the idea of working for a body corporate in the way that people do in local government— of course it's feasible, everybody in local government does it every day of the week— but it is not the tradition that most of us were used to, even those of us who had been outside and worked for a chairman and board.

We started off with a Bill very much modelled around local government but when we got into it with Ministers, the less comfortable we all felt. But by that stage, the Bill had been introduced, so we grafted on to it a Cabinet style structure. It was a bit of a hybrid. If it had been spotted earlier, I'm sure we could have drafted a Bill that set up a Parliament and Executive but I think we would have had difficulty getting the critical mass of people needed to set up the Parliament. I think the Labour Ministers were keen to introduce the Bill straight away, so had we said on day one that we didn't think it would work so we suggest this model instead, I don't think they would have bought it because they were more comfortable with the local authority model. It was only later that we all realised that it wouldn't work and we needed to try a different model. Going back to risk management, maybe we shouldn't expect to get everything right first time: the only way we would have found out what works is by experience.

No, no, no, no, we (the civil service) weren't wrong. The Labour Party was wrong. The Assembly was set up effectively as a large local authority and corporate body status flowed inevitably from that. Just as every local authority is a corporate body so was the Assembly. I can tell you that it took our instructing lawyer and his team all of 5 seconds: 'Is this going to be a corporate body? Well yes, of course it has to be. We haven't got any choice.'

Many politicians and civil servants will admit that one corporate body was the ideal vision but also admit cynicism about its ability to work 'because we know politicians!' Whilst they understand that there may well be different mechanisms in Europe they also appreciate that politicians do not operate in the same way in all countries

and that in Wales, as in the remainder of the UK, each Party has a different agenda and politicians will not collaborate.

One of our sources summed it up with graphic language:

> Politicians engaged with the Assembly prefer the Westminster
> Parliamentary model and wanted to separate the Parliamentary
> and Executive functions. They wanted Committees that were
> Westminster style Committees; the select committee system;
> 'usual channels'; and all the other paraphernalia of Westminster.
> Other countries may not operate like that, and it may work in
> Switzerland or wherever, but this is Wales.

One senior civil servant explained how pragmatism attempted to
overcome the practical weaknesses that were spotted in the constitutional arrangement:

> The corporate body was untenable and we should have seen it.
> Labour wanted consensus and it is true that there is less opposi-
> tion here than in Parliament. Everyone shouldn't have been so
> starry eyed about all parties pulling in the same direction.
> Because of Labour Party discussions and the design of Devolu-
> tion on a fag packet, Ron Davies recognised that given the votes
> for Devolution, and his colleagues' views of the Assembly, he
> could only go so far in untangling the body corporate issue. Civil
> servants came up with a clever ruse that, through delegation, all
> powers were given to the National Assembly, who then trans-
> ferred power to the First Minister, who then delegated powers to
> Ministers, but at any time the Assembly could take away those
> powers. Ron Davies couldn't go any further. We sorted the Cabi-
> net issue as the Bill went through but we were still a corporate
> organisation. The strength of the Cabinet had not been fully
> reflected in the arrangements and there was no recognition of
> Presiding Office power and independence.

And another senior civil servant understood exactly the reason for
the lack of clarity in the constitutional arrangements:

> No government or political party should have come into office
> with a commitment to such a complicated form of government
> without having worked it out in Opposition. We had a blank
> sheet of paper and 12–14 weeks to prepare a White Paper that
> would result in a Referendum. There were many problems and
> we had no time to work them out properly. We were stuck with
> the idea of the Assembly as a single entity and a set of account-
> ability structures. The thing was flawed from the outset and
> experience confirms that it was flawed. It might have worked but
> even if events hadn't provoked things, the problems would have
> emerged.

Armed with five specific theories to account for the rationale behind the introduction of a single corporate, and with a number of people who did not possess a rational explanation, we decided to present these views to Rachel Lomax, Sir Jon Shortridge and Ron Davies. The full account of our discussions with the Permanent Secretaries is recorded in *The Chief Servants' Tale* and with Ron Davies in *The Architect's Tale*. What they said to us concerning the creation of the single corporate body is recorded here in point form only.

When we put the various opinions to Rachel Lomax she reacted quite tersely as she, no doubt and quite understandably, saw our questions as in some way challenging the very integrity, impartiality and professionalism of the civil service she had led. She explained to us that:

- the local authority model which had been used in the 1970s was all that was on offer for Wales

- the broad parameters had been agreed by Labour in Opposition and the job for the civil service was to make it as workable as possible

- tactically, the trick was to introduce devolution and begin to grow a political class in Wales that could get by initially and achieve something better in the future

- some of the people who entered the Assembly had a Westminster model in their mind — it was in their bloodstream

Sir Jon Shortridge confirmed that the single corporate body had been a 'given' and the civil service could not simply 'tear it up'. They had to seek to define what was meant by the idea: it was quite clear that it was intended that the Assembly combine an executive and a legislature and be very much on a local authority model essentially.

Ron Davies's response was fuller in that he broadened the reasons for the introduction of the single corporate body. Whilst he dismissed the 'conspiracy' and 'cock-up' theories he agreed that the reasons for the constitutional arrangement were multi-faceted: 'I don't think they're necessarily mutually exclusive'. His views can be summarised thus:

- it was a legal necessity to create an entity which developed the notion of a corporate body

- as part of the Labour Party's internal agreement there was the plan to follow the local government model

- certainly there was an element of pragmatism.

But, above all, what Ron Davies wanted was inclusivity. That's what he believed in and that is where he was driving. He denied that the Assembly had been designed for a Labour majority as his political project, regardless of what the electoral arithmetic might have been, was to have a new style of government based on a meaningful coalition. He also defended the impartiality of the civil service in the whole process and described their role merely as being part of a process of articulation: the civil servants were articulating emerging ideas.

What is remarkable in this whole examination and series of interviews is the extent to which senior people, politicians and civil servants, take such contradictory views over the genesis of the single corporate body. One is left wondering 'why?': why didn't they ask Ron Davies, why didn't they ask the senior civil servants involved in the process, why did they prefer to believe their own theory rather than understand that the reasons were multitudinous? But, fortunately, many of them were largely right.

Executive Rather than Advisory Bodies

This is a truly fascinating point: did the change from 'Committee Government' to 'Cabinet Government' arise following a sudden and pragmatic change of opinion in an 'away day' attended by politicians and civil servants; or as part of a planned and well thought out process; or only when the political timing and the support of other Parties allowed it to happen; or because it was realised that it was rather naïve to think that political collaboration, of the type envisaged, could work?

Our research revealed that there are many differing views, and sometimes these differing views are expressed rather subtly, and they demonstrate different roles for the civil service. But in all the various interpretations of the policy change the civil service were clearly key change agents in bringing about the change. The degree of actual change management varies, of course, according to the interpretation put upon these events. What follows are different perspectives of the same events rather than a disagreement on what took place.

A senior civil servant came across a report, by the Audit Commission, on the local authority committee system and presented the report's findings at the 'away-day' held at the Glamorgan Building opposite Cathays Park ('We always used university accommodation so that we wouldn't be seen meeting in hotels'). There were a number of such meetings and they were interactive with Ron Davies, junior ministers and civil servants present and it was notable to see politicians and civil servants working together and Ron Davies was seen to trust civil servants far more than many other Ministers they had worked for. A civil servant, with support from other colleagues, suggested that if the National Assembly went the way of local authority committees then it would be inoperable. Those present were taken by the strength of the argument. It started inauspiciously when Rachel Lomax asked a civil servant to make a presentation to Ministers by Powerpoint and the IT system collapsed as he was using it. This was greeted by hooting from Ministers. When the civil servant was two-thirds of the way through his revised presentation Ron Davies said: 'OK. I'm not changing the Bill fundamentally but if we change to a Cabinet system how can that be done?' Ron Davies clearly wanted the change to occur but was not sure of the evidence, or how it should be done, but the civil service gave Ministers a far-reaching solution. One of the civil servants, an academic lawyer by profession, stood up and drew a flow chart to explain how the change could be achieved. And so it was done: a fundamental shift in the way Wales would be governed.

The basic facts of the above account, if not each and every detail, were substantiated in our interviews with the former Secretary of State, the two Permanent Secretaries, other civil servants and it is recorded on the BBC Wales 'fly on the wall' documentary of those devolution events. What is surprising is that the civil servant concerned could not recollect those events when we interviewed him. Such is the self-sacrificing service of the civil servant or was it that he, unlike his superiors, thought that, for a moment or so, he had crossed that very fine line between articulating Ministerial aspirations and undertaking an executive role oneself? As Sir Jon Shortridge emphasised in our interview with him: 'There was nothing manipulative about that. The basic commission was to produce an Assembly that would operate through some sort of committee system. I was always very clear that when you have a committee system, power would always migrate to the political leadership, it was just a question of how it would migrate. Once the politicians saw the illogicality of delegation via the Committees they were happy to have delegation to the First Minister [Secretary] and then to the Ministers.'

However, the intriguing component in the reflections on what took place is the three interpretations that have emerged amongst colleague civil servants and politicians. As with all such explanations there is a degree of overlap but each is sufficiently robust to stand as a separate view.

The first interpretation demonstrates how the issue of being a single corporate body became linked with, and in some instances confused with, the notion of advisory or executive committees and the specific authority and role of Ministers:

Interpretation #1: We were a single corporate body and you must remember that the vision of the Assembly was that it was not a legislative but an executive body, carrying out the former Secretary of State functions. Therefore, it was like a very large county council and so it needed a legal personality to employ staff, issue contracts etc. Someone needed these functions to be given to them and for us to be a legal entity in our own right. The problem was that it became apparent that the Assembly, although it had executive functions, would also be a quasi-Parliament. That's where the single body concept started to split: if it was to be a Parliament holding the executive to account, then how could it be a single body. The Assembly is accountable for a range of functions and 60 AMs couldn't do it as a group. The White Paper said: 'the Assembly would be run by committee' and that was the proposition put to the people in the Referendum. After the Referendum began, and through NAAG, there was a greater feeling that we needed Ministers or, at the least, individuals in charge. But you must remember that there's a difference between a Minister here and a Minister in Whitehall. In Whitehall, Ministers are appointees of the Queen and hold office on that basis and then are accountable to Parliament—but they hold their office by the Queen's appointment. So in London you have two things: executive government—the Queen's Government—and you have a Parliament. We didn't have that. With us, Ministers are people to whom the National Assembly powers have been delegated. The initial vision was that the Ministers would be held to account by the Assembly and this would be the check on those people exercising the power of the sixty. But it became a Parliamentary structure and this was mainly because of the pressure of the Presiding Officer who wanted a Parliamentary system and for the executive to be seen as separate. The 'separability' element became confused with the corporate body issue. It was assumed that the corporate body was very significant but it was intended to give legal personality and not to bind everyone together. There is a difficulty: if you compare local government you can have people acting on behalf of the authority. It works well as the parliamentary/legislative side is minimal and cabinets in local government are acting on behalf of the local authority with little scrutiny and no legislation. However, in the Assembly there is an executive body and a quasi-Parliament, they have debates on policy and they perform a deliberative function.

The second Interpretation is seen through a political and pragmatic lens:

Interpretation #2: Colleagues forget there was a political process and a coalition to be delivered. Ron Davies had to hold this through the legislation and what happened was that all parties favoured a Cabinet model, although Labour had thought that the Opposition would be against a Cabinet model. When it became clear that the other parties would support a Cabinet then Ron Davies went for it. The Parties whose leaders were Westminster Parliamentarians were strongly in favour of it, especially those who thought they'd get power. The Cabinet concept was even stronger after the presentation on the Audit Commission paper on committees. The paper was used to show that committees were good for certain activities but bad for other activities. Also, at this time, there was legislation trying to force the local authorities from the Committee model to the Cabinet model in local government. In addition, as Ron Davies was a Secretary of State he couldn't be seen to be arguing against a Cabinet model. But we had legislation going through Parliament at this time and therefore it would mean a major amendment to the framework.

The third interpretation is a variation on the political theme but also plays up the civil service role in events:

Interpretation #3: Ron Davies needed something that the other Parties could buy into, but 'Committee Government' was seen as a hideous mistake. The single body and the committee system were there because Ron Davies was selling something to the other Parties, to get them on board and to enable them to have a role in devolution. It was shared power amongst the parties and the committee system was a part of that. It was only when Ron Davies could keep the support of the Parties that he could move into the cabinet system. The civil servants played a strong role in getting this changed – it was a civil service inspired process. Ron Davies responded to this positively: he had the vision, the civil servants checked the thinking and it happened.

Ron Davies's View

A fuller account of Ron Davies's view is recorded in *The Architect's Tale* but this brief quote is sufficient to show that in his view the decision was very much his, and that of his political colleagues, and that it was based on the logic of an emerging situation:

> We had a famous away-day, with politicians and civil servants, just to talk about how it might work in practice. We were actually testing the decision-making capacity and we were looking at things like: What happens if you're dealing with inward investment? What happens if you're dealing with policy decisions? You have to have the capacity to make decisions, you have to inevitably move to Cabinet government, we needed to move to Ministers away from the committee systems. Committees have a role, and they ultimately have a role in terms of policy development, but there's a difference between policy development and policy execution and that was the compromise, a sensible compromise, that we came to.

Quod erat demonstrandum.

Conclusion

The story remains an interesting one and one that has not yet finished, given the White Paper. In many ways it illustrates the confused nature of political decision-making. Story telling in many ways brings out that confusion, offering a range of truths.

Chapter 4

People and Change

I am a great admirer of the way in which the old Welsh Office civil servants set themselves up to deliver the institution into existence in a very short space of time (Lord Dafydd Elis-Thomas, Presiding Officer).

Introduction

During the research for this book we interviewed nearly fifty people, held a focus group, read hundreds of official documents concerning the work of the numerous internal committees involved in introducing devolution to Wales, examined various papers on general public policy matters, but there was only one document that caused consternation. It was a minute (internal memorandum) written by a senior civil servant in response to the Head of the Devolution Unit's invitation to establish a working group to examine the impact of devolution on Welsh Office staff and to prepare them for the arrival of the Assembly.

The minute, dated 21st May 1997 and copied to four other civil servants, included these words:.

Welsh Assembly

1. We had a word about setting in train the Task Group ... which will be responsible for developing and overseeing the implementation of the change management elements of establishing a Welsh Assembly.

2. We agreed that the first step should be a meeting of you and any of yours you wish to involve, together with copy addressees of this minute and me.

3. The purposes of the meeting will be:

    i. to identify the things that need to be achieved and the likely timetable for their achievement;

    ii. the mechanisms and processes of the Task Group, including the terms of reference and membership. On the latter, we committed ourselves at the recent Departmental Whitley Council to close consultation with the trade union side from the earliest stages. We will need to consider how to achieve that.

4. You kindly agreed to circulate for the meeting a note on what you see as some of the main things you will be looking for from the Task Group and by when we might expect to have to achieve them.

5. Off the top of my head, here is a list of the sort of things which we will need to cover:

    1. staffing issues, including status, terms and conditions of transfer and the split between the Secretary of State's office and the Assembly;

    2. accommodation for the Assembly, its direct support staff and its policy and programme advisers;

    3. information systems for the Assembly, its direct support staff and its policy and programme advisers;

    4. library, press and publicity services, covering all internal and external communications;

    5. ditto in all cases for the Secretary of State's office.

What is the most astonishing aspect of this minute is not so much what he said but, like Sherlock Holmes's dog that didn't bark in the night, it is what he didn't say. What he said is sparse enough but it is truly amazing that he did not mention training needs, yet alone attitudinal and behavioral change, that there was no sense of the extent to which life in the Welsh Office would fundamentally change and the need to prepare staff for those changes. An astonishing minute and therein, in our view, lay the seeds of the problems that would later beset the people side of preparing for devolution.

In fairness to his senior civil colleagues, two of them, in separate minutes over the next months, did point out the need for behavioural and attitudinal change to be addressed but, to all intents and purposes, the die had been cast.

It is little wonder that when we interviewed the current Permanent Secretary, Sir Jon Shortridge, he expressed this view:

The staff were underdeveloped. We only had two years and we had to cut corners and didn't do enough to prepare the staff. I could justify it by saying that until we knew how it was going to work and what the Members wanted, we couldn't put into place training modules to train people but I don't think we devoted enough time in the early months to supporting staff. We were all under enormous pressure at the time and we didn't really know what to expect ourselves. It was a huge learning process for all of us.

And Rachel Lomax, the former Permanent Secretary, concurred:

I did hold inclusive meetings down to middle manager level but if I had the time over again I would spend less time fussing over the building and put more effort into preparing the staff. We did-n't really have enough time for that. My guess is that they probably felt unprepared.

Given this evidence, it would be quite logical to conclude that not enough was done to prepare the staff but such a conclusion needs to be put in the context of the wider issues that took place in the organisation, including the nigh on heroic civil service achievements between 1997 and 1999 in bringing devolution to Wales, and the fact that so much of the changes were unable to be defined to a degree that would have allowed full preparation of the staff.

As we point out in chapter two, change is a dynamic process, involving many small and large specific initiatives and developments as the process evolves. Clearly as we have indicated we reject the organisational change step models where the 'future state' of affairs has been defined and the staff prepared accordingly. None-theless some sense of the future is helpful. As one Executive Board member said to us:

Both views are right. We didn't know what was coming but we could have prepared people better for not knowing or for dealing with change. I think we didn't do enough. I wanted to develop a new competence framework at the time but colleagues said that it would be too much at that stage. We thought a fair bit about it but didn't think enough about strategic issues. The analysis was fine - we're good at that - but we didn't follow it through. People said that they would do something but then didn't because they didn't have the resources.

Staff Training and Numbers

Although there is overwhelming praise for what was achieved, in making devolution a reality, there were widespread concerns over the number of staff available to manage the process and the consequential work that the remaining complement had to complete. This is in addition to questions over whether the existing staff were prepared adequately within the tight timescales and the uncertainties over what Devolution would mean for them.

These comments represent popular civil service views:

> We had too few staff. Rachel Lomax didn't think there was a need to increase numbers much and invested in IT to achieve savings and greater productivity. (An unsubstantiated view in our opinion.) We didn't have enough understanding of the challenges of Devolution. We should have staffed up beforehand, rather than as we went along, as we needed the staff earlier on. But it was just not acceptable to increase administration costs as Ron Davies had given an assurance that devolution would be great for the country and cost neutral, especially as there would be a bonfire of the quangos. We went into the Assembly with even smaller teams as some of our best people were transferred to the Bay to make that work. Plus there was the tidal wave of work, plus the expectations that had been created. Perhaps we should have shouted louder.
>
> The one regret is that people were driven too hard. People found it difficult to come to terms with the work. There was a lot of pressure on people with very tight deadlines and, even though they were a highly motivated team, we ran too tightly and there was a personal cost. In terms of preparing staff for Devolution, we did this up to a point but we didn't know what we were preparing them for. Communications could have been better but it's a harsh judgement to think we could have fully prepared them.

Numerous training and briefing mechanisms were set in place. The intranet was used extensively and there was a staff forum where staff could post questions and exchange views; they produced charts to show in a simple way what stage had been reached and what was coming next; they held many briefing sessions and discovered that nothing worked as well as face-to-face communication; they responded to the numerous invitations from around the Office to talk about devolution; and the Communications Directorate used various focus groups. There were also question & answer sessions hosted by Rachel Lomax or the Devolution Team and the various Task Groups deliberately included dozens of people who were not in the front-line of preparations who could represent end-users or the staff in general.

A senior civil servant took a less magnanimous view of these events and laid the fault at the lack of staff recruited to meet the needs of Devolution:

I think probably the biggest thing that was got wrong—and this was not accidental—was that Ron Davies and Rachel Lomax were both in denial[1] about how many civil servants the show would need. They wouldn't hear it; it was politically not possible. The selling pitch during the referendum campaign was: this isn't going to cost you very much more. Well, quite a number of us thought you are just not going to be able to adequately service policy development and service the Assembly and service ministers on the size of the Welsh Office you have, and so it has proved. I understand why that was got wrong, but it was got wrong and it put a hell of a lot of strain on people who were working all hours at all levels. I think that a bit more could have been done to educate people in what it might be like but that was countered by the fact that there was very much a feeling that we were bringing this creature into being, it will find its own feet and it will be difficult to be too pre-emptive in telling staff what this thing is going to be like and it is not for the civil service to dictate that. If the telescope had not been permanently clamped to the wrong eye, it could have been seen that we were going to need more staff quicker than we did and then the personnel function of the Welsh Office wasn't geared up, so that even when it became apparent that rapid expansion was needed, the people who had got to manage the rapid expansion weren't there, weren't geared to it.

Not surprisingly, the personnel function denies that particular accusation but when there was a need to recruit more people, in May 1999, there was no recruitment strategy or training plan in place. It has been claimed that the recruitment strategy was little more than a queue of people who waited months for the start of the selection process, because all the focus was on setting up the Assembly. The responsibility for developing such a recruitment strategy might be expected to lie with the personnel department, of course, but it is interesting that recruitment was not even mentioned in that first notorious minute. There was a massive recruitment effort for the Bay and they were, by and large, all new staff. Eventually, a new forward recruitment strategy was introduced 'pretty sharp' but it ran into trouble in many areas.

There was no serious attempt to estimate the changes in 1997 and 1998 quite simply because the devolution teams did not have any idea what they were going into. The only estimate they made was for the purpose of the Referendums Bill in 1997. That had an explanatory financial memorandum stating it was thought that the implications for additional staffing would be 100 for the establishment of the

---

[1]   Something that both would deny!

Assembly, and the 100 staff would be needed in the Bay. The current Bay staffing alone is currently approximately 300! It didn't occur to them that in time they would need a substantial increase to run the government activities. The only defence put forward is: 'No-one had the time, and perhaps the foresight, to ask the questions'.

The politicians were not in any sense better prepared. Some early work acknowledged that an Assembly would need to have an executive arm with civil servants but one of the propositions suggested that fewer civil servants would be needed, in comparison with the old Welsh Office, and that would help to meet the cost of the Members!

Relationships with AMs

The establishment of effective working relationships among key stakeholders was seen as a major factor in the change management agenda. These relationships included those between Welsh Office officials and the incoming Secretary of State, between the Welsh Office and Whitehall, and between the Assembly officials and in-coming AMs. Effective relationships were sometimes difficult, if not impossible, to establish and the fact that the civil servants had served a Conservative Government for 18 years, coupled with the traditional relationship between Wales and Whitehall, was a significant feature.

Rachel Lomax had held pre-Government devolution meetings with Ron Davies and they got on with each other very well personally. After the election Rachel Lomax introduced the senior civil servants to Ron Davies. Ron Davies was seen as a great 'people person' and would ask: '*Who are you*?' '*Where do you come from*?' and then try and build a relationship over some common fact. However, if there was little evidence of a working rapport between him and the civil servant, then the civil servant was not used, as the project was seen as far more important than an individual's feelings. It is interesting to note that when we asked Ron Davies about this he had no knowledge of this process: so perhaps it is a myth, especially as Rachel Lomax pointed out his generally excellent relations with civil servants.

There was also concern about how the sixty AMs would impact on the average civil servant sitting at his or her desk: how do you provide the AMs with the information that they are entitled to, whilst also ensuring that officials, particularly junior officials, were not contacted frequently ('rung every five minutes by a member' as a devolution project manager told us) and maybe put in the position of giving incomplete or incorrect information. There was a serious worry about workload if staff could be contacted on an ad hoc basis by up to sixty AMs for information and so, eventually, it was decided to set up the Members' Research Service, which would be a dedicated resource and act as a conduit for AMs' requests.

With the benefit of hindsight it is felt that more could have been done to support Ministers in the early days. A traditional Private Secretary has an important role to support the Minister: however there were suddenly nine Cabinet Ministers to service and there was an issue at the outset in staffing their offices with experienced civil servants. A better service could have been provided if more thought had been given to placing a sufficient number of people in their offices and also inducting Ministers into the formal ways of administering an office.

There is also evidence to suggest that staff were not prepared properly in terms of their relationships with Members. It has been suggested that some staff, quite innocently, treated AMs as if they were there to support the civil servants! The fact that the AMs were very informal, such as in the use of first names, did not help matters and there was some concern that they were not given sufficient respect. It is interesting to note nonetheless that, whilst many civil servants raised this point of respect with us, not a single politician believed it to be the case when we raised the issue with them.

Numerous civil servants told us that many new AMs, especially those with no Westminster background, appeared to have a deep suspicion of the civil service, especially the 'Oxbridge-types'. This reflected the fact that the civil service was seen to have served 18 years of Tory government and been the bastion of Thatcherism and worse still, in the eyes of many, Redwood-ism in Wales. Some AMs had negative images of certain individuals and met Welsh Office faces whom they felt had stood in their way previously. It was perceived that this reaction was not so obvious from previous Westminster politicians, and some believed that these politicians were able to distinguish between civil servants who had embraced the Thatcherite agenda and those civil servants who had implemented Thatcherite policy with a 'heavy heart' or even 'no heart' at all. These relationships were difficult for some individuals and they had to 'move on' and, for some former Welsh Office officials, it was very tough as they felt tarred with a certain brush.

However, there is more than circumstantial evidence to suggest that some politicians were hostile and viewed the civil service with a deep suspicion. Some of the in-built prejudices even extended to the physiological appearance of some senior civil servants who appeared to be a caricature of the Whitehall mandarin.

Two senior civil servants related their experience of the initial relationship and their views are not unique:

> We were disconcerted to find that the politicians, in general, were desperately suspicious of the civil service as being a kind of fifth party. I think the politicians misperceived the officials. They thought that officials were operating out of their own agendas. They could not conceive of somebody who was disinterested in an intensive political environment, could not grasp the power of analysis that you need in order to do difficult things well in government, could not comprehend the value of due process, high integrity, high work rates. They felt, I think, to some extent intimidated by that. It took a while for Ministers to get it into their heads that we're here to help you, you know.
>
> Under the Conservatives I had been pretty much associated with a policy that was detested by many, certainly at the political level. So I think that (Minister A) and (Minister B) had a little bit of difficulty in having me as their person responsible for this area, as I was, perhaps, persona non grata in some circles. I felt I had to, at one point, really lay it on the line to (Minister B) as s/he felt that I had a personal agenda about a certain key policy. I didn't ever feel that either of them were really taken against me personally, it was rather that because of the baggage, that they felt I brought with me, they didn't want to feel, they didn't want to be seen to be, too close to me you know.

Although this personal antipathy clearly existed and, in some instances, appears to still exist, it certainly was not visible to, and not present in, the majority of politicians. As the leader of one opposition party said to us:

> Although there was no personal antipathy, there was certainly an antagonism towards an approach that sometimes put civil servants on the spot in meetings. Some civil servants had a slightly Yes Minister approach and would say: 'Minister this is not the sort of information we are used to giving out.

The evidence suggests that some politicians were disingenuous when they denied the existence of personal animosity and dealing with deep-seated resentment, in a very small minority, is one of the challenges being faced by the civil service even today.

It can be argued also that civil servants should have developed far more constructive relationships with the politicians much earlier on. Better listening to the needs of politicians would have helped and it took a long time to develop a comfortable relationship as, in the words of civil servants, 'it was a big shock to have politicians on the doorstep'. It was also something of a cultural shock to hear Cabinet members talk about 'my staff' favourably and refer to 'the civil service' somewhat disparagingly.

One senior civil servant, with tongue pressed firmly in cheek, analysed the situation:

> The biggest mistake we made was that from the first moment we should have called the Cabinet members 'minister' and not 'secretary', we should have given them a big office and a private car and also a red box each. Then they would have thought that we were treating them seriously, rather than with the attitude that we were asking them to give us, the civil service, a hand in running Wales as we had done for the past 30 years.

In some instances there was even a need to delineate the respective roles of the Minister and the civil servant. The following dialogue is an impression of what took place in one case:

Official: What do you want us to do?

Minister: Could you tell me? I mean, we've arrived, we've taken ownership of this place. You must know what to do with it. You're the officials.

Official: No, no, no, you're the elected Members, you're the elected Minister. What is your policy?

As one senior official told us:

> I remember asking one Minister precisely that: 'What is your policy?' There was just a presumption that, in some sense, officials, of the kind that they had met in local government, had ownership of particular functions and were in charge of their silos. These officials would simply tell Members what they would be up to. But we were saying: 'We're here to do what is lawful to execute your policy and, of course, along the way, we are your creatures but we're not your ciphers. We will be telling you what the pitfalls are and offer advice about how to get round them and maybe even from time to time be testing you on whether some blue skies policy will fly or will work for you.' This was a level of sophistication which was new for many Members, but not for all.

Relationships with Whitehall

Establishing effective relationships with Whitehall to facilitate the creation of a devolved government was very important and the attitudes of the Whitehall officials were crucial to this and they varied very much. There were those who were: pro devolution and supportive; opposed to devolution and wanted to implement a damage limitation exercise; and overlaying it all there were 'life's complicators' and 'life's simplifiers'.

For people in Wales, devolution was top of the political agenda: yet in Whitehall there was often a battle to get this recognised, especially as A, B and C (three UK Cabinet Ministers who were identified time and again) were against it philosophically. There was a need to fight their opposition and in many discussions where Wales 'sat in the firmament' showed the relative lack of importance of the devolution issue in Whitehall's eyes.

It was fortunate for Wales that both Ron Davies and Rachel Lomax punched as heavyweights with politicians and with other permanent secretaries. The civil servants spent time helping the new Secretary of State for Wales in his interaction with the Cabinet as it was important he got off to a strong start as the Devolution Bill had to be prepared quickly. The Secretary of State went to the relevant Cabinet Committees (where of course most of the key discussions took place) with a carefully prepared brief so that he knew exactly what to do, and what to say, in response to each counter argument. For the transition period, Ron Davies, as with all new Cabinet Ministers, would use the Cabinet brief but after a few weeks reliance on the briefs diminished considerably. The same happened across Whitehall but it was especially urgent for Wales, because of the early scheduling of the Devolution Bill, and if early discussions with Cabinet colleagues had been lost then it could have been disastrous for devolution. However, most of the discussions took place outside Cabinet.

The civil servants developed the Transfer of Functions Order to guide their negotiations with Whitehall and some, apparently, initially even tried for more powers, though as Rachel Lomax and others have indicated to us, this was quickly abandoned and a more considered approach developed. Nonetheless it was a difficult time with Whitehall, especially with two prominent departments. They would not 'give one dot more than we were entitled to' and kept saying: 'It's just this clause from this Act that you are getting and nothing else'. The civil service experience was of many Whitehall officials who wouldn't give a penny more to Wales as they expected that

English devolution would follow and they did not want to set any
unhelpful precedents.

As one senior civil servant told us:

> The Treasury was really constructive, as was the Cabinet Office,
> but with most Departments I dealt with, before and after devolu-
> tion, you wouldn't have dreamt that this was Government pol-
> icy. They clearly regarded this as the Welsh 'getting away with
> something' which they clearly resented.

Without a doubt the relationships have changed and improved as
the comments of one civil servant show:

> Even now, we still have to remind them to involve us but we are
> coming at it from a position of greater strength. We can say that,
> actually, we may do it differently, though you can't afford to dis-
> regard us totally. We are less apologetic than the Welsh Office. I
> don't think Whitehall looks at us as being country bumpkins
> anymore: I think they think of us as being beyond the pail.

The Creation and Role of the Wales Office

The level of interest in the creation of the Wales Office, the replace-
ment of the Welsh Office, was minimal to say the least. Given the
other challenges of establishing devolution the interest in the role of
the Secretary of State was limited and few people were interested in
discussing his role. Some assumed it would be a nominal role and so
it was decided that all the support he needed could be managed by
25 staff. That would never have been enough, in the view of Wales
Office staff, but it summed up the view of the role of the Wales Office
in the minds of many influential people.

The agenda to get the Assembly up and running was enormous: it
was the main priority, what the civil servants were chiefly responsible for, and, understandably, what they cared about getting right. As
a result the Wales Office staff resources were inadequate and it
became a constant struggle to keep their 'head above water' as they
didn't have the resources to establish proper systems and to think
through what was being done. In many ways they existed from hand
to mouth.

As their numbers eventually began to increase, their original Cardiff location, a room in the Assembly building, became inadequate
and as the Assembly were unable to provide more space, the Wales
Office started renting offices in another building in Cardiff Bay.

It is fascinating to observe the relationship between the Wales
Office, the Assembly and Whitehall departments and the extent to

which it is changing and the misunderstandings that have existed along the way. This civil servant quote exemplifies the point:

> Until people deal with the Wales Office they don't really know where we stand. You will get Whitehall departments sending stuff to the Wales Office which they ought to be sending to the Assembly because they don't understand that the Wales Office doesn't actually run Wales. You get people in the Assembly assuming that we are, as it were, the London arm of the Assembly and that it's our job to deliver the Assembly's policies, which of course it isn't. At the very beginning both the Assembly and Whitehall expected it to be our job to deliver what they wanted: so the Assembly assumed that it was the Wales Office's job to tell the Prime Minister 'This is what the Assembly wants, this is what they have to have' and they expected that the Prime Minister would dutifully say yes. On the other hand, the Prime Minister (not personally, of course, but the Government officials) expected that the Secretary of State would come down to the Assembly and say: 'This is what London's going to do; you're going to do it as well aren't you?' And, of course, neither of these pictures was right so both sides thought we were doing a lousy job because we didn't do what they expected.

Typically, the Secretary of State, was very clear that in terms of the reporting structure the head of the Wales Office civil service should not report to the Assembly Permanent Secretary because it was clear that there would be occasions when what the Assembly Permanent Secretary wanted the civil servants to do and what the Secretary of State wanted the civil service to do would be diametrically opposed 'because Jon was working for Rhodri and we were working for the Secretary of State' and the stance of Wales Office civil servants would be unacceptable to Assembly Ministers.

Making a Virtue out of a Necessity: Was Action Learning an Appropriate Approach?

One fundamental question is whether the staff could have been prepared adequately in advance of devolution or whether the action learning approach taken, albeit somewhat unintentionally, was the correct one. Action learning, by and large, allows learning to take place contemporaneously with the activities being practised. Many feel that it was dubious whether training in advance would have addressed the needs in any case and that it was only living the experience that identified and met their learning needs. As more than one civil servant rather cavalierly thought:

People were left to do what they were paid to do and a large part of what you're paid to do in the civil service, especially the senior civil service, is to adapt and to sort yourself out. And different people took different lines on that. One did what one did. But there was no training or development, you know the way you must handle yourself is along these lines, chaps, you know. Come along now. These are the rules of the road. We were making it up day by day, hour by hour on very many different dimensions. And that was as true for the people who were running the constitutional change programme as it was for those who were in the policy and delivery departments, whose environment was going to be affected by these changes.

The sense of action learning seemed to extend even to the writing of the White Paper:

Rachel Lomax had confidence in the Devolution team but there were also some irritations. One irritation was the written work. Shortly before the White Paper Voice for Wales was to be issued Rachel lost confidence in the text; … we were in Whitehall, and she said to certain civil servants: 'You can write. Who else can write? OK, have them start to write.' RL ripped up the White Paper text and told us: 'Keep the same chapter headings and the main ideas but take a chapter each and in 1.5 hours give me new chapters'. We had 5 rooms in Gwydyr House and we took one room each, including the waiting room. It was great fun but scary and there was the feeling 'What if she doesn't like it?' We redrafted it, took it to Rachel and she took it from there and perfected it. We had the White Paper — a new one.[2]

Continuity and Change: Establishing New Behaviours

Cultural change is covered extensively in another chapter of this book but there are aspects of cultural change that were directly relevant to the issue of 'people and change'.

Adapting the culture of the civil service in Wales to meet the needs of the Assembly and a new form of government, whilst at the same time retaining the timeless qualities and values of the civil service, was driven under the banner heading and concept of continuity and change. Changing the culture of the Assembly, from what it had been in the days of the Welsh Office, involved organisation development incorporating changes to structures, systems of work, the attitudes and actions of staff, whilst retaining the traditional values of the civil service.

---

[2]   See also her Tale in chapter seven on this point.

There was a need to keep the on-going business and systems going and to make the Devolution changes happen from a position of nothing – there was no blueprint. As Sir Richard Wilson, the then Cabinet Secretary, had said to the devolution team on a visit to Cardiff: 'You are playing a board game without a set of rules'. There was a small team, who were very close to Ministers and the organisation, and who were imaginative, flexible, practised robust project management, and they proceeded to create the board game and the rules but with flexible systems built in. In many ways it was extraordinary that they managed to pull it off in such a short time and that they did it with a small team of people.

The Welsh Office had become a stripped down machine after many years of Conservative government had reduced civil service numbers substantially and, or so it appeared to the Welsh Office staff, one of their Secretaries of State had done so with gusto. By the time of devolution they were a Government Department that had been serving one Secretary of State, two Ministers, had a policy agenda driven by Whitehall, and had been pared down with what to many seemed like a 10% cut each year in budget (the actual budget cuts in fact were much less). In double quick time they had to create a Cabinet Secretariat, plus all the support mechanisms, and develop made-in-Wales policies to facilitate all aspects of devolution. A vast amount was achieved but they also realised that they could not move from position A to position B overnight, it took time and they had to build capacity gradually. There were also difficulties in understanding the Assembly's powers and resources and balancing the two and when big tests came (such as the Corus redundancies, the foot and mouth outbreak, and the Pembroke oil disaster - though the UK Government led on this one) the Assembly Government rose to the challenge extremely well. All of this would not have been possible without the concept of 'continuity and change' – holding on to previous best practices whilst responding in new and appropriate ways.

However, the fact that a small team of people drove devolution did have a downside as one senior civil servant identified:

> There was an atmosphere almost of disbelief that this thing was happening, you know. Yes, absolutely. You've got a relatively small nucleus of people who had worked night and day on Devolution and they knew damned well obviously that it was happening and their baby was about to be born. But there was an awful, I would say probably a majority, number of people that one came across – of course they knew intellectually what was about to

happen but they hadn't internalised it. I don't think that many people had made the imaginative link to what it was actually going to be like when you had more ministers and they weren't somewhere else in London but most of the time actually right there. If not on your doorstep, as Ron had originally envisaged in the old City Hall, well at least summoning you down to the Bay with a snap of the fingers at any time. That is somewhat negative. Let me balance that by saying I think there was also very much the sense of excitement, mingled with apprehension as all impending major change also brings with it. There were very few nay-sayers, very few really long faces and people who'd say: 'This is going to be a disaster it should never have happened'.

Behavioural change became an on-going process and it has led, to some extent, to changes in the expertise and skills that are valued amongst civil servants. Traditionally, in Whitehall, the ability to 'get on' was based not only on breadth of experience, but also on one's intellect and policy-making ability. In the Assembly, intellect is still important but there are other skills and competencies which people need to bring e.g. an ability to lead and to manage organisations; an ability to deliver, to network and link with other organisations outside the Assembly and outside Wales which enable ministers to do their work. Arguably, Whitehall is also changing rapidly but for many the changes in Wales have been faster.

Certainly, the civil service concentration had been on personal competence whereas, more recently, the ability to work in teams, with others and with ministers has become equally, if not more, important to the organisation. This is seen as one of the most positive descriptions and benefits of the Assembly. The Assembly civil servant is much more of a team player across the public services in Wales. It is also seen as a positive sign that Assembly officials are now in the firing line and accountable for their actions.

Developing and changing the behaviours of the staff has not been without its challenges as one interviewee explained:

> One of the problems at the start was that staff were acting in many ways as though this was still the Welsh Office. I remember very early on, when an AM rang up to make an appointment to see one of my colleagues, the secretary said 'I'll see when he can make it' and the AM said 'I think the important thing is, when I can make it' and the secretary was quite affronted by it but the AM was quite right. We had a whole host of things like that.
>
> The two things I learned early on with Assembly Ministers was that you had to listen very carefully to what they were saying — there was no point in talking at them - and the other thing was to manage the little things: so I always made a point of fixing

the little things and saying ' this is what I've done'. I think there's a strong feeling amongst Ministers that they won't trust us with the big things unless they could see us getting the little things right.

Organisation Development

Any organisation undergoing significant organisational change will move through a number of dimensions – they appear to be common factors of organisational change – and the Assembly's civil servants were no different:

- Quite courageously, they believed that bringing about lasting organisational and cultural change is best achieved through a values-driven approach, built upon a clear vision and mission for the Assembly, and because of this a large people development agenda has emerged to ensure that the values, vision and mission permeate the whole organisation. Understandably, this programme for change has taken place in an organisation already facing an overload of work and so the attempt to change the culture has been an uphill struggle. Many successes can be seen but there are also areas where the change agenda is seen as yet more work.

- Alongside this has been the movement from an administrative culture to one that is dominated by a managerial and leadership ethos. Intellectually the differences and the implications for practice have been grasped but the challenge has been to make it a reality in every aspect of organisation life.

- Then there have been the programmes to meet the development needs of staff. This is especially the case where the staff profile is changing and the increase in mergers and the other issues identified in this chapter have placed even greater pressure on the development agenda.

- Departments are being asked to deal with more cross-cutting issues: issues that do not fit neatly into compartmental-ised – the infamous silo - notions of how business should be conducted. There has been a reduced emphasis on formal organisation charts and a greater reliance on teams to respond to those issues that move across an organisation, or lurk in the white spaces between carefully drawn charts.

- And finally, a variety of 'hygiene' issues arose that appear to be more symptomatic than systemic issues. Examples include accommodation, vacancies and absence and these issues exemplify an organisation that is changing rapidly and requires great care and attention.

All, but the harshest of critics, praise the civil service for what it achieved during 1997–99 and beyond that. Paul Silk, the Clerk to the Assembly, was fulsome in his praise:

> Those who set-up a functioning Assembly from nothing and in very short order deserve a pat on the back. As I understand it, some of the Members didn't know what to do when they arrived but at least they had something to fit into and that was a remarkable achievement.

However, the successful delivery of devolution was not without cost in other parts of the Assembly. Setting up the Assembly became an all-consuming enterprise for the senior civil servants, and others, and although the major things were carried off successfully it had the effect of 'sucking the life out of' the other main parts of the Office and therefore by mid-99 the civil servants were faced with the new structural funding programme and were totally under-resourced to deal with it. They were inadequately staffed and therefore felt that they were not running things properly. As a consequence, when the Assembly had been set up they agreed to wind up the Devolution Unit and 'deploy those civil servants to sections that were desperate for support. In the experience of many the year 1999/2000, when they were negotiating the Objective 1 programme, amongst other things, was the worst year ever.' There was the 'fiendishly complicated European exercise', new AMs who were 'into everything, who saw the government as vulnerable and therefore hammered us, and many of us came into work every day with a stomach knotted in fear'. The last quote came from a senior and highly regarded civil servant who has a very successful track record. For extra effect he added: 'It was hell.'

The decision to close the Devolution Unit, even if understandable, was seen, with hindsight, as an error as the civil servants in Cardiff didn't appreciate the need for a continuing capacity to keep the settlement running. As a result of this many civil servants felt that they were inhibited in developing their institutional knowledge of what devolution meant and how it worked and could be improved.

Civil Service Change Management Systems and Processes

In keeping with civil service traditions and procedures the management of the processes to arrive at devolution was comprehensively managed with an architecture of committees, project teams, boards and the like. It seems that no area or topic was excluded from the minutia of planning — at least in theory — but in practice the subject of people and change was not managed with the skill that all other topics received.

We have examined the change management project team papers, staff seminars, the Critical Path Analysis for the change management team, the skills training plan, the Welsh Office core competence framework, the discussion paper 'Key Changes in Work Practices', the original personnel strategy, the various staff training seminars, the discussions surrounding the Investors in People submission, and much else.

As a result of the impeccable structure of committees and working parties and the various personnel-type activities it would be easy to conclude that all people issues were covered in depth. But that misses the point in at least three ways: the experience of staff shows that not enough was done; the comments of the Permanent Secretaries confirm the view of the staff; and, most convincingly of all, the papers show that although the right words were being uttered there was little to show that the fundamental people issues were being grasped.

On Friday 6th June 1997 the Devolution: Change Management Project Team held its first meeting. Around the table sat eight senior people associated with devolution and people issues in the Welsh Office. The minutes of the meeting are marked RESTRICTED: POLICY but we are giving little away when we say that the meeting started with an update from the Devolution Unit, and then discussed communications with staff ('The need to keep Welsh Office staff well-informed over the coming weeks was regarded as essential. The weekly Staff Bulletin was identified as the most appropriate vehicle for letting people know what was happening.'), guidance to staff in run-up to referendum (a reiteration of the general principles of impartiality, during the period between publication of the White Paper and the referendum), formal consultation with the Welsh Office unions, and a number of technical employment matters.

As we searched through the minutes of the various committees and groups people issues were more noticeable by their absence than by their presence. The one main exception was the Board Directors' Meeting held on the 22nd September 1997:

> Mr A and Mrs B introduced the paper and said the major challenge ahead was to determine what kind of Department the Welsh Office would need to become in the light of the Assembly.

Mr C suggested that the biggest change was likely to be that a far greater number of people would find themselves working closely with elected politicians. The Permanent Secretary said that a big effort would be needed to develop staff management, IT and presentational skills.

The Board (BDM) felt that improved communications would be essential in the run-up to the Assembly; this might involve regular seminars for staff. It was further agreed that BDM itself needed to be more prominent in explaining its role and in communicating with staff. Mr D and Mrs E were asked to look into the possibility of putting abbreviated reports of BDM on to the bulletin board.

BDM welcomed the Personnel Strategy paper; it was agreed to discuss it at the Group Directors' Meeting.

The Personnel Strategy issued by the Personnel Division in October 1997 is a surprisingly (given the comments made at the time and since) impressive document. Understandably parts of it read somewhat quaintly, given what we know of the Assembly today, but its key aims are generally robust:

Here is a possible list of key aims to equip us for the changes we face:

— to improve the Department's capacity for original policy and programme development;

— as part of that , to improve our capacity to develop and implement cross-cutting policies and related programmes to meet Welsh needs and priorities;

— to recognise and respond to the cultural and linguistic diversity of Wales;

— to enable the Department to operate effectively internationally, and particularly in Europe;

— to develop a more open, inclusive, responsive approach both within the office and in our dealings with the general public and outside bodies;

— to help Welsh Office staff maximise their potential.

Their key initiatives included:

— Arguably we need more specialist trained staff as well as generalist staff

— A competency framework more clearly aligned to the Department's needs and used to assess performance and development potential

— We will also need to look carefully at the age and skills structure of the Department

— The Welsh Office needs effective arrangements to recruit, develop and motivate its staff and to ensure appropriate staff are available to allow us to discharge our functions and fulfil our objectives.

The existence of the personnel strategy makes it even more difficult to comprehend why widespread effective action was not taken. Although it is possible to identify much commendable action under the heading of personnel there is hardly any evidence to suggest that there was a comprehensive strategic grasp of the people and change issues and the need to deal with behavioural, attitudinal, individual and organisational learning issues and much else.

As stated in other parts of this chapter, much of the reason for that may be understandable but at the same time it is somewhat surprising.

HR Strategy: From Principal Establishment Officer to Human Resource Management

One of the most senior and influential posts in the civil service was that of the Principal Establishment Officer, the PEO. During the time that we have been acquainted with the civil service in Cardiff a variety of people have held the post: some as a stepping stone or as a development opportunity for a more senior posting; some as a temporary sideways move until another post became available; and some because they happened to be available to undertake the post. Whatever the reason, or the person involved, this senior and important post was not held by a professionally qualified personnel/human resources specialist. The gifted amateur, in true civil service fashion, typically undertook the management of personnel diligently and most performed the role of PEO successfully owing to their experience as a senior civil servant. However, the post was seen as an administrative posting (despite the fact that it was later re-titled Personnel Director), where specialist HR skills were not a requirement and this was one of the factors that led to the problems described at the start of this chapter. As one senior person admitted:

I think it wasn't just a question of numbers it was also a question of calibre. The personnel function had, frankly, very little to do and it became hardly a place where the most able wanted to go and partly a place where the most able weren't put.

The Assembly's first professionally qualified HR director was appointed in 2004 and the first full HR strategy arrived in 2005; arguably, a little late for an organisation employing approximately 2000 staff at the time of devolution and approximately 4000 staff in 2004. In part this reflects the Whitehall traditions, with many Departments not having professionally qualified Directors of HR. Nor does this mean that there were not a raft of personnel and employment policies covering recruitment, reward, equal opportunities and much else, or that there no attempts to construct personnel strategies at earlier times, but it does mean that there was no comprehensive HR strategy aligned to the core plans of the organisation and there was no HR professional sitting on the executive board of the organisation.

The senior civil servants realised that this was an unacceptable position and in 2003 the most recent holder of the Personnel Director post imaginatively introduced a holding position until the arrival of the Assembly's first HR Director. In September 2003 the Executive Board was presented with *A PEOPLE STRATEGY – THE WAY FORWARD* and, in what was clearly a short-term document, recommendations were tabled regarding: behaviours, roles and responsibilities of line managers and individuals, training and accreditation, the decentralisation of the Personnel Division to the Group Directors, and the development of a HR strategy that would:

> ... explain what people can expect of the Assembly and what the Assembly can expect of them. It will explain how we will bring in, bring on, develop and use to the fullest extent the Assembly's greatest resource – its people. It will define and describe the types of behaviours we expect of the people who work in the Assembly and explain what the Assembly will do in return. It will also include an explanation of how people issues will be delivered and what can be expected from line managers and HR staff.

An admirable set of objectives but, arguably, four to five years after it should have been tackled. The full HR strategy was finally agreed and introduced in 2005 and for the first time the Assembly civil servants had a strategy that was based on the key objectives of the Assembly and presented under the five headings of:

- Delivering a leaner, sharper, results-driven organisation
- Equipping managers for delivery
- Driving up performance
- Developing our talent
- Moving our culture on

Many of the earlier Principal Establishment Officers would never have used such management-speak but the new and current HR strategy represents an impressive attempt to bring the management of the Assembly staff into the modern world.

June 2002: Senior Civil Service 360 Degree Appraisal

The Permanent Secretary was aware from the earliest days of devolution that work was needed to raise the overall leadership and management performance of the senior civil service (SCS). As a result, the consultancy firm CPCR were commissioned to oversee 360-degree appraisal of the SCS. At the simplest level 360 degree appraisal involves an individual asking their 'superiors', 'subordinates' and 'peers' to assess them against a set of organisational and personal competencies. In the CPCR analysis respondents were asked to rate the perceived importance of the following six SCS competencies to the participant's job:

- Giving purpose and direction: creating and communicating a vision of the future
- Making a personal impact: leading by example
- Thinking strategically: harnessing ideas and opportunities to achieve goals
- Getting the best from people: motivating and developing people to achieve high performance
- Learning and improving: drawing on experience and new ideas to improve results
- Focusing on delivery: achieving value for money and results

The ratings were on the scale 1–4 where 1= quite important and 4= very important. Comfortingly, the resulting average rating scores by the SCS all fell within the 3–4 range and their collective view was supported by the scoring of the non-SCS civil servants. What is far more revealing is the scores for the more detailed level of behaviour items within the overall headings.

The CPCR report examined the highest and lowest rated behaviours and found these to be:

Top Ten (highest first)

1. You act with honesty and integrity
2. You accept responsibility for your decisions
3. You use knowledge and expertise to get things done

4. You don't give up when faced with problems or obstacles

5. You give objective advice based on sound evidence and analysis

6. You monitor financial performance against budget

7. You make people feel comfortable to approach you

8. You build productive relationships with people across and outside the organisation

9. You make decisions which reflect wider political and organisational priorities

10. You give difficult messages to senior people when appropriate

Bottom 10 (lowest first)

1. You spend time coaching individuals so they give of their best

2. You take action to harness the potential of technology

3. You talk about the future in a way that makes people feel motivated

4. You seek feedback to improve your own performance

5. You deal with the consequences of changes in technology

6. You adapt your leadership style to different people, cultures and situations

7. You seek out what is new and different

8. You seek out and take account of diverse views

9. You welcome challenges from other people

10. You know when not to intervene in the team's work

As the management consultant's covering note highlights:

> ... it suggests a picture of people who are very good at managing themselves and being excellent as individuals, but less effective on some of the collective and longer term things including leading and managing others, change, learning and developing.

The Board had evidence to support their earlier belief that action was needed on a number of issues but were also able to draw considerable comfort from the results as many of their development measures were having a positive effect.

Leadership Development

In keeping with the practice of organisations throughout the private and public sectors in the UK, and elsewhere, it was agreed by the senior civil servants that they needed to invest in leadership development and to ensure that leadership responsibilities were cascaded throughout the organisation.

In November 2002: the CPCR consultancy reported on the leadership development programme it had carried out over the past year, which included both diagnostic and development activities with the Board and the SCS. The purpose of their report was:

- to reflect their perception of the position reached after further work and

- to outline our views on the way forward, for the Board, the SCS and generally for the ongoing management of leadership development for the Assembly.

The summary of their report concluded that:

> The senior management group in the National Assembly has developed an increasingly clear understanding of leadership and development, and the connection between personal development and organisational capability ... At this stage however there is neither the infrastructure nor impetus to match the needs and expectations that exist. This report provides some specific areas that could be addressed to ensure that development does not stall just as it has begun to gather pace.

Their report went on to note and recommend, amongst other things:

- The Directors as a group have developed considerably more awareness and acceptance of their corporate leadership and management role but still face significant barriers, some very practical, to making the lasting changes needed to make that role work well in practice.

- Many Directors are likely to benefit from individual coaching to enable them to make the transition from functional head to corporate leaders.

- The SCS have begun to clarify the message about the future of development in the Assembly and need endorsement and support to continue the process already started following the development event.

- A framework for an SCS development programme has emerged from the recent development event and needs a decision to move forward. In particular there is an urgent need to equip the SCS with core personal effectiveness skills to enable them to provide leadership when the People Programme is rolled out.

- There are some very good processes already in place — performance management, EFQM — which need protecting and bedding in.

With regard to the role of directors in the Assembly the report commented:

> The Board has made considerable progress on the establishment of a Management Plan which focuses attention around a prioritised set of themes. It is our view that there is also a greater appreciation and acceptance, in principle, of a greater corporate leadership role alongside their functional roles, amongst members of the Board. There are, however, practical barriers, mostly related to time pressure and Ministers' expectations, that we believe will continue to work against the Board becoming really effective in leading and delivering the Management Plan.

The report went on to suggest ways in which these issues could be managed and highlighted the importance of coaching:

> Whilst most recognise the importance of collective leadership and of playing their corporate role effectively, it is also true that for most to do so in practice is proving extremely difficult to achieve, and many would benefit from focused support to help make the transition.
>
> The transition for any individual from being an excellent functional head to being a corporate leader is huge. It is likely to include some or all of the following

- developing the people around them to a degree where they feel able to delegate large areas of work with confidence,
- developing strategies for managing ministers' and others' expectations, and
- learning to stop doing many of the things for which they are currently valued and developing skills for making a difference at the corporate level.

The report also identified a number of measures to support the ongoing development of directors.

'Modernising Government: Leadership — the Key to Better Government'

Alongside the Assembly's own initiatives they had to respond to central government initiatives for the whole of the civil service, such as the Modernising Government agenda. The initiative was launched in the Assembly with a certain degree of razzmatazz and central funding support:

> Better leadership across the Assembly is the key to Delivering Better Government. That's the message that is coming out of the European Foundation for Quality Management (EFQM) Action Plans and the Staff Attitude Survey.
>
> Barbara Wilson, Director of Research and Development Group, has responded to the challenge and become the Leadership Champion. Barbara will be working with the new Executive Board to make sure that leadership skills are developed across the Assembly. To work alongside Barbara, a Leadership and Teamworking Group has been set up to look at ways to support and develop leadership in the Assembly. The Leadership Group is chaired by Chris Bamford of the NHS Directorate and aims to pool ideas from inside and outside the Assembly.
>
> To help fund its work, the Leadership Group has been given Better Government funding for either major projects or for pilot studies that use different approaches to tackling key leadership issues.

An internal publication announced that *Barbara Leads the Way!* and Barbara Wilson explained to readers that:

> Leadership is about knowing where you are going and taking people with you, and helping them achieve what is needed. The work of the Better Government Leadership and Team Working Group will help to develop a broader understanding of what we mean by leadership in the Assembly and how to foster it. We all have a part to play. My own role is primarily to work with the new Executive Board. Our intention is to adopt a more focused, decisive and open style. We hope to become better leaders. We hope the staff will notice the change, be clearer about their role and feel better supported. This should make it easier for us all to deliver the objectives of the Plan for Wales and its supporting strategies and plans. We won't get there overnight, but by looking at ourselves honestly and helping staff do the same, we can all move in the right direction.

A Leader in the Assembly

As a part of the *Modernising Government* initiative the Executive Board set about establishing what the Assembly wanted from its leaders. Demonstrating its understanding of the fundamentals of leadership it explained that 'leadership can be exhibited at any level; it does not have to be related to grade or position — and may be based on informal structures as much as formal ones'.

Six main principles of leadership for civil servants in the Assembly were agreed and the initiative set out that:

All civil servants in the in the Assembly can demonstrate leadership in their work. A leader:

- Sets visions
- Builds teams
- Values people
- Motivates
- Earns respect
- Gets results

We are not saying there is a single 'one size fits all' style of leadership that we wish to clone, but a leader needs to do all six elements. It is not an exhaustive list, but it is the basis of leadership.

Conclusion

In many ways there can be no conclusion as the challenges of 'People and Change' continue day by day. Obviously, more could have been done on this front up to say 2001/2002 to prepare the staff for devolution. While issues of staff development, spreading leadership and enhancing communication arose, were considered and certain actions taken, the evidence suggests that initially at least, all of these became 'second order' to what were seen as more pressing matters. The impact on culture and on the attitudes of junior and middle management are discussed in the next two chapters. But those days have been consigned to history and current HR practice in the Assembly indicates considerable learning and contains an ever-improving range of initiatives.

Chapter 5

Managing Cultural Change

Introduction

Chapter two has indicated our view that culture, while a vague and in some ways unsatisfactory term, remains important as a way of understanding change, not least because managers see it as a useful vehicle for understanding and explaining what is happening (or not). There we have articulated our views on the concept. Our research approach, given our grounded theory philosophy, was to allow our interviewees to tell us their understandings of the term and its implications. Most of the civil servants and politicians we spoke to about the culture of the Assembly, and how it differed from the Welsh Office culture, asked us to explain what we meant by the word *culture*, or told us that their answer to our question depended on what was meant by the word *culture* and then proceeded, sometimes at great length, to explain to us what they understood by the term.

When we explained our understanding of the term we deliberately eschewed the comfort of an accepted academic definition and rather explained that we were looking for their views on 'how things are done around here?', 'what is valued as important?', 'how people behave and relate to one another?', and 'how things have changed since the arrival of the Assembly?'.

We recognised for reasons articulated in chapter two that it was unlikely that there would be just one culture present in the Assembly and that it was far more likely that different people, reflecting their different roles and status, their former employers and personal experiences, would explain what they thought was the *culture* of the organisation in different ways. This we anticipated would give us a clearer picture of the complex organisation we identified in earlier chapters and which we were researching.

In each of the sections that follow we present the views of the politicians and the views of the civil servants. Although we identify 'who said what' with some politicians, with others we have referred only to their roles. The views of civil servants, in keeping with tradition, are always anonymised and were expressed by a range of senior, junior, current and former staff even though they are shown as if spoken by one person. The one exception to this civil service rule relates to the current and former Permanent Secretary whose comments are shown as part of a wider analysis in *The Chief Servants' Tale* (chapter 7). The following text has been edited and occasionally expressed in a form suitable for the written word, rather than the spoken word, but the views are always presented faithfully. Where the views of a number of people have been merged into one voice we have ensured that the views are representative of the wider constituency we interviewed.

PART 1: THEN AND NOW

The Culture of the Welsh Office and the National Assembly for Wales

A Supine Position?

First Minister Rhodri Morgan summed up the views of most politicians in his observation that prior to the advent of the Assembly the role of civil servants in Cardiff was reactive (to use the kindest interpretation placed on it) to the direction being set by Whitehall politicians and that senior civil servants in Wales knew that their career progression depended on towing the civil service party line and defending the interests of their Secretary of State:

> I may be biased because obviously I'm an ex Welsh Office Civil Servant. Jon Shortridge and I have had many discussions about this: how much change was there between 1972, when I left, and 1999 when I returned as a Minister, and then how much change has there been from 1999 to 2004.
>
> Although it had trebled in size in the 27 years (1972 to 1999) I'm not sure its culture changed very much. It was still quite dependent on Whitehall because it didn't generate legislation. It had an Act of Parliament to do once every 5–10 years. It would occasionally write White Papers, but really it was a paragraph inserted in what was, for example, a Secretary of State for the Environment's

White Paper.

So I always thought that the Welsh Office culture that I left had not changed all that much really — though others take a different view — even though the numbers of responsibilities had enormously altered. So it was a much bigger office, with much bigger promotional opportunities, but not really an ability to generate policy ideas: it was a lobbying office trying to make sure the voice of Wales was not lost in Whitehall and trying to make sure that the Cabinet Minister- the Secretary of State - was well informed and briefed, received deputations, delegations and played his full part in Cabinet and so on. You could administer Wales, rather than develop new policies, and you could lobby for Wales in the big wide world in Whitehall.

It was quite a different culture from the Scottish Office, which was legislation driven and 'give Whitehall a bloody nose' driven. Whereas, in Wales, I always had the impression — and I don't think it was different in 1999 — that, in your mind, you had to have the approval of Whitehall to be promoted, (whereas) the Scottish Office was driven by: 'Have you given Whitehall a bloody nose in the past 2 or 3 years?' If you had, you had a very good chance of being promoted for having done so. I would see big meetings in Whitehall when all the different Ministries were represented - to discuss the impact of defence or steel closures, or whatever - and you'd be able to see the different styles and attitudes of the Welsh Office and the Scottish Office. The Scottish Civil Servants were very aggressive, not personally aggressive. They'd say: 'This could cost you North Sea oil if you push this policy too hard or if you fail to satisfy Scottish demands on saving a factory or building another big steel works', or whatever it might be. And if challenged they would reply: 'Don't forget the vast subsidy the UK taxpayer gets from North Sea oil.' The Welsh Office civil servant would never treat Treasury civil servants like that. You would just never dare use that language and if you did you wouldn't be promoted in 30 years. A totally different attitude.

Two points might well be made in reply. First, the Secretary of State was of course a Westminster politician and so civil servants had no option but to take this into account, unless they wanted to propose a novel constitutional theory. Second, senior civil servants would object strongly to the allegation that they were merely reactive to Whitehall initiatives, and cite various initiatives that support or defend their position, including various 'battles' they took part in to secure money from the Treasury.

One senior civil servant appeared to strike a balanced position when he told us:

Then you had a Secretary of State who depended very heavily on officials to brief him on what the line was, but actually, in many cases, not knowing Wales in depth: certainly it was impossible to know the whole range of policy considerations and the Government's policy on everything. He was quite heavily dependent on civil servants to keep him out of trouble and therefore there was a heavy emphasis on being sure you're in touch with the latest developments in Whitehall.

I think the culture of the old Welsh Office was pretty relaxed: people knew one another; links with Whitehall were close and easy; there was hardly any contact with opposition politicians. So there was a pretty good team feeling and everyone knew what everyone else was doing. But it was very much within a framework of:

- 'How will this go down in Whitehall?'

- 'How could we do this differently?'

- 'How could we convince the Prime Minister or the Chancellor of the Exchequer to do X?'

There was rather more of a dependency culture.

Becoming More Proactive

The arrival of sixty AMs in 1999, determined to demonstrate to a Welsh public, who had given them the slightest of mandates, that they would make a difference to Welsh life, plus the politicians' belief that the civil servants in Cardiff had enjoyed a fairly comfortable existence, meant that *pro-activity* was the order of the day.

The leader of one of the Opposition Parties expressed this view cogently:

In 1997 there were two types of civil servants:

1. Those for whom regulation-making is everything and they go through the hoops and making sure there is a judicious approach to all issues is their primary motive;

2. And others whose role in life was to say how to make this happen: a 'can-do' mentality.

And the balance between these was very much skewed towards the regulators, and what scrutiny, openness and policy direction has done is to alter the fulcrum much more in favour of the 'can-do' mentality. It isn't by any means perfect or far enough along that track. There is still a very essential role for regulation and guardianship of the public purse, but even within that role the desire to be an implementer, a policy change agent is crucial for us in the National Assembly.

> The culture has shifted. There is much more of a sense now that
> we have to find policy solutions to issues and where a solution
> has got difficulties, a route has to be found to make it work. It is
> by no means perfect but there is a genuine desire, particularly
> from middle management people who see their future in the civil
> service, to try to find solutions to issues: policy initiatives that
> will work.'

Although civil servants would not use the exact language of the politician there is more than a tacit agreement that their culture was far
more balanced towards regulation and that there was a need to
introduce a new equilibrium:

> The culture in 1997 was good at making things work, good at
> fixes, so in that sense quite nimble. We were less good at big
> ideas, less good at hard thinking for policy answers and much
> less focused than we are now on delivering things out there.
> More of a perception that it was important for us to look as if we
> were doing what we ought to be doing, as opposed to actually
> following it through and getting things done. Looking back on it,
> it was a lot more stodgy, with less of an appetite for risk, quite
> hierarchical, and inward looking. If you go to our committee
> rooms — still — none of them have got any windows: it just seems
> symptomatic of the organisation we were then.
>   We have more rigour in our policy analysis now and we're get-
> ting better at thinking for ourselves: one of the things the Welsh
> Office was never allowed to do was think for itself but we have
> freedom to do that now, which is a great help. And we have more
> targets and delivery outputs but we are much more focused on
> what we are trying to achieve out there.
>   The other side is the feeling of pace. There's a far greater
> emphasis on doing things quicker, better, faster now because I
> think the Assembly Government feel the clock ticking at any
> point in time, and in a way that wasn't there before. The feeling of
> accountability for having delivered on a clearly Welsh manifesto
> is palpable. And that sense of the need to be accountable, the
> need to be able to deliver, and the need to be able to deliver some-
> thing tailored to the circumstance of Wales, can give rise to pres-
> sures and tensions within the teams that perhaps weren't there
> before.

Policy-Making Capacity and Capability

However, while the civil servants are willing to accept the charge of
having been somewhat reactive in their work, they do not accept that
they were seriously deficient in their policy-making capacity and
capability. It may well be that their capacity was hindered by the
severely reduced numbers of civil servants in Cardiff but they never

doubted their capability to develop policy as they had practised that for decades under previous administrations.

The charge made against them is clear and widespread and was summarised by an AM:

> When I came here, the first thing that struck me was their lack of policy-making skills. In 2005, as far as the civil servants' own career structures are concerned, they appear to be remaining more within their own sphere of interest, probably reflecting the increased policy-making. I think that is a good thing, as it takes a long time to develop skills and expertise in a policy area.

When we put this charge to numerous civil servants their disagreement was clear and the two most entertaining and illuminating rebuttals from senior civil servants highly regarded for their achievements in Wales pre and post devolution, were:

> It is not true that basically all we did was 'top and tail' London policies. Actually, I don't think it would have been possible for the Cardiff-based civil servants to have made such a success of the devolution project if those skills had been absent. 1997-99 was the period when those policy-making skills broke cover for the first time. Prior to that, I think it's true to say that a lot of what went on in the Welsh Office was visible only to lobby segments: particular parts of the health service, particular aspects of housing or whatever, who were affected by the policies.
>
> Because the Welsh Office wasn't subject to very close and sustained political or media scrutiny it was possible for many Civil Servants here to say: 'Well, we'll let the Whitehall Department do these two things, this third thing is dormant at the moment (but likely to become live downstream) and that leaves us with the option to pick or choose as to how much priority to give to the remaining two'. So people, here in Cardiff, had a significant degree of control over what they would commit to in terms of policy development or implementation. They had the capacity to be selective.
>
> In addition to that what Cardiff based civil servants did in Whitehall was not visible to many in Wales. I mean, on the whole, what Welsh Office civil servants were doing for Wales was - you didn't crow about it OK, you would not get your way with Whitehall if you were crowing about it down in Cardiff and kicking up the dust, making people take notice in Whitehall and making them feel that it was all rather inconvenient. If you wanted it negotiated effectively you needed two things: one, a thumping good argument and the determination to see it through and the clout and the savvy; and the other thing you needed was a deal with Whitehall, which was essentially 'go with it' or 'come with me' otherwise I can make your life a mis-

ery. But I'm not going to crow about it back at the Welsh Office because there's no machinery in which I can crow. So 'them out there' didn't see to what extent what was being done was the same Government slogan but a different policy. They also didn't see it because the Welsh Office was serving segments rather than being visible as a coherent whole. Nor did people see what was being achieved, for example in relation to housing where at one stage we were spending something of the order of £250 million on private stock renovation when that same sum was being spent for the whole of England. How was that achieved? People don't ask because they didn't know much about what was happening. I think there are a number of instances where a limited number of officials were picking and choosing which policy; and officials chose very well and very effectively and made a really major difference both to the patch, to Wales, and indeed, in some instances, to Government policy in England. But perhaps I would say that!

The second rebuttal caused mild disarray in the interview as we laughed out loud:

The way I feel about this is a bit like after a divorce: the one thing you can't do with a new wife is talk about the advantages of the old one.

'She was a cow wasn't she?'

'Yes dear! She was.'

You don't point out that she had many fine qualities.

So when a Minister says: 'You lot just sat in here in your rooms doing nothing.'

The answer is: 'Yes, that's quite right Minister.'

You can't say: 'Do you think that no roads were ever built? Do you think we didn't introduce Enterprise Agencies? That inward investment never happened before you came?'

The divorce analogy is relevant: there is this myth that policy did not exist, that we were just stuck in here doing nothing. What is different now is a far greater expectation that we would be more skilled policy analysts because it wasn't a well grounded or understood skill and one of the reasons for that, and especially for people who hadn't worked in Whitehall as I had, is they didn't understand that you could go through the process of policy and development in the same way as you would go through any project.

Rebuttal number three was far more clinical in its assessment and built a bridge between the view of many politicians and the civil servants:

> The old Welsh Office was wrongly seen as purely just being a colonial outpost of Whitehall. It was always much more than that. I mean the old Welsh Office created the Welsh Development Agency, the Wales Tourist Board, the biggest land reclamation scheme in Europe, worked on the new M4, created Cardiff Bay Development Corporation, had a number of Valleys initiatives and Care in the Community. It was much more than just being an outpost of Whitehall, but nonetheless it didn't have the ability to be able to think freshly about the big political issues and policy issues of the day. It worked within a prescribed framework and tried to develop its own solutions within that framework, but they were always fairly closely proscribed. The Welsh Assembly Government has much more confidence and I think that confidence seeps through to the civil service and a range of other players - but it remains early days.

Many Cabinet Ministers recognise this point, even if they believe that the policy-making capability owes more to the arrival of the Assembly than to some dormant or partially hidden existing quality:

> It has been a huge change and a big shock. We've had to develop massive policy making capacity and expertise and I think the civil service has responded remarkably well in just six years, while being under intense scrutiny.
>
> Ministers do take points forward and the civil service have confidence in coming forward with radical and exciting policy ideas. The 'Assembly Civil Service' is largely driven by lot of the SCS having the space to think, in liaison with ministers. This was stifled previously.

However, improvements remain to be made in achieving the correct balance between the politician's role and that of the civil servant in policy formulation as First Minister Morgan pointed out to us in a lengthy analysis. These are his main points:

> The broad ideas for generating policy shouldn't come from a civil servant anyway. This is always the most interesting thing for anybody who, like me, comes quite late in life to be a Minister: how much do you do because the civil servants ask you to do it, and how much do they do because you've asked them to do it? A civil servant's ideal expectation of a Minister is one who does his box every night, brings it back in the morning, tied in a ribbon, and everything has been signed.
>
> So if you have been on a visit which generated what you think is a bright idea, they seem much more likely to either lose it in the

depths of the machine, so you never see it again, or to just simply say: 'I don't think we can do this' or 'It's already been tried' or something like that.

It's totally subconscious; it's not obstruction. It's just not knowing how to deal with a Minister who has an idea for a policy that we don't already have, or for improving an existing policy. It's not helped really by this physical divide between the Ministers and special advisers mostly working in the Bay and the main administrative machinery in Cathays Park. We don't see sufficiently frequently our administrative civil servants. We don't bump into them in the canteen, in the corridor, or in the toilets, so we don't have those chances, those chance conversations to say: 'Have you thought of doing this, can't we push this a bit more because that's going really well', or 'can't we change course slightly on that?' It's a damned inconvenience being three miles away and it's even more inconvenient for the civil servants as they've got to catch the shuttle bus down and the shuttle bus back. We've got to live with it but I think it exaggerates that problem of trying to make sure that Ministers' ideas can be transmitted into generating policy ideas, not merely following administrative good practice.

Greater Openness and Scrutiny

Arguably, the greatest change has been the introduction of a far greater degree of policy scrutiny and a greater openness in the way that business is undertaken. As three civil servants, representing the views of most colleagues, explained:

It's much more open: I think one of the things which gets under-mentioned is that the whole culture of openness and scrutiny has meant a change inside the heads of the civil service. I think that the culture of openness didn't come in with The Freedom of Information Act; it came in with the greater scrutiny and committees and that's made the quality of decision-making, lower down, more effective than it's been in the past, because everyone knows that there's a greater interest in what we do. Political involvement and decision-making have permeated much further down the organisation and external scrutiny is hugely greater, and that means that intellectually one doesn't cut corners so much, so the quality of decision-making evolved hugely.

I think as an organisation we are becoming less stuffy and more informal, and I think one of the great things about the Assembly as a whole, which I think reflects one of the things I like best about Wales, is that it's just not pretentious. People from outside might think that we have a long way to go — and I'm sure they're right — but it's better than it was.

It's a much more political world. I mean there's more politics around. You are associated more closely with leading politicians, particular as the head of a department, than you would have been in the old Welsh Office. In the old Welsh Office I might have had in any typical week, if I was lucky, an hour's worth of time with a Secretary of State or Minister on issues. Here it's enormous multiples of that figure. You've got a full-time Minister. So this makes it much more political, and the breadth and level of understanding of the issues by politicians now is significantly greater than it was before because they can specialise more.

What we've actually got now is an organisation that engages more obviously in the outside world, that looks at stakeholders and officials in a way that officials now are judged in essence as providers, at best, of advice to senior politicians. Because the senior politicians in the Welsh Office days spent only a limited amount of time here they truly weren't able to examine things from as many different perspectives as they do now.

What has become clear to the civil service is that if they wish to preserve their reputation then they must engage with the outside world and the key stakeholders in their portfolios. If they fail to do that then they will not be credible advisers, or deliverers, or providers of advice to senior politicians.

Developing Effective Relationships

When the Assembly began to function it was noticeable that the relationships between many politicians and certain senior civil servants were influenced by their previous encounters. This issue is dealt with in more detail in the *People and Change* chapter. The impact of these relationships on the culture of the organisation was contained in the comment of a prominent 'back-bencher':

There was a level of distrust, although it was in no way malign; it was an inevitable symptom of what had taken place before. There had been a huge cultural change — and issues were subjected to a level of scrutiny that hadn't been experienced before. Therefore, the civil servants' attitude was always quite defensive, but there was no question of any lack of respect. As AMs we were quite inexperienced in asking questions and needed to learn how to frame questions much more effectively.

This tension was also recognised by a number of senior civil servants:

We were there working for ministers, and trying to convince ministers - that proposition was not always very easy because I think quite a lot of them, not all of them, came in with some sort of

> opposition baggage: you know, they inherited this crew who had
> been working with the Tory administration for 18 years, promul-
> gating Tory policies — trying to actually convince them that we
> now owed our professional loyalty to them, and we were actu-
> ally going to do our damnest to implement whatever policies
> they wanted implemented. They had some difficulty in internal-
> ising that. But I think, by and large by the end of the first term, we
> hadn't completely cracked that and I think the higher up the tree
> you were the more difficult it was to crack it. But I think we were
> getting there.

Most senior civil servants were also conscious of the need not to
overstep the line between being politically sensitive to the environment and becoming political themselves. For most this was seen as a
very narrow line, especially in a country as small as Wales, but the
civil service felt that there were occasions when Ministers did not
really understand that distinction. There was almost a Thatcherite
resonance in the unspoken question: Are you one of us? Also, and
because of the close proximity of working relationships, the culture
developed where, for very pragmatic reasons, if a civil servant and
their Minister did not get on - on a personal basis — it made life very
difficult for both concerned, and that was quite a different set of
dynamics from the position that existed in the Welsh Office where
relationships were far more distant and infrequent.

The various aspects of *culture* vary from portfolio to portfolio and
as one civil servant revealed to us:

> Obviously I'm not going to name individual senior officials or
> politicians but there are no two members of the Cabinet and no
> two members of the Executive Board team who see business in
> exactly the same way. And there are different styles, particularly
> driven no doubt by the individuals themselves, and their politi-
> cal or managerial background, and partly driven by the subject
> matter that they're responsible for.

Becoming Assembly People

One thing that surprised us as researchers was the extent of the support amongst civil servants for the Assembly. Inevitably, and as in
all organisations, there are some people who disagree with the fundamental concept upon which their organisation has been formed
but in the Assembly, and at all levels, there is an overwhelming support for the institution. One would expect senior civil servants to
support the organisation—that is, after all, what they have been
trained to do irrespective of their personal views—but the personal,

even visceral, support for the Assembly amongst the most senior people was quite clear.

> I think that despite the fact that, notionally to this day, the Assembly civil servants are national civil servants by the end of the first term, in reality, the culture had changed very much to thinking of yourself as a civil servant of the National Assembly and that it would actually be odd to think of yourself as something else. By the end of the first term we were all feeling, very much, that, like it or loathe it, this creature, this Assembly, was what we were working for.
>
> I don't think there's any single member of the senior management team at the moment who would feel less comfortable now than they were in the Welsh Office. Everyone that actually was a senior official in the last days of the Raj felt it was the last days of the Raj. It had been time expired. We knew it; every single person knew it. There are different views, strongly held, on how one takes it forward but no-one felt: 'Oh, wouldn't it be good to back those days again'.

PART 2: PAST AND PRESENT—THE CHANGING NATURE OF THE CIVIL SERVANT ROLE

Greater Confidence and Visibility

Cabinet Ministers saw one of their roles to be the instilling of a greater confidence and visibility within the civil service. As one minister told us:

> I get the impression that between 1979–1997 the staff of the Welsh Office were seen as part of the occupying army and that led to a certain defensiveness. That has changed now and I saw one of my roles as Minister to encourage my officials to be less defensive and engage with the private, voluntary and public sectors. So the civil service hasn't just changed in size, its changed its role: its not just making policy but making policy ahead of the UK and Western Europe. It's much more engaged and engaging. Although we have a statutory responsibility to consult, we do it anyway. I'm very keen that we develop services that are genuinely customer/consumer focused and commercially orientated. That means that the civil service must be more proactive, tuned-into the needs of the users and less focused on the needs of the provider and the pressures and trends in the UK Government. It happens elsewhere but the imperative in Wales is stronger because we have to prove our right to be here - particularly because of the referendum result - we need to prove our legitimacy as an institution.

The civil servants recognise this sea change:

> Our Cabinet is not at all accountable to the Whitehall Cabinet
> and, although they obviously don't want to be put in the position
> of rubbishing Whitehall policy, they have a great deal less inter-
> est in 'What is the Whitehall line on this?' Their interest is in: 'Tell
> me about this subject'; 'What do I need to be doing?', 'What are
> we doing?', 'Are we responding to … ?' So the emphasis has
> shifted from people who were well known for networking in
> Whitehall, which is in many areas not counted a whole lot these
> days, into people who know the subject. There's a greater confi-
> dence and our Ministers are very well networked.

Whilst most civil servants have welcomed this change, for others it
has been a painful experience:

> Initially, there was suddenly a very greater visibility of civil ser-
> vants. There were more senior civil servants, and sometimes
> quite junior civil servants, sitting next to Ministers in a commit-
> tee with the cameras rolling with the public sitting there. Some
> people thrived on that; other people earned a lot of respect for
> that; and others struggled with it.
>
> For those people who struggled with this, some aren't with us
> any more. They have retired or gone on somewhere. Most people
> adapt, learn and others … there are still people around who just
> keep as low a profile as possible and steer clear of that sort of
> stuff.
>
> As it has evolved and further changes have taken place - a
> move more to a parliament and executive model - in some ways
> people have found themselves working in a situation they're
> more familiar with, with no accountability directly to a commit-
> tee but accountability clearly to a Cabinet Minister. That's easier
> for people to cope with.

One of the very welcome spin-offs from this greater self-confidence
has been a slackening of the grip exerted by Whitehall departments:

> I love the greater independence from Whitehall! I really couldn't
> go back to being a Director for a Government Department, hav-
> ing Treasury or whoever crawling all over my back, telling me
> what to do. It's hugely stifling and unnecessary. We have free-
> dom to decide our own high standards and what is important. I
> still go to regular meetings with Directors in Whitehall, and the
> relationship is still very positive, but we just do the sensible bits
> of what the Treasury advises. In terms of career, devolution is
> much more fun.

Made in Wales – A Personal Commitment

Across the Assembly there is a commitment, even if not a 100% success rate, to develop policies that are relevant to Wales. As a Cabinet Minister said:

> There's been almost an unwritten law that what we are trying to do here is make sure we have Welsh solutions to Welsh problems, and to do that we need to find and measure what you're trying to do in terms of the Welsh outputs. Also, I think people now see much more of a professional career in the civil service, with an opportunity to develop, than before.

That principle is entirely supported within the civil service and their rationale was captured eloquently in this comment from a senior group director:

> I think that in the senior management of the Welsh Office there was a cadre of people who were first of all very committed to Wales. They wouldn't make a great song and dance about it but for one reason or another, whether Welsh speaking or not, whether born and brought up in Wales or not, they were by habit, by cast of mind, very committed to territorial administration. They also shared many of the presumptions, expectations, habits of mind of the Civil Service in the way in which people think about that: a preference for analysis on the basis of very honest assessment of the facts; a strong commitment to 'speaking truth to power'; a determination to pursue the right course, within the context of Ministerially expressed priorities, to a vigorous conclusion; and to do it on a basis of tolerance, a certain character of understanding. A lot of the old virtues survive and are alive, kicking and very vigorous. And you simply cannot get by in the public service if you are not committed to, if you're not resilient, if your integrity is flawed, if you're not capable, don't have a certain intellectual capacity and real weight, if you're not courageous, if you're not determined to look after the interests of a variety of different stakeholders and make sense of competing priorities and these are difficult and very privileged roles and they're still around.

Far less eloquently, but with just as much enthusiasm, a newer Assembly civil servant added:

> I really like working for the Assembly. I joined as a deliberate act. I believe in devolution and want to be part of it. It's a great tribute to all who were involved in setting it up. My own experience of the organisation is: it is more enabling, more encouraging of ideas, but there are still some frustrating hangovers of the past. We have been slower to embrace the people changes than the process changes. People are much more of a mix than before,

more varied. The old certainties have gone and establishing new certainties has been a bit difficult. There is still something of the Civil Service culture but it is changing fast, and the mergers will accelerate it exponentially. Being a member of the Assembly civil service will be even more different in the future and I welcome that.

Initiative and Accountability

Alongside the greater freedom has come a greater accountability and as this quote from a member of the Executive Board demonstrates putting in place an infrastructure to support the growing accountability has been an on-going challenge over the life of the Assembly:

> At more senior levels you are more accountable. As of this 1 April, most of us with large budgets and working portfolios have become sub-accounting officers. So the Permanent Secretary has spread his accountability to the heads of the major departments. It's also more managerial, far more managerial. If you've got an organisation with a £13–14 billion budget and 4,000 staff that would probably, certainly in terms of turnover, put the Welsh Assembly Government in the FTSE 100, if it was in the private sector. We haven't yet got FTSE management systems in place, but the big breakthrough is that we recognise that we haven't and are doing something about it to focus the new organisation as a management organisation on a number of key themes including top-class policy development, top-class delivery, either directly or indirectly, creating centres of excellence, and where there are shared services crying out to be pulled together creating shared service centres.

Continuity and Change

Throughout the period of change the Permanent Secretary's leitmotif had been *continuity and change* and this guiding principle can be seen in many of the actions. Such an approach can attract the opposite reactions of *too far, too fast* or even *too little too late* but, as a guiding principle, it has much to commend it and its effects are quite easily observed within the Assembly as one civil servant explained:

> Lot's of things have changed. If you'd been away for the whole devolution period, you'd still find a lot of familiar landmarks. You would find a number of top officials still sitting in offices along this corridor, that some of the Departments you would find had pretty familiar shapes, though some have been significantly reorganised, and a lot of the names and titles might look pretty similar, but behind that a lot has evolved in terms of the way we

do things and so on. I think it's the process of professionalisation, and nothing big happens now without expecting to see a framework of the project and programme management around it, and an emphasis on delivery.

I suppose the other great change is who we are. We had a colleague from the Cabinet Office talking to the assembled senior civil service. He was talking about the traditional matrix of the Civil Service where you can have people who came in from university and spent their career in the service and retired at 60. As he came over to our table I said to him: 'You may not realise, but I'm the only person in this place to answer your description and actually I look around this room and I can see very few people who do'. He was quite taken aback by that. And we do have a huge number of people coming in since the Assembly, from all sorts of backgrounds and we are a much more diverse organisation. I think the culture primarily has been evolving.

And, as with all change initiatives, and especially one based on *continuity and change*, some issues have to be resolved as they arise:

I have had occasions where either I or my staff have had to say to senior civil servants: 'We can't do this because it will put the Permanent Secretary in an impossible position' and they have said 'I can't do anything about that, it's what my Minister wants'. We must never allow ourselves to get into that position, nor must we say to a Minister: 'You can't do that because the Permanent Secretary won't let you'. We must keep all the balls in the air.

An Increasing Burden

Without exception civil servants will say that devolution, despite the increases in staff numbers, has increased their workload substantially:

What has changed is firstly the volume of work. Now everything's a priority. Every single one of the functions on your ticket is 'GO'. There are very many more hands around, commissioning hands or many more voices to take account of, many more people who want to get their 'sticky fingers' on this, that, or the other than there were in the time of the Welsh Office, which I think has been, in some respects, very positive. A large number of people who felt locked out of government have been 'outreached' and they have brought a lot that is lively and positive to the processes of government.

One of the adverse and unfortunate aspects of this is its effect on the ability of senior people to 'get out and about' in Wales—an important part of their role:

I think to some extent they have weakened the capacity of the most able officials to be outward facing. One of the odd things about the old Welsh Office was that people were able to get out a lot more than they are now. The key policy making, the key budget setting, the key implementing officials are actually sucked in to the processes of the Bay in a way that can often be all-consuming and they're less able to get out there to go see, go fix than they were 10 years ago.

Benefits of 'New Blood' and Development for New Challenges

In round numbers the staffing of the Assembly has increased from 2000 (pre-Assembly) to around 4000 today and with the merger of more organisations the number is likely to reach 6000 or more. Although much of the increase has been associated with absorbing other public sector bodies, such as Tai Cymru, there has also been the recruitment of new staff who have no civil service background and who have a personal commitment to working for the Assembly. The traditional senior civil servants have welcomed this with open arms:

> We have a lot of good people coming up, some fairly new, who want to go places - dead right too - and we're starting to get away from the assumption that you can't be promoted until you've served your time. So it's a real opportunity both to bring on the new talent and have a fusion of people from outside who can bring some new, bright ideas.
>
> Both the Assembly Government and Parliamentary Service have benefited hugely from the influx of new people: a whole lot of people have joined the Assembly who wouldn't have dreamed of joining the Welsh Office. That's had some difficulties in terms of trying to bring on a new organisation but it's been really, really good for us. A lot of the best people that I would have confidence in are new to the Assembly. Conversely some of the people who I worry about more are some of those who have been around a long time and are getting slightly world-weary. I've heard a different take on this from some people: 'We have had this influx of new people and they don't know how we work' but I think it's great. Because they don't know how we work, they come in with fresh ideas and they're not cynical. So when I roll-up and say 'these things are important' they believe it and they go off and do it, as opposed to thinking: 'That's what he would say' and go off and do what they were going to do anyway. We have a mixed economy: some people who have been here for years have really taken off with the Assembly but others have been left by the wayside. Some of the people coming from outside haven't worked out so well but overall I've been delighted with them.

Since Jon Shortridge became Permanent Secretary he has been committed (and in many ways has led the civil service field) to using open competition to fill senior civil service vacancies within the Assembly Government, whenever practicable. At the time of writing (late 2005), since the Assembly was established there have been 91 SCS recruitment exercises of which 75 involved open competitions and nearly 40% of these competitions resulted in the appointment of successful candidates from outside the civil service. This demonstrates a policy of opening up the top of the Assembly's civil service to competition and the attraction of high calibre people to the civil service.

Alongside this opening up of the recruitment gates has been an accompanying investment in developing the senior cadre of people especially:

> In terms of development to undertake the role you're dragged through a hedge backwards before you're even head of a department in this place these days. You've got the full battery of leadership courses, psychometric tests, assessment centres, you name it, to be able to get any of the senior jobs. Quite rightly so, too. Most of the senior jobs here are openly advertised so there's contestability on the system and that's going to be a continuing feature of it. I contrast that with the days when if in fact you were appointed to equivalent of what I am now, the Under Secretary or whatever they are called, that would largely be on the basis of a tap on the shoulder. You would come in on the Monday morning, having done a decent job on a couple of areas, and somebody would say: 'The Permanent Secretary wants to see you.' He'd say: 'I'm delighted to tell you, you've done a wonderful job and you're now Under Secretary.' There was no preparation for that whatsoever, whereas today, there's the full panoply of development for senior managers.

There is also a need to merge the traditional civil service virtues of cool-headed, impartial advice, being able to manage and interact with a political agenda without becoming political, but on the other hand not acting in a politically naïve way. These skills will always be required and many of the people coming in may not have that skill. The civil service has not traditionally focused on delivery, or the customer, so they have learning needs also. So the new civil servant needs a synthesis of old civil service values and grafted onto it the customer focus and sense of delivery that the new recruits bring.

PART 3: HERE AND THERE—THE CULTURE OF 'THE BAY' AND 'THE PARK', AND THE IMPACT OF THE CRICKHOWELL HOUSE BUILDING AND SYSTEMS ON THE CULTURE OF THE ASSEMBLY

The creation of the Assembly building and its infrastructure, and the use of the infrastructure as a part of the development of a new form of government, played a major part in helping to forge parts of the culture of the new organisation. The refurbishment of Crickhowell House, and the disagreement over City Hall (detailed in *The Architect's Tale*, see chapter 7), loomed large in the minds of the public. In terms of culture and change it is interesting to note how the building and, equally importantly, its systems played a significant part in bringing about the devolved government and new styles of operating.

Project Managing the Building and its Refurbishment

The project management approach followed was 'Game Playing' where the team said: let's have a pretend library, a pretend chamber, and so on and this approach, they claimed, introduced a greater dynamism and immediacy into the process than typical project management.

The decision was taken that everything should be established on electronic systems - electronic chamber, Hansard system, papers and voting, and AMs speaking into wires where a typed version would be available the next day. It was a brave decision; some might even consider it foolhardy, given the time available to them.

As the project managers were appointed they were made responsible for their part of the project: they had to design and develop and implement their own features. They would also take on other responsibilities and each project manager was committed to obtaining the very best for the Assembly. The project director's quality measure for day one of the Assembly was that he wanted a building that would be seen as the equivalent of a 5 star hotel: a place where AMs wouldn't notice the systems but would just 'glide around' (to use his phrase) as in a 5 star hotel. As the projects went forward the project team met every day at first and then once a week. Real responsibility and authority was handed down to the individual project managers. They started with just three people and then further middle managers were appointed and given specific responsibilities. They also ran a matrix organisation in order that individual project managers could be line responsible for one project, such as the Committees structure, and also responsible for staff training across the organisation. As there was so much to do and deadlines were tight it was imperative that everyone had to be clear about their personal responsibilities.

The major concern was whether the systems were resilient and robust? So they decided to embark on total destruction testing and even ran trial plenary systems and, on one occasion, they even had someone jump over the security barrier to test the reactions of security. They wanted to see how they would react. They ran and ran the systems to see if they crashed. They even held mock debates, with Hansard recording, and senior civil servants played the roles of the AMs and Assembly officials. As you might expect, and mostly tongue in cheek, the civil servants claim that the quality of their debate was better — or at least it was more impassioned. The sense of urgency was such that a mere twenty-four hours before the AMs arrived men were still putting the finishing touches to the place.

They tried to run the record at speed, they had mock security incidents, and they did their best to 'wreck' the system. And bits of the system did crash, one a mere three days before the Assembly Members arrived and overnight the computer company had to remedy the systems.

The team put on a good performance and the first day of the Assembly was seen as very successful — they felt that the project team had got them off to a flying start, better than they had thought possible only a few weeks before.

The Presiding Officer expressed his gratitude for what had been achieved. He was insistent that a modern democracy must have electronic systems and there were no complaints from AMs. The Presiding Officer even called for technical adjournments and he introduced a new parliamentary language when he said: 'Would all members log on or log off'.

The Permanent Secretary, Rachel Lomax, also gave her full support. A senior civil servant, later reflecting on her support said:

> Rachel led first with her emotions then with her intuition and then her intellect, in that order, which is actually a very powerful way of forcing through change. You know, this is what I feel about the work, this is what I sense should be done, for these reasons. Whereas, of course, we were the opposite way - the old Welsh Office was the opposite way: analyse things to death and then say something publicly about the whole thing. Really, I think she just felt that her organisation was bound up: an unwillingness to confront difficult issues, an unwillingness to act strategically.

The project team comprised a mix of civil servants and non civil servants and the most important criterion for selection of team members was to find practical-orientated people and to layer on top of that the discipline of the project management processes. The people selected were confident that they would get things done. Where it was not possible to select each person on the team there was a need to identify, very early on, those who would thrive and feel comfortable with change and working in such a way: people who would not get over-stressed if they were dealing with a 'bag full of risk'.

Another principle important to the team was that they had to talk to each other constantly. As the project director said to us:

> One thing I've discovered recently is one of the major causes of project failure is people don't talk to each other. You've got a major project going and the project has failed because people don't talk to each other.

In order to set up the Presiding Office the team met frequently and then as the project grew the same approach was strongly encouraged for each of the project teams and the subsequent operation teams. They all sat down and collectively worked out whether the business process was designed and tested, and they collectively decided if they wanted a system to support them. It had been decided that every system in the place would be electronic and so the teams went out and selected their own electronic rating system. Similarly, the records people selected their own electronic record editing system because they were the ones who were going to have to use it.

The line management of the project teams was based on three principles. The *first* was total loyalty between the director, team leaders and team members. The director acted on the basis that anybody who inappropriately attacked any member of the team, attacked him. Alongside this, if there was any line management issue to be resolved then that was sorted out promptly. This was an important principle as experience had taught that when people were involved in a 'scary project' then one way in which people often react is to go for the team. The *second* thing is a reverse expectation: the team members had to give back that loyalty. This was essential in order to work through difficulties when something went wrong. If a team member had done something that clearly should not have been done, then there needed to be an openness and mutual respect to resolve the problems. The *third* principle was to embed a culture of achievement based on a set of challenging interventions such as:

- Are you thinking about … ?

- What are you doing about ... ?
- Have you thought about doing ... ?
- Would you like to do ... ?

The project leadership was based on those three principles and was an overwhelming success, as the building and systems testify. The project also stressed continually the importance of learning. The lessons of learning were not seen as something to be put on the file; they were something to be discussed and talked about and shared. Risk management was seen not to be keeping a log: it was talked about constantly.

If a member of the team was not contributing, and the project director felt they would never contribute, then he 'just got rid of them. Otherwise, my project is a mess'.

The team decided that the culture of the approach would be a well-oiled set of Secretariats and process systems supporting Members. That was the embedded culture, which would enable them to perform. The process systems and infrastructure of the building, through the introduction of Standing Orders, on which the process is based, meant that people had to behave in a certain supportive way. That became their 'culture'. As far as they were concerned the Members were the most important issue in their working lives: the democratic process, they actually believed, was the most important piece of government and they had to make it work. Encouragingly, if one asked most of those project team members they could not envisage doing any different kind of work or working anywhere else.

The Influence of Information Technology

Our interview with the Presiding Officer, Lord Dafydd Elis-Thomas, was informative and entertaining and he articulated clearly his views on the Assembly, as we had expected. But when we asked him about his commitment to information technology he took on the enthusiasm of a young lad anticipating Christmas.

> The National Assembly for Wales could not have been brought into being without ICT. Back in 1993, when I was at the Welsh Language Board, it emerged that I couldn't send emails to the Welsh Office. I said: 'You mean if I want to tell (he named a civil servant) where to get off because we haven't enough funding, I can't do that?' In fact it was explained to me they couldn't email each other in those days. So I became interested in ICT, multimedia, and my head was full of all this stuff before I came here, and when I saw the Osiris system I thought 'great'. So the project was

then to make e-democracy work—it would mean we were as
paperless as possible—we worked in chamber through electronic voting, and by making clear that anything that happened
electronically had the same authority. I lost one big argument
over electronic signatures for legislation—they wouldn't have
that (even though it's OK for banking) but hopefully we'll get
there sooner rather than later.

   We have an IT sub group and Alun Cairns, who Chairs that, is
brilliant because obviously he was an electronic banker for years
and years. Let me give you one very simple example: during the
Foot and Mouth crisis, it was amazing really because most farmers are on ICT, so when there was a problem they used to email
me, and I would then email the Minister, and Agriculture
Caernarfon (the people dealing with it on the ground). I remember I was sitting in a cottage in Betws-y-Coed on the weekend
and my wife said: 'Why are you logged on, it's the weekend?'
and I said 'I'm sorry, but I'm moving sheep - I'm moving sheep
electronically - there's these sheep on this field in Anglesey and
the officials are saying we can't move them, but I know there's
this other field, which is fenced off, 'cause the farmers told me
about it and what we want to do is get those sheep there and they
won't be affected' and of course eventually it happened. That
sort of thing could never have happened without ICT, so I reckon
the fact that we have got this means that we are able to function in
real time all the time.

Extraordinary, and yet the development of IT is an inherent feature
of the systems and, in turn, has impacted on the development of the
Assembly's culture.

The People in 'The Bay' and 'The Park'

Anyone who has spent time in Cathays Park and in the Bay
(Crickhowell House) will appreciate that the two places are quite
different when compared against a number of factors.

   A senior civil servant in the Bay seemed to sum it up:

   In the Bay there are more new staff, and younger people than at
   Cathays Park. There's a lightness about the way people work in
   the Bay—partly the physical environment and partly because
   they are younger and fewer have a long civil service background.

A senior and influential civil servant from 'the Park' was even
more direct:

   Well, they're more energetic down here aren't they, in the Bay?
   It's difficult to capture something more than that but I think in
   the Bay people have got particular jobs to do and they get on with
   doing them. In Cathays Park, the civil servants who work for the

Welsh Assembly Government have a huge agenda, they're people who are good at setting and directing policy and, with Ministers, they have an enormous, enormous agenda and so people have to prioritise. Most people can't do all the things that they have to do and so there is somehow an acceptance that people at best will get by and if people can't manage everything then they're not held to account.

Not all of the Park's senior staff see it in such terms and believe that the responsibilities of supporting the Welsh Assembly Government, in 'the Park', are far more onerous than the role of supporting the Assembly Parliamentary Service in 'the Bay':

> Amongst the Civil Service there's a generally held view that they are under less pressure in the Bay. I think at the end of the day, I mean the sharp end accountability for driving down hospital waiting times, doing something about schools, dealing on a day to day basis with industrial closures or making tricky decisions about grants or something rests with the people in Cathays Park.
>
> In the Bay they are younger, buzzier, slightly fresher, a bit green and wet behind the years, they don't know what it's like to deliver stuff, and they are 'dancing to a different tune'. In Cathays Park they are older, stuffier, they have more history and experience, also some baggage, but they are delivering over a much longer timescale to a wider audience. When you walk into Crickhowell House it is fresh and young and quite exciting. This is partly because it's new and there are simply younger people who don't come with the same baggage and they have a cushier life in the Bay with no pressures from ministers. In contrast, the Cathays' building is miserable and grey, tired and falling apart.

Proximity to Politicians

One of the other noticeable differences between 'the Bay' and 'the Park' is that in Crickhowell House there is a somewhat free mixing of civil servants and politicians, whether it is in the dining areas, the corridors and lifts, or, as one person told us, in the private and somewhat secret areas where you can go and have a cigarette.

One politician, with a degree of bravado, highlighted this difference for us:

> I remember walking into that wonderful place in Cathays Park with the islands and the water - the coffee bar in the middle. When I arrived, it was full of civil servants having coffee but within two minutes it was empty. Here in the Bay there is an almost total intermingling of politicians and civil servants, which has led to more openness than you might expect in the Park, although it has also led to recruitment difficulties as I think

people don't want to have their bosses too close to them. Though some people find it invigorating.

PART 4: CURRENT CULTURAL ISSUES AND THEIR IMPACT ON THE EVOLVING CIVIL SERVANT PROFILE

Delivering the Goods

Despite the emphasis on policy development the issue that appears to dominate discussion is the focus on the delivery of better public services for the people of Wales. Politicians understand that it is this issue — better health services, better education, and the rest — that will earn them the support of the public and so the civil servants understand that their political masters will expect them to deliver, or set in train, better services. And therein lies a problem; a challenge.

As one influential senior civil servant said to us:

> We've got to learn how to be proper managers. Colleagues in senior positions in the Assembly Government are very good thinkers, very good at being creative, energetic at generating policy, but we're much, much less good at 'operationalising' it and I think we have to learn how to work in partnership with colleagues outside to help do that 'operationalising', and inside we've got to learn how to be better managers, to be more effective managers. We're good at creating, we're much less good at doing and I don't think we can carry on being like that anymore. I think we really do have to change - and that doesn't mean that you need to have the same people doing all those things but between us we need to get the right set of skills and the right way of working so that we can make things actually happen and to do that I think we need to look where good things are happening now and to build on that. But the main thing is that we really need to make things work, it's not good enough the way we are doing things now.

As in all organisations the focus on delivery places the major operational departments under pressure and, in turn, they complain that the centre of the organisation is not supporting them adequately. This tension is common to all such organisations.

> What hasn't really caught up is the infrastructure within 'the centre', that's still working in the old kind of way, for an organisation which was much smaller, much more intimate and needing much more control because people were less able to do things. We need to skill-up the policy areas so that they can take control of their own management, organisation, finance and personnel, and all those kinds of arrangements in the centre, so that we can

actually get on and 'do-the-doing', because there's so much frustration around at the moment, we can't get on and do-the-doing
because of the seizing-up in parts of the centre.

One of the styles of the Welsh Office was to be quite paternalis-
tic from the centre; 'just do as we say'. The bigger we get and the
more complex our business gets, the more impossible it is to hold
everything in control from the centre: you have to devolve
responsibility by making clear what's important for the organisation.

Another issue to cause concern is the potential outfall of a performance driven Assembly civil servant. Managerialism will produce
successes and failures, that is the very nature of taking a more entrepreneurial approach, and this causes concern:

> I hope we will become less risk averse but that's tricky in a very
> small, pressurised, political atmosphere. It easy to say that the
> civil service needs to take risks but you know you'll have a pretty
> hard time in the press and in front of your committee if some-
> thing you undertake does go wrong. There needs to be a bit of
> give-and-take with the media and the political side: there's a dif-
> ference between having a greater appetite for risk and eliminat-
> ing risk altogether: sometimes things will go wrong, you'll have
> bad luck, but there's no room for bad luck in government
> accounting.

Being a Specialist for Wales

The growth in the size of departments and the development of portfolio departments with civil servants mirroring politicians will inevitably lead to emphasis on specialist civil servants and a diminution
in the generalist—the gifted amateur—civil servant.

The other implication is that as people concentrate on developing
the Welsh agenda it will inevitably place pressure on the traditional
links with the Home Civil Service. What surprised us was the extent
to which senior civil servants welcome such a development:

> I'd say probably most of the senior team in the Executive Board
> are sceptical about the added value at this stage of us being part
> of the Home Civil Service. We can see the attractions of it but if
> we're serious about developing a Welsh public service where
> there's an easier interplay between people, management people
> in the NHS, maybe local government, certainly organisations
> such as the Environment Agency and a range of others. If we're
> serious about that then the Home Civil Service link strikes me as
> a bit of an obstacle to that.
>
> The idea of dropping the civil servant is a good idea: call our-
> selves 'officials' instead. I think we've made more strides

towards that than we realise: we have a lot more meetings in partnership with Chief Executives of Local Authorities or ASPBs. It's easy to forget what a citadel the Welsh Office was, we tossed press notices or glossy brochures over the wall. We have learned to trust each other and share ideas. That is much more important than having formal processes.

Conclusion

Summarising the (changing) cultures in the devolved world is a complex task. There are a number of conclusions that can be made nonetheless. First, it is obvious that notions of culture are widely used as explanatory vehicles by managers and politicians. It is true that they may mean different things, but for many it was a term used to capture a broad sense of what was deemed important and how business was undertaken. Second, is is also obvious that much has changed. The civil service is more open, more Welsh-focused, more aware of the interactions with politicians and a more exciting, less stuffy, more informal place to work. That is not to say to it is informal: just less formal. Third, is is also clear that there are different cultures at work. The Bay and the Park is an obvious tension (see also the Tale from the Bay in chapter seven), but it is also true that the many current civil servants who came from outside the service have brought new styles of working, while seeking to accommodate themselves to the civil service. Fourth, geographical separation, the nature of the task and personality all play their part in recreating the culture that was there previously. We found pinning down the cultures difficult but however complex the notion of culture is, it is obvious that it describes something real.

Chapter 6

Structural Change

The Executive Board

Introduction

The changes to the civil service organisation, and its methods of working, can be seen best through the introduction and development of the Executive Board and its role in directing the Assembly's management agenda.

The Executive Board is highly significant in that it represents a substantially different way of managing the civil service in general and integrating senior civil servants in particular into that process. Furthermore, it constitutes an attempt to employ more business management approaches in these activities. It is therefore an impor tant change management vehicle well worthy of examination.

This chapter sets out the various configurations and amendments to the board arrangements and does so with little commentary: the changes and the participants, as described, speak for themselves. The board has faced many challenges as it has adapted itself to 'do business' in a new way and through new organisational frameworks. Most of this has been successful and any so-called failures are typical of an organisation committed to a systematic evolution, rather than revolution, to the way in which it conducts its management affairs.

The Executive Board is the top management team of the National Assembly and is chaired by the Permanent Secretary. The Board holds a short weekly meeting, without the Clerk to the Assembly, to consider operational issues relating to the support of Cabinet business and a full monthly meeting, to which the Clerk is invited, to consider corporate management issues concerning all parts of the National Assembly.

As with all Boards it has produced a vision and values statement which it calls its 'Ambition Statement':

> Our *commitment* is to the success of the Assembly, excellent public services in Wales and putting the citizen at the heart of everything we do.
>
> Our *goal* is to be an organisation that sets the standards for the public sector: innovative, confident, open and agile.
>
> Our *values* are:
>
> • Impartiality and integrity
>
> • Delivering results
>
> • Valuing people and their diversity
>
> • Listening, learning and improving.

The work of the board has been set against the most recent backcloth of major political initiatives emanating from the Assembly such as: the Welsh Assembly Government's intention to merge the Welsh Development Agency, the Wales Tourist Board, ELWa (the Training Council in Wales), the Welsh Language Board and Curriculum and Assessment Authority for Wales, with their sponsoring Assembly Departments; the White Paper *Better Governance for Wales*, setting out the next stages in the development of the Assembly; and *Wales: A Better Country*, the strategic agenda of the Welsh Assembly Government.

The Board's principal role is to support the Permanent Secretary by taking collective responsibility for:

- defining corporate strategic aims, anticipating potentially difficult issues and developing solutions;
- allocating and managing financial and human resources;
- monitoring and managing corporate performance, and aspiring to best practice in public sector governance;
- expediting Assembly Government business and the delivery of cross-cutting Assembly Government objectives;
- overseeing a transparent system of prudent and effective controls;
- assessing and managing risk;
- leading and driving internal change;
- bringing on internal talent and bringing in wider experience and broader perspectives from outside the Assembly;

- ensuring that appropriate measures are in place for the health and well-being of staff, and for the safety of staff, Members and visitors

- protecting and enhancing the Assembly's reputation, and

- helping the Assembly to set the standard for the public service in Wales.

The Establishment of the Executive Board

The description of the Executive Board and its functions appears orderly and typical of executive arrangements to be found in large organisations across the country. The story of how this was achieved and the challenges associated with developing this form of leadership amongst people with a tradition of acting as senior civil servants, rather than senior executives, is fascinating.

At the launch of the National Assembly for Wales, the Permanent Secretary was supported by two bodies—a Management Board (probably an inappropriate descriptor) and a Group Directors' Meeting comprising principally the heads of the large operational groups.

The Management Board's role was to support the Permanent Secretary in taking decisions in the exercise of his formal and statutory responsibilities for the management and administration of the office. It also guarded his role as accounting officer.

The Permanent Secretary chaired the Board and its membership comprised: the two Senior Directors, the Counsel General, the Clerk to the Assembly, the Personnel Director and the Principal Finance Officer. The Board met monthly, unless there were special issues to discuss, and its agenda comprised items related to the responsibilities of the Personnel Director and budget and performance management of the Assembly's administration. Summaries of the Board's discussions were posted on the Assembly's Intranet in an attempt to communicate with the remainder of the organisation.

The Group Directors' meeting provided a forum for an exchange of views between the Management Board and the Group Directors and senior professional staff on management and policy issues that affected the organisation as a whole. It had no formal decision-making or advisory function and met approximately every month. The Permanent Secretary chaired the meetings and its summaries of discussions also were posted on the Assembly's Intranet.

By mid 2001, the Permanent Secretary had concluded that he needed a new group, with more of a managerial focus. Most members of the senior civil service shared this view, commenting on the effectiveness of the Management Board (a.k.a. the Senior Management Team) during subsequent interviews held by one of us in mid-2001:

> The current Senior Management Team is old fashioned and has simply evolved. The accounting officer role is strong: finance, probity, effectiveness. The Board has not changed in 12 years even though the individuals in the senior structure have changed a lot.
>
> There's no framework, they don't know each other's role, minutes are not read, no information/communication comes in or out of it, there's no asking: 'what type of people do we want to be?' There are no management type issues, nobody knows what they are doing, why they are doing it, and no-one has respect for them as a group. They're too similar, too cosy and need external challenge.

A senior civil servant, speaking in 2001, who was not a member of the Management Team, summed it up:

> Our 'old mandarin' group is sincere about values and integrity. They are lovely people, we respect them, they have integrity, but they will not grasp the nettle. They are too gentlemanly — they're sometimes reluctant to deal with incompetence. We need to change their behaviour.

The Permanent Secretary needed and wanted a new group, one with a managerial focus, and he commissioned one of his senior people to present him with a set of options. The terms of reference were:

> To review and propose options for the functions and structure of the top corporate management team of the National Assembly for Wales which would provide leadership and an outward looking vision for the Assembly's next stage of development.

The commissioned Director would compile a set of options and established a Review Team to take forward the development work. The Director encountered opposition from a small minority of colleagues, who were reluctant to change and who employed classic stalling tactics — 'we need to work these things through'; 'we need to develop ideas' — before proposing to the Permanent Secretary three possible models for a new structure and supporting arrangements.

July 2001: Review of Senior Corporate Management Functions

Within the overall Review, the Review Team also considered three categories of senior corporate management functions in detail:

1. Strategic management of staff, resources, performance and corporate governance, plus

2. Strategic management of the arrangements for the development and delivery of policy, plus

3. Proactive engagement with Ministers and others on policy

Senior Managers within the Assembly and individuals from other organisations were invited to give their views on the current organisation and the vast majority felt that the time for change was overdue. The principal views on improving the leadership role of a board were presented in the report as:

- Being clear about the board's function and role.

- Setting the vision and giving more strategic direction.

- Providing greater clarity to staff, politicians and the outside world about its functions, decisions and role.

- Setting an example in its approach to performance management and delivery.

- Creating greater diversity in membership of the senior corporate structure.

- Providing greater openness and authority to internal communication throughout the Assembly.

- Showing by the example of its own development a willingness to improve and learn.

- Improving links with the Assembly's Cabinet

The Review Team's final report, probably in an attempt to illustrate its contemporary nature, resembled a balanced scorecard approach with definitions of vision and purpose, values and culture, and change surrounded by the following four key roles for the proposed Executive Board:

1. *Stakeholders*: cabinet relationships; diversity; external directors; statutory responsibility.

2. *Body Corporate*: board's role; functions; structure; corporate behaviour; leadership; collegiate.

3. *Growth*: learning (individual/organisational); development; thinking; challenging.

4. *Management Systems*: performance management; information systems; risk management; delegation; governance; managerialism; communication; reward systems.

To translate these principles and roles into effective action the report suggested three alternative organisational models:

1. A board with a membership involving all the present members of the Management Board (MB) and Group Directors' Meeting (GDM) and with 3 sub-groups, (an option which represented little change to many aspects of the structure of executive management).

2. A small Executive Board with all current GDM members involved in sub-groups. (These options made the group directors feel excluded and was reminiscent to them of the 'bad' old days when the inner sanctum would decide all major issues.)

3. A sole board containing directors who reflected ministerial portfolios. It would have no sub-committees.

The report highlighted that for a management board to take on a more strategic management role, it would need to:

- strengthen its capacity in relation to corporate performance management;

- appoint one of its members to drive forward the operation of performance management;

- be accountable itself to the Cabinet;

- ensure that there were processes in place so that individual Group Directors knew what they were expected to deliver each year, include those things in their Personal Responsibility Plans and are regularly called to account for delivery;

- formally delegate to individual board members, group directors and sub-boards or committees matters that could reasonably be determined elsewhere; the Permanent Secretary should consider issuing formal delegations for those matters;

- improve the articulation of its role in the governance and management of the corporate body;

- strengthen its approach to risk management.

The report also recommended the introduction of a communication strategy and a development agenda for the board and its members.

26th July 2001: Facilitated 'Away Day' for the Creation of an Executive Board

To consider the report in depth, and to allow the most senior civil servants an opportunity to inform and influence the Permanent Secretary's decision, a facilitated away-day was arranged.

The brief to the facilitator was that the Permanent Secretary wanted an Executive Board:

- That supported the First Minister and the Cabinet, with effective relations between Ministers and board members.
- With an improved competence in dealing with cross-cutting issues.
- To strengthen corporate governance arrangements.
- That improved internal communication systems.
- With a focus on professional delivery of the agenda consistent with civil service values.
- As a mechanism that communicated corporate leadership and promoted accountability.

The away-day provided an opportunity for all to contribute and concluded with the Permanent Secretary telling colleagues that he would consider the issues during his summer holiday and announce his decision on his return. At that stage he informed his senior people that he had decided on model 1, that the Management Board would be replaced with an Executive Board, that there would be three sub-groups and that they would appoint two non-executive directors for the first time.

'Transforming the Management Board'

The changes were announced to the staff of the Assembly on 6 September 2001 via the document *Transforming the Management Board*, which declared confidently that the new board must:

- Give clear leadership and direction to the staff.
- Build closer links with Cabinet, addressing its pre-occupations and providing stronger collective support.
- Work as a team and act corporately.

- Be proactive and forward-looking, not simply reacting to events.

- Concentrate on strategic issues, not become enmeshed in detail or matters that can be settled bilaterally.

- Focus on delivering results and performance.

- Address the management of policy as well as resources.

- Be outward-looking.

- Place internal communication and responsiveness at the heart so that it has a clear profile and is in touch with staff.

- Demonstrate by its own development a willingness to improve and learn.

It set out in detail the role of the Board and its committees.

June 2002: Board and SCS Development

To address the development needs of senior people, the cpcr consultancy were commissioned to produce a set of recommendations. As their report identified:

> The Executive Board has identified the need to develop their leadership, role and effectiveness as individuals and as a team, in order to meet the challenge of developing the organisation. This recognition arises from several strands of diagnostic work, including a Peer Review and EFQM Self-Assessment process. Further diagnosis (at both collective and individual level) has been provided through the 360 degree feedback process to Board and SCS managers.

From feedback coaching sessions, the consulting team identified several themes and organisational characteristics to inform its proposals on the next stages of the process:

> The development construct: In general people do not see development as particularly important, nor is there particularly deep experience of personal development. Past experiences of development have tended to focus on technical or professional skills and development to overcome shortcomings.

The consultancy found a 'very strong appetite for development' amongst the people they met and believed that a key issue would be 'helping the more senior managers develop the appetite, skills and confidence to start operating within a different construct'.

> *Stress and workload management:* We have encountered high levels of stress amongst the senior managers in the Assembly. The key

underlying causes appear to be work being done by people at too senior a level. This is linked to the relatively weak development culture ... (and) ... as demands have changed and grown, managers have coped by absorbing workload rather than by developing new capabilities in their teams. There is also a culture of saying 'yes' to new requests and additional work without challenging and without tackling the resource implications.

And their *'other findings'* section makes for fascinating reading:

- very high levels of intellect and problem solving capability
- the tendency to be very inward looking. This corresponds with a general lack of self-confidence.
- specialists feeling undervalued.
- (in some instances) poor relations with Ministers.

To tackle these identified needs a number of appropriate and conventional (in terms of senior executives) development activities were proposed.

July 2002: Pause and Review:
The Executive Board and its Sub-Groups

In July 2002, the Permanent Secretary commissioned a review of the effectiveness of the new Executive Board arrangements.

One-to-one discussions were held with board members and others, taking the challenges set the board in the *Transforming the Management Board* document as the standard to judge effectiveness.

These extracts from the *Pause and Review* report demonstrate the significant progress that had been made in a mere twelve months and the willingness of the senior team to learn (within the meaning of organisational learning) and to improve its performance:

> The new Executive Board arrangements meet with the overwhelming support of colleagues. They are seen as a substantial improvement on the previous Management Board and Group Directors' Meeting.

> The involvement of group directors in tackling corporate issues is a major plus point. However, the amount of time spent by group directors on Executive Board activities can result in a larger workload being passed on to heads of division and others.

The following comments should be read against the background that the new arrangements were considered to be a substantial improvement on what went before.

The Business Meetings (Tuesday) are thought to be a great success. They are seen as effective and providing: quick feedback, a
link to the Cabinet, an opportunity for colleagues to meet, discussion on common issues, and an understanding of the wider
agenda. The presence of advisers is a major advantage.

The Management Meetings (Friday) are seen as less satisfactory. Although they are thought to be a vast improvement on the
previous meetings they are considered: too long, too infrequent,
often indecisive, and, for some, too large. To balance this view
they are seen as improving teamwork, an essential part of acting
corporately, containing stimulating discussions, and an important part of building a greater understanding of each other's portfolios.

There is also a feeling that at times what is a virtue can become
a vice: 'we analyse, cogitate, talk up something we don't fully
understand, and something emerges which has little effect on the
main stream'. One colleague said: 'Everyone has to make a
speech. Our business around here is words and we admire a carefully crafted speech'. As another colleague put it: 'Everyone's too
clever by half. We need to move away from talk, talk, talk, talk to
talk, decide, do, review'.

The work on vision and values is highly regarded by most and
should be developed further.

The significant and interesting difference identified by the *Pause
and Review report* lay in the three perspectives that emerged on how
further changes should be made. Whilst everyone accepted that the
three perspectives were not mutually exclusive they did reveal significant differences in approach:

- The *structure and roles perspective* believed that most effective
  change came from the reordering of the organisation and the
  appointment of key posts. Those holding this view had three
  alternative, but related, models:

  a)   the appointment of a chief operating officer (COO), chief
       financial officer (CFO), etc under the direction of the Per-
       manent Secretary in CEO mode;

  b)   the creation of a Departmental Government model mir-
       roring ministerial responsibilities, far closer to the North-
       ern Ireland structure, with a clearer sense of devolved
       responsibility and accountability;

  c)   an Executive Board which acted in a manner resembling
       the board of a major plc., where there is far greater
       accountability, clearer decision making, including voting
       on issues, and a concentration on delivering the bottom-
       line.

- The *values perspective* believed that true change would come from an emphasis on shaping the values of the organisation, by working on behavioural change, developing people and personally acting as a model of the new order. They recognised that this was the hardest way to bring about change but considered it to be far more effective in bringing about fundamental and longer lasting change.

- The *systems perspective* believed in plans, milestones, targets, co-ordinating, and ticking-off checklists of achievements, etc.

All three perspectives were important and necessary: some appointments should be made; values should be emphasised continually; plans needed to be drawn up. Where the perspectives were unhelpful was when one position was adopted at the expense of another perspective and with criticism of another's viewpoint. As the holders of the different perspectives agreed that they were not mutually exclusive positions, recognising the different perspectives and the value of integrating them strengthened the organisation.

A perennial problem in all organisations is the relationship between the centre and the operating units. Although this existed in the Assembly's management organisation it rarely manifested itself, as the overall culture commendably encouraged colleagues to behave in a civilised manner to each other.

However, tensions existed. Some group directors saw the organisation as 'the Centre and the Rest' rather than as one body, the amount spent on corporate overheads was considered disproportionate by some who thought the amounts should de devolved to operational activity. As one might expect, the Centre took a different view: it pointed to the substantial growth in civil service numbers and the relatively modest growth in the Centre; it was also understandably leery of the development of, what they called, 'Group Barons' without a correspondingly strong, but not necessarily large, Centre; and it felt that there were times when carefully drafted central policy documents had rocks thrown at them, by Group Directors, quite unfairly.

An overwhelming majority of senior people accepted the need to appoint an HR Director and probably to increase the number of professionally qualified HR practitioners within the overall organisation.

September 2003: The Portfolio Study

The Permanent Secretary asked one of his senior civil servants to examine the possible impact of introducing portfolio departments — that is, departments that mirrored the Ministerial responsibilities — within the context of the Executive Board arrangements.

The interim report was mainly concerned with highlighting the arguments for and against various proposals and, as its findings indicated, it:

- set out the high level risks and benefits of a further move towards a strengthened departmental structure aligned with Ministerial portfolios;
- described 'where we are now', recognising the steps already taken corporately to tailor our structure and the way we work to deliver the devolved Government's agenda;
- held up the mirror of experience elsewhere, and
- invited reflection on the emerging issues to inform further work and the preparation of a final study report.

The team undertook structured interviews with Executive Board members and two local authority chief executives, and visited the Scottish Executive and the Northern Ireland Civil Service where they met a variety of colleagues.

The benefits of portfolio departments included:

- To clarify existing arrangements and processes and to specify new ones;
- A wider spread of formal accountability was made on the basis of alignment of operational responsibility and personal accountability; strengthened 'managerial grip'; and concern around the sustainability of the current arrangements;
- Stronger departmental identity was reported as a benefit identified by the First Minister, and was more generally acknowledged as important for staff and customers;
- Greater focus on delivery

There were certain risks in the opinion of those interviewed:

- Fragmentation was the risk considered most likely and potentially most serious in its effect on the overall capacity to deliver the policy, services, objectives and values of the Welsh Assembly Government.

- Inflexibility was expressed mainly in relation to the inevitability of portfolio change and a consequential requirement to re-structure.

- Inefficiency, and in particular poor value for money, was predicted if central service functions were duplicated as a consequence of further delegation of financial and HR responsibilities.

- Reputational risk arising from control failure was identified as the main risk of transition from the existing arrangements to a new business model.

The final portfolio study report, intriguingly called *Shaping Up To Deliver*, was made on 26 November 2003. The focus for this second phase of the study was to mitigate the risk of the fragmentation inherent in a strengthening of portfolio departments. Their renewed discussions and consideration were therefore directed at

defining the role of a strengthened corporate centre and its relationship to operational delivery and at arrangements for the corporate leadership and management of the Assembly.

The report also set out a new Assembly business model to:

empower delivery of the Welsh Assembly Government's strategic agenda for public service delivery through strengthened departments working individually and together, supported by high quality central service functions and a strong corporate centre, delivered within existing resource levels and facilitated by stronger partnership with the wider Welsh public sector.

The *Shaping Up To Deliver* report made an important qualifying comment:

… addressing these consequential implications, together with the strengthening of departments, in a holistic way leads beyond structures and into a very significant re-engineering of the way in which the Assembly undertakes its business.

Shaping Up To Deliver saw the role of the Corporate Centre as critical:

The new Assembly business model requires a close working relationship between the political and corporate leadership of the Assembly. It also provides a unique opportunity to help develop that relationship.

Working to the Permanent Secretary as Cabinet's principal policy adviser, and drawing its authority from Cabinet, the principal role of the corporate centre is to work with Ministers to develop the Assembly government's strategic agenda and to communicate it clearly.

The effectiveness of all other activities within the model is dependent on an effective corporate centre, which needs to be authoritative and strong enough to balance strengthened operational departments.

Shaping Up To Deliver recommended that the corporate centre should: 'own' and develop identified cross-cutting issues on behalf of Cabinet; play a role in informing strategic thinking/policy making and delivery through horizon scanning; ensure a stronger focus on delivery; provide strategic horizon scanning and better analysis of future business and customer needs; continue to play a role in improving overall capacity within the Assembly to deliver the Government's strategic agenda; and other similar strategic activities.

In terms of the roles of Heads of Department the *Shaping Up To Deliver* recommendations revolved around a new business model and claimed, with justification, that:

> The stronger departmental identity which will flow from the new business model and the publication of departmental budgets etc, has the potential to provide staff with a focus for organisational loyalty, to their Minister and department. Externally, it affords an opportunity to clarify and brand sectoral delivery within an overall Welsh Assembly Government branding. This carries forward the First Minister's drive to make clear the role of the ASPBs as part of the Welsh Assembly Government's delivery. Stronger departmental identity has consequences for the role of the Head of Department.
>
> Overall performance management needs to be strengthened and the delivery agreements between departments and the corporate centre will form the basis for personal performance agreements between individual Heads of Department and the Permanent Secretary.

December 2004: The Permanent Secretary's Changes to the Executive Board's Structures and Procedures

At the Executive Board (EB) meeting on 17th December 2004 the Permanent Secretary announced changes, some already implemented and others in the pipeline, to the board's structures and procedures.

Some of the changes were ones that had been in mind for some time, whilst others were drawn from the Cabinet Office draft Code of Good Practice for corporate governance in central government. The aims of the changes were to:

—   streamline and focus EB business, facilitating informed discussion and incisive decision-making with a stronger emphasis on planning and on the organisation's fitness for delivery purpose;

—   distribute corporate governance responsibilities more equitably, using Board Directors' more sparingly but employing their particular experience and expertise across a wider range of EB responsibilities, whilst ensuring clear reporting lines back to the main Board; and

—   continuing to raise staff awareness of the Board's role, functions and deliberations.

The Executive Board structures and membership were streamlined, which mainly affected the overall agenda and the corresponding persons who would attend, and the sub-committees were to be amended. The proposals were:

• To retain the Corporate Governance Committee (chaired by a non-executive director) and the Policy Committee (chaired by the senior director) in their present forms, although the proviso 'for the present time' was added.

• To retain the Remuneration Committee, again with a provisional 'for the time being' attached to it. A need for greater transparency around the process was also signalled.

• To create a new sub-committee on HR issues and property management to quality assure the operational and non-strategic HR and accommodation issues which have to date been submitted to the Board, and to oversee the development and implementation of a property management strategy for the WAG estate. The committee would be chaired by the HR director.

• To abolish the Senior Staff Management Committee and subsume part of its remit into the monthly Executive Board agendas. The monthly Board would consider such matters as SCS recruitment and performance management, succession planning, training and development, and related issues. It would also be responsible for talent development.

• To create a new sub-committee on investment issues (the Investment Board/Committee). This committee, to be chaired by a non-executive director, would be the forum for decisions on the funding and prioritisation of all capital investments.

The Permanent Secretary also indicated his intention to take action on the oversight of the change programmes, through his chairmanship of a Change Board responsible for overseeing co-ordination and delivery of organisational and individual change, an induction programme for all new Board members whether internal or external, to improve their leadership capacity, to take stock of the skills/expertise balance on the Board and to put continuous professional development on a more formal footing.

Board members were invited to note these proposals and to write to the Permanent Secretary with any substantive comments, copied to colleagues, and it was added that subject to their views the above proposals would be introduced within the next 3 months.

Spring 2005: Comments Made by Senior Civil Servants Regarding the Executive Board

In the light of the attention paid to the creation and further development of the Executive Board and its sub-groups we were intrigued to ask representatives of the most senior civil servants for their views on the role and effectiveness of the board. The four sets of comments, made by members of the Board in 2005, concern different aspects of the board's function.

The first two comments compare the role of the Executive Board with earlier days in the Welsh Office and with the role of the old Management Board:

Comment #1: There's a big difference from the Welsh Office days. When I came here there was no top management structure. There was nowhere, explicitly nowhere, where senior officials sat down and talked to each other about policy. It didn't exist. There was a Management Board and 5 directors, I think, would meet.

There was no sense of direction, no idea that we needed to strategically think about the development of the organisation. I think the creation of the Executive Board, in its policy mode, set up some antibodies, and I don't know how far those suspicions have been fully dispelled, but it was obviously very important to have corporate direction. It's now very hard to see how you would do business without that sort of structure.

Comment #2: It's better than the old Management Board, which had five members. It was pretty well an exercise in deconstruction in that papers went up to Board and they would pick holes in them. It didn't lead or set an agenda. The Executive Board still doesn't do enough leading or agenda setting and I think Jon sometimes gets quite frustrated in trying to move us on.

The third view assesses candidly the need for the board and identifies some of the reasons for the grudging acceptance, on the part of a minority, for its role:

Comment #3: Do I think that this is an effective body? In some respects I feel I have to say 'yes' and in some respects 'no'.

Jon clearly has to struggle with an organisation which is extraordinarily disparate in terms of: function; components; staffing; and the political dynamics, which are very volatile and very tough; and to maintain coherence, and corporate collective focus, to ensure that departments' portfolios are supported from the centre; to strike the balance between tight and loose and all the rest of it.

I think Jon, I was going to say errs but I don't mean errs, I mean his cast of mind is more centralist than mine ever would be but I'm not the Permanent Secretary, I'm not the Principal Accounting Officer and there is this personal responsibility of the Principal Accounting Officer which it's easy to overlook. It's a very exposed and vulnerable position so a lot of what the Executive Board has done - to build a sense of holding hands, a sense of purpose — is important, even though I have my reservations about the product and the scale of the agenda that we visited on ourselves.

The agenda is so immensely complex - quality management, performance management, culture change, the equivalent people and project management skills, developing the skills and capacities of the workforce - a huge amount has been done and, you know, we wouldn't be in the condition we're in, we wouldn't be as successful as we are, if it hadn't been for the work of the Executive Board, and the centre, and Jon in particular. The leadership is real. I mean the fact is that it has to be exercised in this fierce micro-political context where staff imagine that the Chief Executive can just do what he thinks right. Oh no he can't! Very suddenly, if you become the story you're a liability to Ministers and the politicians so the way in which leadership is exercised, in this context, is very subtle, very tough, I think.

The fourth comment examines the link between the Executive Board and the politicians.

Comment #4: I've never been a believer that leading politicians and leading officials are in entirely different camps. They have clearly distinguished roles but you're only actually going to make a success of education, health or economic development policy if in fact the Cabinet and the Executive Board, or equivalent, of its senior officials are clear on what the objectives are and clear on how those objectives are going to be achieved. And that, on the Cabinet's behalf, the senior officials should be looking at that dashboard and not having any trepidation about approaching Ministers, either individually or corporately, if it doesn't look as though the metrics are going in the right way.

Conclusion

This chapter started with the comment that 'the changes to the civil service organisation, and its methods of working, can be seen best through the introduction and development of the Executive Board and its role in directing the Assembly's management agenda'. The Executive Board truly shows the transformation that has taken place in the leadership and management role within the Assembly's civil service. The organisation has changed substantially and is continuing to experience transformation.

Postscript

As we were writing the final draft of this chapter (September 2005) the Permanent Secretary announced a further change to his Executive Board, including that, in future, it would be called the Management Board.

The purpose of the new Management Board is similar to that of the Executive Board:

> To support the Permanent Secretary in the exercise of his responsibilities for:
> — the management, development and organisation of staff;
> — the stewardship of Assembly assets;
> — the use of public money;
> — the development and delivery of the Assembly Government's policies; and
> — the service provided by the Assembly civil service to Ministers, Members and the citizens of Wales.

The membership of the board is also similar and the introduction of the Senior Business Team, which meets every week to review and take forward Assembly Government business with most of the civil servants from the Management Board sitting on it, provides a distinctive name for what was before the weekly business meeting of the board. The Head of the First Minister's Office and a Special Adviser are also members of the Senior Business Team, as is the Chief Medical Officer and the Head of the Culture Directorate.

Other significant changes include the Management Board undertaking at least four away-day meetings each year, for consideration of major strategic issues, to undertake strategic review and/or to develop solutions. The Management Board may also establish ad hoc working groups, on a task and finish basis, to take forward particular issues or develop solutions, and report back to the Board. Individual Management Board Directors may also undertake a 'champion' role, at the Permanent Secretary's request, in respect of key corporate or cross-cutting matters.

Sub-Committees of the Board have been established to oversee and develop operational-level corporate issues. These are the Policy Committee, Corporate Governance Committee, Human Resources Committee, Investment Board, Change Board and Remuneration Committee.

Chapter 7
The Tales

The Prologue

Stories are powerful. They tend to capture and hold the attention of the hearer and a good story, especially when accompanied by a good storyteller, evokes the very essence — the 'feel' — of the events that took place. A 'story in its external aspect is something to be observed, analysed, and dissected into its component parts. Story in its internal aspects is something that is experienced, lived as a participant' (Denning 2005).

We have sought to defend our approach and the value we have put in story telling earlier as well as in Appendix one, but this seems a useful place to remind ourselves again of our arguments. For most of us, trained to believe that analytical is good and anecdotal is bad (Denning 2005), there can be a discomfort in listening to someone relating their views and recollections of an event that took place six, seven or eight years before, but for the people telling the tale, for those who lived through dramatic days, the tale is as fresh as if it had happened to them a matter of weeks before. That is what we experienced with a number of politicians and civil servants when we asked them to tell us about the events of 1997–1999: the days when they played an important part in bringing devolution to Wales.

One person responded to our storytelling approach by questioning the veracity of what we describe and whether the search for a 'good story' and 'a good storyteller' meant that we departed from 'truth and accuracy'. All we can say is that these stories represent 'truth and accuracy' for those telling the stories, that as authors we have done our utmost to maintain that sense of 'truth and accuracy' when merging different people's views, and that, above all, the art of the storyteller is to provide insights that others have to reflect upon and measure against their understanding of 'truth and accuracy'. In any case, notions of 'truth and accuracy' are, as is well recognised, highly contested terms and increasingly interpretive approaches to organisation studies, politics and policy-making are seen as important (see for example the special edition of The British Journal of Politics and International Relations 2004, Vol 6, No. 2).

These then are our *Canterbury Tales* — our Crickhowell Tales — a vivid set of recollections concerning the successful attempt to bring devolution to Wales. We do not wish to push the metaphor too far, and talk of a pilgrimage, but it is true that for those concerned this was an unprecedented mission that they knew would have a lasting effect on the people of Wales. Whether that effect would be for good or bad was too early to say.

In *The Architect's Tale* we record our two marathon interviews with the former Secretary of State and Assembly Member, (the Rt. Honourable) Ron Davies. Our second tale, *The Chief Servants' Tales*, sets out what Rachel Lomax and Sir Jon Shortridge, the former and current Permanent Secretaries, told us. The third tale records the extensive discussions we had with civil service staff from grades below the most senior levels; we call this *The Middle and Junior Servants' Tales*. The fourth tale sets out the experiences of those bodies previously merged with the Assembly (or the Welsh Office) and the fifth tale provides insights on devolution from those employed at the Bay.

We believe that their stories shed light and provide great understanding on what took place in those days and since, and so they are provided with as little commentary as possible from us. Albert Einstein is alleged to have said: *If at first the idea is not absurd, then there is little hope for it.* These people took what, for many, was an absurd idea and made it work. This is their story and it is only over time that people will be able to judge properly the efficacy of their vision and work.

A — THE ARCHITECT'S TALE

Preamble

Meeting the Rt. Hon. Ron Davies, the former Secretary of State for Wales and the architect of devolution, was an essential part of the research and we were pleased to discover that he was keen to participate. As he said to us:

> I think there's a huge amount of work that's not been done yet in terms of devolution so I very much welcome what you're doing and I'm prepared to co-operate in whatever way I can in order to

make that a success, even if it means that we have a series of meetings.

We interviewed Ron Davies on two separate occasions, with one of us present at both interviews and two present on one occasion. The two of us who interviewed him initially had met him previously, when he was Secretary of State, and therefore it was difficult to judge the relationship we would form with him when he sat there, relaxed, casually dressed and speaking as if to two friends in a pub. We found him good company, ready to assist, and full of anecdotes about devolution. The lengthy interview was taped.

The second follow-up interview was conducted at the University and was intended to check any details from the initial interview, to raise any further points of interest and to allow Ron Davies to elaborate.

In keeping with our research protocol, we wanted to know his views on the civil service's change management role in bringing devolution to Wales. We stuck to the brief despite temptations to drift further afield. In the narrative that follows we present his comments as spoken: the only editing has been the occasional need to turn relaxed conversation into something more suited to the written word; the removal of the inevitable umms and ahhs (ours as much as his); the exclusion of offers of tea, biscuits and water during the interview; the exclusion of two or three political anecdotes where names were given; and, most significantly of all, the deletion of the interviewers' comments except where retaining our words is needed to make sense of the flow of the conversation. The interviewers' words are shown in italics, Ron Davies's words in plain text, and the occasional post-interview comment also in italics. Both interviews have been integrated.

The Interview

Would you say something about the political context and how you think that affected things?

My role in it was quite interesting because I had the Welsh, and therefore the Devolution, brief put very firmly in my lap by John Smith. I was elected to the Shadow Cabinet in the autumn of 1992 after we lost the General Election; Bryan Gould had contested the leadership and he lost the leadership, and resigned from the Shadow Cabinet in the autumn of 1992. Hence, as a result, I was elected to the Shadow Cabinet: Anne Clwyd was moved to Shadow the Culture portfolio and John Smith asked me to become Shadow Welsh Secretary, which I did. He made it clear to me, in the very first meeting, that he wanted me to deliver devolution for Wales. So those were my marching orders. I immediately knew that there were huge issues to be faced because the Labour Party in Wales was not enthusiastic, to say the least, about devolution. At that stage I had a little bit of a breathing space because the Government introduced what became the Local Government Reorganisation Act, which had two effects: first of all, it put the structure of the Welsh Government on the Party Political agenda which was helpful. It meant that in Government time the issue was raised, not only on the floor of the House of Commons but in the public generally. So that was helpful, it also gave me the opportunity to start talking to local government and local leaders about how they saw things moving ahead. It allowed us to start the process of talking and we actually produced a document in 1993, or thereabouts, which set down some broad principles, on which I managed to get agreement with local government leaders, basically saying that none of us would co-operate at any level with Local Government Reorganisation unless they addressed the issue of devolution. And that was quite an important lever for me, for it started getting people to acknowledge and to acquiesce at that stage to devolution and also it bought me some time. That was quite a valuable period of time, but then, unfortunately, John Smith died.

Following the Local Government Reorganisation, the Labour Party announced a commission to explore devolution. Ken Hopkins was the Chair and that took evidence around the country. I started working with the Commission and it became clear that what I had in mind about devolution was not what the Labour Party had in mind about devolution. So, in a sense, I was in a bit of a quandary. I was personally committed to devolution, so it was a question of making it work under these circumstances. Suddenly, I had two issues: I had the prospect of trying to win public support, and I had to manage Party issues.

We talked to people on the industrial side, and in quangos, and there was no conceptionalising; there was no nation building, there was no desire to enter that debate at all. It was all: what's in it for us? how can we protect our position? So what do I do? It really was about trying to do some nation building, identifying the strengths of Wales, building up its own identity and that meant dealing with issues like the language, for example, like the culture, like having the strength to say that we wanted to develop our own tourism, our industry, that we would look at issues about the environment, and we would have to look at it from a Welsh perspective. That was all for me part of nation building, so these were the big issues: big issues about sustainability, about equality, about partnership, about culture, about a new inclusive way of working. So, those were the sort of issues that I had to get around and the other signpost was: what is going to be the views of the other parties? The other Parties, for me, were the critical issue.

At the time, there was an emerging — not a Welsh chattering class — but there was emerging a pro-devolution mood amongst academics and environmentalists and radical political thinkers and so on. There was a developing mood for devolution. I felt that could be captured.

In looking back, do you feel you achieved your vision? How do you think things have stacked up against that vision?

In my mind, the arithmetic was always going to be a hung Assembly and I took the view that you could actually deliver the new politics, you could deliver a new inclusive way of working, if the Labour Party was prepared to lead that process and not demand exclusive ownership, which would mean literally trading a new side of politics. For example, you might well have senior figures from other parties in a Cabinet, in administration, you didn't say: well that wouldn't work, what about collective responsibility and so on? Well, why can't you have a system where you reach agreement on what you can reach agreement on, and you recognise that there are other areas of disagreement. But you take a pretty mature view: because you can't agree on everything, doesn't mean to say you shouldn't agree on some things. So I took the view that it would be possible to develop a style of government based on: where we can agree we will agree. And bear in mind that the sort of Assembly I wanted to see was one based on openness, a completely new relationship between the civil service and ministers, with committees having full access to all the information and advice which ministers traditionally have. A system underpinned by a new culture based on openness, on partnership, on equality, on sustainability, all of these principles to be actually written in.

I'd like to talk briefly about the civil servant relationship with politicians and with Whitehall civil servants. Then I'd like to move on to the development of the model of devolution.

In the immortal words of Barry John to Gareth Edwards, 'you throw them and I'll catch them'.

Let me tell you what I think is an amusing little anecdote which sums up entirely the way in which relationships change. I'd had a number of meetings prior to the election with Rachel Lomax and with June Milligan, and I had a 'phone call on Friday from No 10 to say that the Prime Minister would like to see me the following morning (Saturday). So I rang the Welsh Office and asked if it was alright if I waited in the Waiting Room of the Welsh Office, because I was not yet sworn in as a Member of Parliament so I didn't have access to the House or to my office—I didn't want to sit in a cafe on the embankment waiting for the call to go into No 10. So June said, 'Oh, I'll have to check'. She rang me back, very embarrassed, and said 'You can't come in.' So I did actually go to a fish and chip shop on the embankment and waited until my allotted time before nipping across to No 10. I wasn't in there for more than a moment, came out and, lo and behold, there was a Ministerial car waiting for me, with a Ministerial chauffeur, 'Welcome, Secretary of State'. And I was a bit bemused, so I got into the car with my special adviser, Huw Roberts, and they took us all of 100 yards up Whitehall then back down again and dropped us off at the Welsh Office. When we went into the Welsh Office it was like 'hail the conquering hero' because there was everybody there. They took me up to the Secretary of State's room with a bowl of fruit and 'how do you like your car?' Only ten minutes earlier they dared not let me across the portals to sit in the waiting room and now there was my empire. So that was slightly amusing.

What was your relationship with the Civil Servants like in your first few weeks as Secretary of State?

I felt that I had a good relationship with Rachel Lomax because I'm fairly irreverent and I think Rachel was fairly irreverent as well, so I think we got on well personally, which is quite important. I'd had contact with her predecessor, actually on devolution—the whole incident was quite amusing. About twelve months before the Election, a letter appeared in the Western Mail in the name of a Welsh Office civil servant saying that Labour's plans were unworkable,—impossible to achieve in the timescale. I thought it was a bit odd but didn't do anything about it.

Then, a couple of days later, I had a phone call from the then Permanent Secretary in the Welsh Office, who sounded embarrassed and asked if he could come and have a word with me about an important matter. 'I have a problem with one of my Civil Servants who has written a letter' he said. Apparently the official had written a letter to the Western Mail, giving his name and address but saying 'name and address not for publication' but the Western Mail made a mistake and printed his name. I told him to do what he would normally do. I think the Permanent Secretary was mightily relieved but clearly he was trying to check whether I was going to make a fuss about it.

Tell me more about your working relationship with Rachel Lomax.

When Rachel's predecessor left I had some contact with Jonathan Powell, Tony Blair's Chief of Staff, we were still in opposition, and I was given a number of names that were in consideration as Permanent Secretary and asked if I had a view on any of them. I said no and then shortly after they came back and said they were proposing to appoint Rachel Lomax as Permanent Secretary.

So that duly happened and then in January 1997, under the Convention, we were all told as members of the Shadow Cabinet that access would be granted to the Permanent Secretaries and that they would contact us. So I was contacted and asked if I would like to meet the Permanent Secretary. I went along and had several meetings with her in the Welsh Office. This would have been in winter/ early spring '97. I got on quite well with her; we just chatted. What she was particularly anxious to know, as I recall, were two things: first of all, about how I saw the administration functioning in terms of Cardiff, in terms of the Welsh Office in London, and I think that Rachel had guessed correctly that, unlike the Conservatives, we would want Cardiff to be the centre of things. If we did want to change it then it would have implications for staffing, accommodation, all sorts of working arrangements, and I confirmed that indeed it was the case and I would very much want to reverse the arrangements: the main base would be Cardiff and that Gwydyr House would be the point of operations mid week.

So we talked about that and then we talked about devolution and I remember giving her a couple of Labour Party documents that we had. And I think she looked rather askance and I remember her asking: 'Is that it or is there anything else?' — although she didn't ask it as directly as that.

And we chatted and then, fairly early on, Rachel and I found that we had a very good working relationship, I think that we had an affinity, and we, quite properly of course, gossiped about politics: I would gossip about political politics and then she would gossip about civil service politics, and I think that was very helpful from both points of view. First of all, it helped to establish a relationship of confidence and a bit more than mutual respect, a sort of an understanding that we could work together, not as fellow travellers, or like-minded souls, because we had different roles, but very compatible in terms of our approach to work and so on. That was a very important part of it and I think it helped to underscore the fact that she started to understand what we wanted to achieve through devolution. So I think those early meetings were important.

Was there any bad feeling between politicians and civil servants about 18 years of Tory rule and the fact that the civil servants had been serving those governments? Because, there were stories about personal antipathy.

Personally, I thought that was extremely foolish. It was the fact I'd been in Parliament, from 1983, and I had occasional meetings with the Permanent Secretary and I muse on the fact that after a week in government my Parliamentary Private Secretary had more contact with the civil service, and knew more about the civil service, than I did in coming as Secretary of State after 18 years in Parliament—because of the division. So there was very much of a very steep learning curve for me in terms of understanding the dynamics of relationships and so on.

I've no clear views but I knew I couldn't take a book off the shelf which would tell me how to do it. And I certainly was aware of many people in politics, obviously mostly in the Labour Party because that's where I was, who used to curse the civil servants for being party political and you would hear Ministers saying: 'My civil servants wouldn't let me do this' or 'They frustrated me from doing that' and I always thought that was a load of tosh. I took the view, even before I had the experience of the civil service, and it was confirmed afterwards, I took the view that if a Minister was worth his salt, if the policy was any good, if the Minister was any good, then no civil servants in the world would stand in the way. So that was the general view that I took in with me and that was subsequently confirmed, and the issue of political prejudice never entered my head. I took the civil service at face value; I mean we are told that the civil service serve their political masters and I accept that line. My initial judgement was confirmed by almost all my dealings with civil servants.

You had to bring a team around you and you knew you had to deliver devolution against a very tight timescale. What were you looking for in the civil servants who had to assist you on devolution?

Things moved very quickly and bear in mind that when I went in I had a steep learning curve about the civil service process, as well as about my particular project. I can recall being given a red box, on a Saturday morning, and travelling back down and going through the red box they had prepared. As I recall, there was a draft policy paper on devolution and I wasn't aware of that. I thought that might be the case and certainly, at one of our earlier meetings, Rachel had intimated that during the course of the election some civil servants would be looking at what the implications would be for them. So I was pleasantly surprised to see the volume of the work that had been done and the speed of the process, because decisions needed to be taken the following day. I went into the Welsh Office on the Monday but I was distracted all the time by calls from No 10. Rachel and I were dealing with issues about the Private Office and it was all a learning curve for me.

I've heard a couple of stories about you and people have said: 'Ron was very much a people person, he was very good at judging people and he knew that he had to deliver devolution quickly, so he wanted people that he felt he could work with'.

Well in terms of this, that's absolutely true. I did feel it very important, I felt very much that the trust of loyalty, because of the pressures that I knew we were going to be under, was very, very important. That was a crucial principle. And therefore I was testing in a sense the system (this was on the Bank Holiday Monday after the Election), testing Rachel when I said 'I'm not sure about this guy' and Rachel would challenge, but would come back very quickly to say: 'Well, there is someone else'. This only happened occasionally but the process, and this is why I raise it, was very important in establishing the relationship between Rachel and myself because I didn't know where the boundaries were. I didn't know what I could say. I vaguely knew that the Private Office had more influence on decisions but Rachel indicated that she would co-operate and I think most of our developing relationship was based on almost testing each other, discovering is a better word, discovering where the boundaries were and how to work together.

But it was interesting for me because a week ago I was a backbench opposition politician and now I'm Secretary of State and they're here as a team of civil servants, and we sink or swim together. But I had a pretty clear idea in my mind of what I wanted to do. But it wasn't written down, there wasn't a manual, and I knew that it was a question of not letting the 'urgent' squeeze out the 'important'. I mean it really was a question of me trying to focus on what was the big issue for me, and that was devolution. I realised that if I got side-tracked on other issues then devolution was actually such a difficult concept. If I got side-tracked, if we didn't get that right, everything would collapse.

So I was very focused on that and in terms of the disposition of Ministerial portfolios, for example, and in terms of my attitude towards Ministers, I took the view that I would only take personal responsibility for devolution initially, and for general strategic direction of the Department. By that time I had Peter (Hain) and Win (Griffiths) as my junior Ministers. And again, Rachel was very, very good. Because I had a broad idea of how I wanted things to work I'd say: 'I'd like to put education with economic development' and previously they were considered two of the big portfolios. She'd ask: 'So do you want to develop them?' Then we'd talk about putting health and agriculture together, and then the environment and we talked that through and she obviously was thinking in terms of how she could deliver through the civil service mechanism what I was trying to do in terms of Ministerial dispositions. And that all worked very well and then I made it clear about my relationships with my Ministers and the relationships with civil servants. I wanted to devolve responsibility to Ministers: I will discuss with them, I will have my own political reporting arrangements with them, but I had to give confidence and trust to the Ministers so that if they made decisions everyone could assume that those decisions were made in my name. Now that has implications for the civil servants and I know that there were one or two civil servants who were a bit reluctant to accept that initially and who felt that they needed to have a meeting with the Secretary of State. They were not trying to undermine the Minister, but they were trying to get me to take a view which was different from the decision taken by my junior Minister. On each and every occasion I backed my junior Minister, not least because I knew what the issues were anyway and we had discussed issues or they had flagged-up things.

But that was important for me in terms of establishing that rela-tionship. I went back to that Monday meeting and lo and behold there was the Devolution Unit and it was a question of where do we go from here? We just had a general chat and talked through where we were and I was surprised to be told that there was a meeting of DSWR (Devolution to Scotland, Wales and English Regions commit-tee) the following morning in the Cabinet Office in Whitehall.

I was very surprised to think we were moving that quickly and that there was an agenda. It meant that there was a lot of work for me to do but fortunately Scotland was taking the lead because of their constitutional issues.

I should say in passing … I don't know if you know this, but Rachel Lomax and June Milligan created the Secretary of State's Office out of what was the Conference Room or Board Room, because they saw that as a very symbolic act in terms of having the Secretary of State in a proper office rather than in a side office.

I went in and we went into this board room, with Rachel Lomax, and we were talking about accommodation and I went in and there in the board room, at the far end, was a portrait of Prince Charles at his Investiture (and pictures of other Royals), and I don't think this room had been used since then. I looked at the portraits, and I looked at Rachel Lomax, and she said: 'We'll move those'.

I was thinking all the time of my period in office, but I was trying to lay down circumstances bearing in mind what it would be like post devolution. So I always took the view that this was going to be my office as Secretary of State but I wanted to make sure that I left arrangements which could be picked up post devolution. So that room was very much my office but it was also the Cabinet Room post devolution.

It was a joint decision, you know, and we talked about how it should look and what decorating should be done and what paint-ings. I wanted the room made as a working room and I used it for two purposes. I had part of the room, the top end of the room — what has unkindly been called Ron's leathers — I used that as a place where I could sit and talk with civil servants and other people who came in; it was like a reception area for me.

I'd leapfrogged on to the Tuesday but I was still answering your question about the Monday. I was surprised that the process had advanced that far and I was about to say that fortunately the Scottish business was taking precedence, which gave us a bit of a breathing space really. That allowed me then to experience the briefings which the civil servants were doing. It was a novel experience for me having civil servants saying: 'These are the issues' and subsequently, you know, a relationship developed. They would say: 'DTI are going to oppose this' or 'These are the arguments which will be used against you and these are the counter arguments'. This practice led to a highly amusing incident in one of our early Cabinet meetings when one of our Cabinet colleagues, who subsequently got the sack fairly early on, read out his brief but he read out the wrong page of the brief!

And it was by a process of this sort, by discussion with your own civil servants that you worked out those things. But I found out very early on that civil servants appreciated the fact that I was as honest as I could be with them and I had no desire to withhold anything from them and that I would explain about this and that and I'd always report back to them straight away.

Did you find that civil servants in Cardiff had some difficult times with civil servants in Whitehall? Were some Whitehall Departments helpful and others unhelpful?

My relations with my civil servants were always, I think, highly professional even though I encouraged first name terms, but that was a hurdle they couldn't get over and I understood that perfectly well. I could see, in terms of the process within the Cabinet Committee, I could see in the Committee, in terms of my political colleagues and the debates that we were having, where people were coming from. I'd been in politics for a very long time, and I'd been shadow Secretary of State for Wales and I'd thought through a lot about devolution, so I knew where the sticking points were, I knew the difficult issues, particularly in terms of the constitution, but I'd had a lot of discussion with Blair and with Straw particularly beforehand and I knew that the support was not universal. So I knew what the difficulties were and then I would pick up from my civil servants their concerns because they would say things like: 'Well, we think that there might be a debate on this issue', and that would be enough. I wasn't going to press and say: 'What do you mean when you say that there are difficulties?' because I knew that there would be difficulties. And I could well imagine where the difficult areas were.

Others have told us that there was a feeling that Wales and Scotland had somehow got away with something and there was resentment.

I can well imagine that because it paralleled what had happened in Scotland in politics. Bear in mind the political context, where

John Smith had given a very clear lead in '92/93 — the Labour Party was committed to it, and Scotland was committed to it — and my task, from '92 to '97, was to make sure that Wales slipstreamed and created the political climate that we could do it. So even within party politics there was a sense that, well perhaps, we have to do this for Scotland but, you know, does it really matter for Wales? There was a sense of that. But I wouldn't be at all surprised if that sort of political view had reached down to the civil service because civil servants do reflect those prejudices. So I could well imagine that civil servants, in some of the unhelpful departments, were reflecting that political atmosphere, if you like, over the previous five years.

And I knew enough to question the civil servants and they would answer my questions. And I got to understand that they had their official committee. They never told me, they never said: 'Look, we actually had meetings beforehand with so and so and we know exactly what is going to happen on the agenda, where people are coming from.'

Within days, it was abundantly clear to me that that was happening and I took the view that civil servants were the best allies, in fact they were the only allies, that I had. Therefore I had to work with them, as best I could, and as part of that I had to have trust in them, I had to try to ensure that they trusted me and that I ensured that there was a free flow of information of whatever sort I could bring back to them. Because Rachel had a wider agenda, obviously, in fact it was Jon Shortridge I spoke to extensively and within weeks I was speaking bilaterally. If I knew that Martin Evans was the person, or Hugh Rawlings, or Ian Miller, then I would deal with them. It was a formidable team.[1]

And as part of that process I had regular meetings with the Devolution Team but also with Rachel. I wanted to create a sense of unity and purpose, if that's not too dramatic, by making sure that Rachel was there and the whole of the political team so my Ministers, my PPS, and my special advisers — everybody would be there, so it was a complete learning process. Nobody had to try to second guess where the other influences were because I wanted to encourage an environment where if anybody had any reservations or doubts then we needed to talk about them in the meeting. So we agreed that everybody should know everything and that we wouldn't have to worry about internal machinations, or trying to side-track or second guess

---

[1]   Martin Evans, Hugh Rawlings and Ian Miller were members of the Devolution Unit.

people, because we knew where everyone was coming from. And in fairness, my recollection is that it worked because I don't recall us going out from meetings thinking: 'Oh well, we've got a real division of opinion on this'. I think we understood where everybody was coming from and I think it worked in that sense.

I think it did. If we can come on to the mechanics: you had to make this happen. The idea's got to happen. We've asked civil servants: what were the main change management issues you had to deal with? From your perspective, what needed to be put in place?

I think there was a political change. There was a transfer of sovereignty, a transfer of decision making out of London to Cardiff and that was a very difficult political management challenge because I knew that accompanying that there would have to be much further cultural change on my side.

And we can see it's commonplace now. Devolution has meant education policy, for example, is in Cardiff and therefore Cardiff is free to make its own mind up on education policy. But in 1997 that was challenging because we had unitary government, and all that goes with that, and the Welsh Office didn't have much of a culture of policy development and initiation, that was broadly London. So I knew that there was that cultural shift which was necessary, which was going to be a problem, but I actually felt all the time that there was an opportunity as well which came from both the shifting in political power and the cultural change which would hopefully liberate people in Wales in terms of initiation of policy making and so on. And I felt that there was always a huge opportunity there to create a new approach which was inclusive, that was the word that I always used, and latterly it became commonplace, but at the time, certainly in 1996/97, the word inclusive was met with: 'What does that mean?' It was challenging. Blair, for example, only used the word inclusive for the first time in 1996 because inclusive meant a different style of government. What I was trying to do was to lead by example. It sounds pompous and grand but I don't mean it like that. I was trying to test the ways in which that might be done by creating a better interface, by making sure that decisions were widely canvassed, were widely discussed. We took account of all views. It wasn't just a single Secretary of State making decisions and laying them down but it was opening up the process of government so civil servants could debate, could give their own best advice, they could build links outside with universities, with pressure groups, with trade unions and with the voluntary sector, whatever, and at the same time we would have a culture which was non-discriminatory, which was based on the things which subsequently were put into the Act, of commitment to equal opportunities, commitment to partnership, commitment to consultation. All that in 1997 was quite new and quite radical and I took the view that my responsibility was to handle the politics of it, to understand that there was going to be this huge cultural change, and try to facilitate that as best I could. I always tried to keep looking up there rather than opening the bonnet every day to look at the spark plugs. That wasn't my job.

People have said to me that your style was highly pragmatic in the sense of saying: 'We'll take what we can get easily without frightening the horses too much'. That you took the Secretary of State's powers, devolved those with an intention to build on those.

Well, yes. You make pragmatism a virtue and I think sometimes you've got no alternative and I don't think you're being particularly pragmatic if you accept that for which there is no alternative. There was a discussion on the meaning of pragmatism. The issue of taking what I've got was influenced by two things: first of all the pre-devolution discussions, which was a very long and very painful process and, you know, the Labour Party still haven't come to terms with devolution. There are still very strong reservations about the whole devolution process based on identity and Labour Party traditions and, you know, 'what are we doing this for?', giving jobs to people who speak Welsh and a lot of prejudice and a lot of bias and malice and so on. And I've had to deal with all of that right throughout the period from 1992 to 1997 and at all times in my mind was the need to make sure that I managed the Party and therefore there were certain battles that there was just no point in fighting, because if I had to fight those battles with, for example, the Home Office I would find out that I'd be dragged reluctantly to the compromise that we had. So, in that sense, I had to stick to that compromise. But there was also the other practical consideration that I realised that if I started a debate with the Ministry of Agriculture about the extent to which animal health powers should be devolved to the National Assembly we'd still be sitting here and I realised that I was arguing from a position, relatively speaking, of weakness. Where I had the strength was the manifesto commitment and policy documents. That was in the bank and based on my Secretary of State powers. I can say to MAFF, or I can say to the Department of Education, that in future I will have these powers anyway, so it's no skin off their nose. But I realised if I then started saying: 'We wouldn't mind that to be transferred', that would mean that the whole process was open for a revaluation and they might then say: 'We're not going to release any of our animal health powers'. If I'd opened up the discussion it would have actually weakened my political position. It would have meant that I was offering up for discussion something which I had already had in the bank and that might have resulted in two things: first of all, re-opening the debate about what's to be devolved and it would have lengthened the whole process, and I really wanted to get the General Election buzz for the referendum. It would have lengthened the process but also it might have meant a re-examination of those things which had been devolved. And at that stage I was quite clear in my mind that devolution was a process and once we'd started this it would go further. How or when, under what circumstances, I didn't know but it was clear to me that the creative process had started. Therefore I was comfortable. What I had to do was get the legislation on the statute book, create circumstances for further change, win the referendum and hey presto off it goes. Therefore, during that initial period, when we were framing the White Paper which underpinned the subsequent legislation, it was winning the referendum that was the key thing. At the time I knew that there were two big issues: time in terms of the September deadline we'd set ourselves, and unity in terms of keeping the Labour Party on board and not giving too many hostages to fortune.

How interesting. We're discussing the mechanics but it seems also opportune to talk about this notion of the single corporate body. Your brief, as you said, was about creating something fairly new for Wales but partly, I guess, there was also this point of taking things forwards step by step and not creating too many 'vibes' in terms of negotiating new arrangements. Is that what happened?

As I recall, my judgement might by faulty, but as I recall the big issue was actually, unlike Scotland who were creating a parliament, we were transferring powers. Well if you're transferring powers then to whom are you transferring them? So you must create an entity. I think it was that legal necessity of creating an entity which developed the notion of a corporate body, because if it's not a parliament, what is it? And I think that a survey during our earlier discussions, and as part of the Labour Party's internal compromise, there was the idea that there would be a sort of local government model. If you have primary powers it means you have to create a parliamentary-type process and if you create a parliamentary-type process it's about the institutions for empowering it. The notion of having a cor-

porate body drew on local government and for me the importance of
it being functional. The idea of having a more collective approach, a
more corporate approach through committees and so on, was facilitated by the corporate body argument.

*We've been given various explanations for the single corporate body and in
no order of priority they go from: it was a mistake; we were naive if we
thought politicians of different parties could work together; it was highly
imaginative, it was inclusivity; it works on the Continent, it works in local
authority; it's the only thing the Secretary of State could negotiate with
No 10. What's your view on this?*

It's interesting that we should be faced with those views now. I don't
think they're necessarily mutually exclusive because certainly there
was an element of pragmatism. We did have to have an institution.
Certainly No 10 was saying 'God, what's going to happen in Wales?'
but is much more relaxed now about devolution, but they were very
twitchy at the time. So they weren't flag-waggers for us, if you'll
excuse that expression. The one extreme which you said would be: it
works on the Continent and it was highly imaginative and you can
have that inclusivity. That was what I wanted, that's what I believed.
That's where I was driving. And I think the committee systems, for
example, could have worked that way and certainly I think that had
the Assembly itself not gone off on the disastrous way that it did get
off we could have created that. But my view of inclusivity was quite
different from other people's, even in my own party, but it was
something on which I found common ground with certainly Plaid
and the Lib Dems. What I always had in mind was the creation of
some left of centre coalition of ideas. That was always what I wanted
to see, co-operation across political parties but there were those who
didn't want to go down this strange, radical Celtic route. I think it
might have happened but the political system didn't give it a chance.
I think that had things happened differently in the creation of the
Assembly in 1999 it could have been made to work. But it didn't and
the committees are very different: civil servants have gone back to
the old road and civil servants are now the mouthpieces of their
political masters and the opportunity to give the advice to the committees, that they would have previously given in confidence to
Ministers, that has completely, the opportunity completely disappeared.

   It's not true that the Assembly was designed for a Labour majority. I think that constitutions are remarkably robust and capable of
withstanding changes and responding. No it wasn't designed for a

Labour majority. We had a famous away-day, with politicians and civil servants, just to talk about how it might work in practice. It was captured on the BBC Wales fly on the wall documentary. We were actually testing the decision-making capacity and we were looking at things like: what happens if you're dealing with inward investment? What happens if you're dealing with policy decisions? You have to have the capacity to make decisions, you have to inevitably move to Cabinet government, we needed to move to Ministers away from the committee systems. Committees have a role, and they ultimately have a role in terms of policy development, but there's a difference between policy development and policy execution and that was the compromise, a sensible compromise that we came to.

There were various things to resolve at the Whitehall end but my political project, regardless of what the electoral arithmetic was, was to have a new style of government which was going to be coalition government. Now, whether that coalition government came because we wanted coalition government, or the electoral arithmetic required it, was neither here nor there. So I assumed that there would be, if I can use the term, a 'majoritarian' government. I assumed that there would be the capacity within the Assembly to carry the Government's work but that might have been based on a three party grand coalition of the left.

A grand coalition of all parties perhaps? Who knows? Once you go down that road of inclusivity, I mean, is there anything particularly wrong in having a Conservative Minister for Agriculture, for example, provided that the Party has bought in to the rest of what you're trying to do. I always took it to mean that the political differences in Wales were always grossly exaggerated and you have, if you like, if you take an issue like the countryside, take an issue like transport, take an issue like housing, and you would have to spend half an hour with the political parties. You could quite easily create a coalition of what needs to be done and it was that that I was after. I always felt that devolution would impact on the Conservative Party and they would have to 'get real' in Welsh terms and they've done that now by their policy shifts. So I took the view that the idea of number crunching and trying to get a majority through was never a big issue because we'd have a new style of government and whether they were coalitions of desire or force majeure didn't really matter because you would have sufficient people there to sustain an administration in government.

I had good personal relationships with the other leaders. Once you go through a process of discussing and understanding people's issues I think you build up a degree of confidence.

How active a role did the civil servants play in this?

Well it's interesting. There was a process of articulation really and they were articulating emerging ideas and we had many meetings — the away day, it would have been in Octoberish, perhaps even a bit later because it required an amendment to the Bill. So it might be later than that but certainly it was well post referendum. And it was clear during the course of the referendum that there were issues emerging. One of them was, for example, decision making in relation to investment, and that was causing us to rethink. And certainly behind the scenes strong representations were being made to us about the decision making capacity, which was then causing me to think. I'm not sure when we started it but I started general discussions, got the Assembly to think about it, what their view would be on whether we were to move to a lot of informal soundings and those informal soundings would have included talking to senior civil servants at that meeting. So when we had that meeting it was in the sense that we knew that there was an issue that we had to resolve. It wasn't a question of us sitting down, as naive and innocent politicians, and suddenly being told of a problem, or it emerging through discussions.

The one civil servant, referring to the need for executive decision-making, said: 'This is the reality of what we are faced with'. It didn't come as a surprise to any of us and I had discussed it politically, certainly prior to that with my political colleagues, and thought about what we were going to do.

Will you tell me something about NAAG (National Assembly Advisory Group) and its workings? What was its role as far as you were concerned?

It was about binding the whole thing together and that was what we created initially. It was about getting a mechanism out for resolving what might be a squeaky referendum result. It changed, yeah it changed. It was a learning process for all of us. I'm not sure where the idea came from now but it was about: how are we going to make the Assembly work? We appointed a Chairman who had these people and I think the civil service had a difficulty at the outset, because they (NAAG) were very professional and would say: 'Well, what are we supposed to do then?' And it certainly meant you had to do more work and prepare papers because unless they prepared papers they'd have loose style thinking from 15 well-motivated people sitting round the table. It had to be properly serviced. I think that that was a learning experience for the civil service because they had to start to get involved in the work of NAAG, which they did very well. Once you start to get involved in the work you know that you must and will retain your objectivity, that you have to start making judgements about how things should go, or what are the important issues, or what the advice is to the committee and so on. And I kept a close eye on them, what NAAG was doing, and I wanted them to come to a consensus. I wasn't worried but where there were issues like, for example, movement towards Ministerial government, then I did take a close line. I spoke to key people.

Then there is the referendum. The very famous speech: 'Good Morning Wales'.

Well, I tell you what. I mean, what came as a surprise to me was the quality of the speech that they'd written. I knew things were not brilliant and in the course of the mid part of the evening it was very dodgy although I always believed that we were going to win. I could see a pattern of results so I could see the size of the majority and I was confident. There were one or two civil servants from my Private Office who were very close to me and encouraging me whenever. And at one point, it must have been about half past eleven, I had a quick word with Huw, my special adviser, and Dave Hill, who was there at the time to represent the Labour Party.

'What happens if we lose? Have we got a speech?' Because the great thing about the civil service is they always produce a speech. If you go somewhere there's a speech. In many cases it's bloody awful. I had long discussions with the civil service about the quality of the speeches. One senior civil servant once famously said to me: 'Secretary of State we don't know what you want'. That summed up my sort of relationship with them on many occasions. But it was clear that I didn't have a speech about what I would say if we lost, so I put my mind to it, but fortunately the pendulum started to swing at that point in time. So I didn't worry about what I was going to say if we lost. What I didn't say was; 'Let me have a look at the speech that I'm going to use if we win' because I was too concerned about the politics and there was the adrenaline rush.

Well I went on a walkabout, because at that time it was just a short time earlier that I'd thought things were looking grim, and word was going round that at last I was going to resign. And there were some good friends of mine in the counting area, so I went down to shake hands and say: 'Hi, everything's fine and OK' and that was just to reassure people that I knew, who were there, who were concerned about me. And it was then that some people were saying: 'Resign, you've lost, we've lost, we've lost'. But I knew that we'd actually won but I kept a very straight face and I was just reassuring my friends. At that point I knew that we'd won and that was when Peter Snow announced on BBC that we'd lost.

As good civil servants they arranged the announcement with the Returning Officer and it was literally about 30 seconds beforehand that I was standing behind the curtain waiting to get the result of the Referendum that I actually said: 'Where's my speech?'

It started off 'Good Morning' and then it just went into some sort of dry and arid civil service-ese. I looked at it, then the curtains opened and I went forward and said 'Good Morning'. And then it was just lips moving ... because I couldn't think of anything else to say but I did need 30 seconds.

It's been said to us that the success or failure of the Assembly, to a large extent, was driven by the Standing Orders. Do you agree?

Yes. I certainly knew the importance of having Standing Orders because we were creating a constitution for Wales. I mean it's not a constitution as we would necessarily want it but it's the best thing that we had. And I knew that it was the legislative framework and the Standing Orders that was going to be our lynchpin.

Buildings are of great cultural significance – the creation of your office in Cathays Park, Crickhowell House or City Hall. How do you look back on those discussions and decisions?

That was a politically driven process and that was very much down to me. I'd always assumed that the City Hall was available. I wanted the City Hall, seemed to be the sensible thing to do. I didn't want to get involved in an argument about a building, because whereas there is a strong argument to say that you should have an icon which represents the new style of government, I didn't believe that it was necessary. I felt that it was the processes and it was the delivery that was my project. And so we had the whole business about negotiation with City Hall. We tried to negotiate with Russell Goodway and he wanted a lot more for it than we could pay. I think I was well advised by my civil servants and they said: 'You know the state of the building and if we pay £17 million for it, or whatever they're asking, you're going to have to spend a lot of money on that building'. The key thing for me was that you can have a possibly defective heating system if it's the City Hall but if it's the home of the National Assembly for Wales you can't have a heating system, one which is 100 years old, and may be defective. I insisted that we needed from Cardiff either a quality assured building or them pushing the price down, as I wasn't going to pay more than the District Valuer's price. There were a series of negotiations and the fact is that I shook hands with Russell in the presence of his then Chief Executive, or whatever, and my special adviser. We did the deal for £4 million and when I got off the train, at 6 or 7 o'clock in the evening, in London there was a 'phone call to say the deal was off. He'd obviously thought about it in that two hours and for whatever reason the deal was off, which was hugely discomforting. The big thing for me was the political news management about devolution, because we'd had a narrow squeak in September and what I was trying to do was to create a sense of enthusiasm and to make sure people knew what was happening. If devolution was to happen it was going to work, be safe and go forward.

So the building saga was unfortunate because it was sand in your eyes time. It gave good ammunition for critics to say that, yeah it can't work. So I was pretty disconsolate about that and we then immediately started to look for alternatives and the difficulty that I was in was that we'd said it's got to be City Hall, and then suddenly City Hall wasn't available. So then my choice really was either to pay more for the building than I could justify or look for an alternative. Now if you looked for an alternative the judgement for me was: do I say it's got to be in Cardiff or do I say it might actually be out of Cardiff, and if it's not this City Hall, then why not somewhere else, why not another City Hall. And once you move and say it might be outside Cardiff the only thing you could do is to say if we've got to consider alternatives, we've got to let everybody have a say, so therefore it's got to be a public competition and certainly Swansea rapidly emerged as a strong option, but there were practical difficulties. I think they were overstated; it could have worked. What I was looking for was what would now be called, I suppose, a virtual network but I strongly believed at the time that it could work if we had Swansea as the home of the Assembly with four or five other places throughout Wales acting as regional centres: for public administration, for the WDA, for ELWa, for universities perhaps, for local government, whatever, all linking into the Assembly. But that idea

wasn't sufficiently worked up for me and I didn't have anybody to
do it. My time was preoccupied. I didn't have anybody with the
same sense that I had that it could work, to work it up for me, and
there were a couple of people that I asked who were just talking a different language. And then we went down, I think it was on St
David's Day, to Swansea to receive their presentation. They said:
'Oh yes, it could work because we've got video conferencing' and
they put on a video conferencing exhibition which was absolutely
abysmal. There was flickering and flashing, and this was their pitch,
this is what they were going to sell. They had the Assembly, and I
hadn't told anybody, but it was that experience of sitting down and
seeing this exhibition — it was just a disaster. End of story. So it was
back to: 'Okay, what are we going to do?' Back to Cardiff or if they
hadn't got any building what do we do? Have a competition! And
the first competition was for sites and then we looked and it was
clear then that there were no other buildings in Cardiff and that was
part of the first competition, so I decided then that it would be a new
build somewhere in Cardiff and the two sites were Bute Square or
where it is now. And it was a strong competition between the two.

When we were choosing between the two, Bute Square was a PFI,
which was a very workable PFI. This never happened. And there
was the public build option down in the Bay and we canvassed opinion, and had a meeting of my Devolution Unit. Opinion was
divided. Some were strongly in favour of the Bay option and others
were strongly in favour of the Bute Square option. I listened to the
debate, and I was about to declare that my preferred option was Bute
Square when in came a very grey-faced civil servant, who had been
negotiating up until that very moment on the PFI, and he came in
and said the PFI didn't stack up. He's retired now but he was a very
good civil servant and he came in, literally grey-faced, just moments
before I was about to announce.

So we had the site, it was okay, but what were we going to do
about a building? I couldn't say that I would decide what it would
look like, even though as Secretary of State the responsibility was
mine, but you couldn't make that decision — there had to be a competition. There was no alternative. I was conscious of what had happened before with the Opera House and so on but it was partly a
calculated risk. I suppose I thought: we must show that we can do
this; we mustn't be frightened of the challenges. So I was quite
relaxed to say we would have a competition for an architect.

Many have said to us that not enough time was spent preparing the staff for the change. That the extent of the changes was under-estimated, that the new ways of working were under estimated – if we had our time over again we would have spent more on preparing the staff.

Yes, I mean I have got to take huge responsibilities for these things and I was very conscious of the need to keep staff involved when I started doing a series of newsletters at the time. I have no doubt at all that my resignation was hugely damaging to everybody and there is no doubt at all that the hiatus that it caused must have been dramatic in the Welsh Office amongst staff, and then having an in-coming Secretary of State who was probably the complete opposite of me, in every sense, would have meant that the momentum would have been lost. There was a sense of direction, which I had formed at that time – I knew what needed to be done. I think that had I been there those issues would have been addressed, because then the agenda would have still been the inclusive agenda. The fact it wasn't was probably, like many other things, a casualty of me.

Thanks ever so much.

Let me tell you a little anecdote. I was pushing a supermarket trolley around a couple of weeks ago, not too far from here. People look at me all the time, and you often recognise when you have been clocked, because you see them coming back around the other way. A little old lady looked at me – and you know it is coming – and she said: 'I know you don't I', and I said: 'Yes, probably'. 'Didn't you used to be somebody?' she said and I said, 'Yes, and I still am'.

B – THE CHIEF SERVANTS' TALES

The interviews with the former Permanent Secretary, Rachel Lomax, and the current Permanent Secretary, Sir Jon Shortridge, were conversational in style: they didn't know what questions we were going to ask, they had no papers available for reference and they were not accompanied by colleagues or minders. As interviewers, we wanted to participate in a conversation, one that flowed naturally, one that might capture their most vivid memories and feelings, although we realised, only too well, that both interviewees were far too senior and clever to be unintentionally indiscreet.

What follows is a record of the two conversations. Both of them used everyday informal language, and were certainly not speaking from a brief, and the narrative explains, with refreshing style, the role of two Permanent Secretaries in bringing devolution to Wales.

In much the same way, the questions we asked, or the prompts we made, were part of a natural conversation and are shown in this text, in a deliberately abbreviated style, solely to help the reader appreciate the flow of the conversation. We also restricted ourselves to issues pertaining to the civil servants' role in change management no matter how great the temptation to wander into other areas of interest.

Our questions and prompts are shown in italics, their responses in plain text, and any subsequent comment from us is also in italics.

Ms. Lomax's Tale[2]

When I arrived in Cardiff the Welsh Office was like an outpost of Whitehall in Wales, rather like a slightly old fashioned version of several Government Departments. It had been created from the Welsh offices of a number of Whitehall departments and it had grown over the years as different bits were added to it. It was organised under different Under Secretary directors who, although they didn't all have exact counterparts, related closely to Whitehall Departments. A very large proportion of the activity was in health, and we were also very heavily engaged in running quangos, so 'fund distribution' was a core activity. The Welsh Office was a bit embattled after nearly twenty years of Tory Governments because local government in Wales had remained mostly Labour. Those civil servants who had been there before 1979 were scarred by their previous (failed) attempt at devolution. And the staff in general were very apprehensive [at the prospect of a change in government] and, I thought, very sensitive to the possibility of criticism from the local press, and very concerned as the election approached about how they would get on with a Labour Government with a devolution agenda.

You have been described as a 'whirlwind'

I could see that change was bound to come. It was clear that we would have a new Government that would come in with a devolution agenda. Either we grasped that agenda and ran with it and made a success of it or we would be in for an extremely bruising and difficult time.

---

[2]   Rachel Lomax is currently Deputy Governor Monetary Policy at the Bank of England. We met her in the marbled halls of the Bank and she gave freely of her time. Her impressive CV is well known to most people interested in politics and the public sector. She was born in Swansea.

I also saw devolution as an opportunity to modernise what was going on in Wales.

Devolution gave us the opportunity to think about problems in a holistic way, from a Welsh point of view, to look at the needs of Wales as a place, and to think more strategically about Wales. One of the attractions of the job for me had been the challenge of economic regeneration. That calls for a joined up, strategic approach to policy and a deliberate refusal to see any place as just the provincial back office of some metropolitan economic power. I thought we needed to re orient our thinking: to look at problems from the Welsh perspective and focus on what suits Wales rather than adapting London policies to Welsh circumstances; to show more intellectual boldness and grasp the opportunities of having health, education and transport under one roof; and to exploit the synergies between them rather than treating them as lots of small businesses which we effectively ran separately. Departments in Whitehall often have great difficulty in working together but in Wales, because everything was on a more human scale, it was practical to look at economic regeneration in all its aspects- social, and economic, both transport and education policy. So I saw devolution as a wonderful way of unlocking what we should have been doing anyway. But this approach required a bit more self-confidence, for people to think imaginatively outside the boundaries of the work they were immediately engaged in. To be frank, I did think that people in Cardiff were a bit timid: some of them were very bright, it wasn't that there was any serious lack of capacity, but I felt they tended to be a little constrained by their past experience.

Why was that?

Civil servants respond to what their Ministers want. I don't think John Redwood spent a night in Wales: his political ambitions were very, very clearly focused to London and that influences the civil service, and affects the way it looks at life. And I had the advantage of coming from outside—I wasn't even from London, I had just come from Washington, I'd had this liberating couple of years in the World Bank—so I suppose that gave me a degree of boldness.

Is it fair to say, as some have told us, that Labour hadn't thought through its policy on devolution in Wales?

I think that's a little harsh but thinking about devolution for Wales had not been as fully developed as it had been in Scotland. There had been a constitutional convention in Scotland, whereas in Wales it was pretty much the 1970s' model of devolution. I don't think it was ever regarded as likely to be wholly satisfactory. But it was a case of taking what we were given and making the best of it – as Ron used to say: 'devolution *is a process not an event*'. So the challenge was to make the devolution model which was on offer as workable as possible, in the time available; and not to let it get picked apart, as happened in the 1979.

Ron and I had at least two key meetings before the election and a couple of important things were secured during that period. The first was agreement that the major work on devolution would be done in Wales, rather than by some gigantic team at the centre (ie in Whitehall) which is what happened in the 1970s. That gave us more control over our own legislation. The purpose of the machinery which was set up at the centre of government was to facilitate and coordinate devolution preparations in Scotland and Wales (and Northern Ireland). It was relatively lightweight, at official level, with a Cabinet Committee to oversee things at Ministerial level. This agreement was secured by negotiation with Sir Robin Butler (then Cabinet Secretary) and the Scots and the Irish. I had little plotting meetings with the Scots and Irish Permanent Secretaries before the election and then regularly thereafter during the devolution debates so that we were all working together as closely as possible.

The other key agreement – this time with incoming Welsh Office Ministers – was that we would not attempt to get more powers devolved to Wales than the Secretary of State already had. So devolution was essentially about changing the political arrangements for exercising the powers that had already been devolved to Wales. I think that limited the scope for boundary disputes and 'argy-bargy' with Whitehall Departments and it made it feasible for us to draft the legislation and pass a Bill in double-quick time.

There was a third big issue which wasn't addressed before the election but became clear during the first year: the decision not to re-open the Barnett formula.

Those three key agreements meant there was so much less to argue about. Our aim was not to get bogged down. To be successful we needed to move fast: and stick to the same timescale as the Scots. To have re-opened the Barnett formula, or argued for more powers to be devolved to Wales, would have opened a can of worms and risked sparking disagreements that could have become incredibly bitter and maybe even scuppered devolution itself.

In which ways was the civil service changing?

I thought the experience of doing devolution was itself a tremendous confidence builder for the Welsh Office because it wasn't being done *to* the Welsh civil service, it was being done *by* them. We had a task force consisting of senior people like Jon Shortridge, Martin Evans, and Hugh Rawlings as well as some really quite junior people, who worked their socks off and were very, very good. The fact that a small group of people, most of whom had spent the bulk of their career in Wales, could design and execute this completely new policy — from drafting the White Paper, to holding a referendum and enacting the Government of Wales Act — from a standing start, in record quick time, was a great demonstration of what they could do. It was a great boost to morale. (*Some senior civil servants do not see this as such a great confidence builder as they never doubted their ability to 'deliver the goods'.*)

My own contribution was to choose people for the devolution team and in that I relied on advice from people like Jon Shortridge and John Lloyd.

Yes, it's true that I took a hand in drafting the White paper. We were all in Gwydyr House the day before the White Paper had to be circulated to the Cabinet Committee. I didn't think the draft was compelling enough — it didn't have enough 'oomph'. Devolution was by no means a done deal in Wales, and there was a lot of scepticism among the people who would be most immediately affected by it. To put out a limp, confused document would have been proof of all their worst fears. They would have said: 'That's exactly what we'll get if we get devolution'. So a decent draft was one way of showing that we knew how to do things properly.

I probably had more self-confidence in dealing with Whitehall. The other area where I felt I could make a contribution was in dealing with the incoming Labour Party, because I hadn't been part of the past. In fact, I'm pretty certain Ron had already made up his mind to get along with the senior civil servants, whoever they were, but I did put a lot of personal effort into that relationship because I thought it was absolutely key.

We've been told, many times, that certain politicians had a strong personal antipathy towards certain civil servants. Did you feel this?

Not at all. When I was in the Welsh Office, the Ministers were Ron, Peter Hain and Win Griffiths and then Jon Owen Jones. They did not strike me as suspicious or antagonistic to civil servants. Rather, I felt that this was their big moment, devolution was the one thing they really wanted to do — that was certainly true of Ron — but they knew they couldn't do it without us, so they had to get on with us.

People say that Ron Davies was very much a 'people person'?

Ron was a very good Minister. He was very easy to work with when he wasn't being wound up by politics. He really knew how to chair a meeting and get through the business: he once said to me: 'There's one thing you learn in the Labour Party and that's how to chair a meeting'. Most ministers have their likes and dislikes when it comes to civil servants but I thought Ron was relatively catholic in his ability to get on with civil servants. And I would be surprised if you found anyone who had worked in the civil service during that period who didn't have great respect for him. The reason was that it was all great fun and we got through an enormous amount in a short space of time — and we could do that because we had good working relationships between the Ministerial team and the key civil servants. We had regular and very open meetings, both at Gwydyr and in Cardiff.

In the run-up to the election, we turned the best conference room into a Secretary of State's office, overlooking Cathays Park. Tory Ministers had used a flat and a small office, but there wasn't a proper Secretary of State's office in Cardiff. We thought that if we were going to do devolution then there needed to be a proper Ministerial office where the Secretary of State could set up camp. We had meetings there and people used to mill in and out of the outer office, and it was quite a hub of activity. I can't tell you how it takes the soul out of a department if the Ministers who are in charge of it never come near it. June Milligan and I organised that, we had to re-jig some of the other rooms. I don't know if Ron appreciated it, but it was one way of saying welcome. It's not enough to write 'we're on your side, we want to work with you, if you trust us we won't let you down'; sometimes actions speak a lot louder than words.

Can you talk about the initial process of securing devolution?

There was one major strand of work in getting the constitutional arrangements worked out, negotiating them through Whitehall and the House of Commons, and then developing the standing orders for the Assembly — the NAAG and Standing Orders Commission. It was a long piece of work, and an important one. There was a party in the House of Lords to celebrate the passing of the Government of

Wales Act in July 98 — that was a big moment, but after that there were many other work streams, to set up and prepare for the Assembly itself. I remember Bryan Mitchell saying to me, in a rather tetchy way, when I put him in charge of it [establishing the building and systems]: 'We've started far too late on this', he was right in a way, but we had to give priority to the legislation.

I don't think we could have got very far with developing 'ways of working' until the AMs themselves arrived. There was a lot of stuff that was always going to have to wait until the Assembly Members were there. The AMs needed to feel it was their Assembly, not something that civil servants had created without consulting them and they were just being slotted in. You can be too slick; it would have been like moving into a house and finding that someone else had already furnished it. So the building had to be ready enough but not too ready.

So it was a conscious decision to allow the AMs to mould the Assembly building and systems?

I felt the Assembly needed to take ownership of the whole project and if they felt everything was too fitted-up in advance they would rebel against it. That said, a lot of what was done was based on the tacit assumption that Ron would be the First Secretary. He was taking decisions that he thought would clear the decks when he was First Minister. The business with Ron in autumn 1998 disrupted everybody's planning.

On the issue of civil service culture, preparing for devolution was itself a huge exercise in change management. It led the Welsh Office to do new things: the first time I suggested having an 'away-day' it caused great shock — anyone would think we were off on a junket, 'What if the Western Mail got hold of it?' I did hold inclusive meetings down to middle manager level but if I had the time over again I would spend less time fussing over the building and put more effort into preparing the staff. We didn't really have enough time for that. My guess is that they probably felt very unprepared.

Given limited time and resources, I focused on the senior managers and essentially said to them: 'When the AMs arrive it'll be for you to show leadership to the staff and forge the right relationship with the AMs. If AMs do go round you and approach your staff directly, remember that you are the Director, it is for you to protect your staff from excessive demands and manage the relationship with the AMs'. In one sense, until the senior managers had got their heads around all that, trying to prepare the junior staff was a bit premature. And imagining what life would be like under the Assembly wasn't easy — for any one.

To sum up, there were three major work-streams:

- the constitutional work-stream — which went well;
- the practical arrangements and the building — which was good enough in the circumstances, despite the to-ing and fro-ing over the choice of location.
- preparing the civil service — where, looking back on it, I suspect we only scratched the surface — though maybe living with devolution was always going to provide the most valuable learning experience .

To what extent did the civil service influence the adoption of the single corporate body?[3]

Not at all: it was not our choice. It was the local authority model which had been used in the 1970s devolution debates; and that was all that was on offer for Wales. I don't think any of us thought it was ideal, but it was the only legal framework of devolution that the Labour Party was prepared to offer Wales. As civil servants, we felt the broad parameters had been agreed in opposition, and our job was to make it as workable as possible. The aim was to get devolution on the statute book — and rely on the fact that devolution is 'a process not an event' to secure something better in the future, if need be.

A senior civil servant has said that the model works in Birmingham, and that a continental politician would recognise it.

Birmingham City Council wasn't operating this model when we were contemplating it for Wales. The Cabinet model of Local Government post-dates the Government of Wales Act. And there are two reasons why Wales might be different from Birmingham:

Firstly, the local authority model didn't entirely fit the ambitions of people in Wales who were in favour of devolution; and secondly some of the people who entered the Assembly had cut their political teeth in Westminster — so the parliamentary model was in their

---

[3] At this point, and for the only time in the interview, Rachel Lomax became quite abrupt in her manner. It was her indignation that we had suggested civil service interference in what was clearly a political decision. We were putting to her a point that had been put to us on several occasions.

bloodstream. Both groups might have been more comfortable with a devolution model closer to Scotland — or Northern Ireland.

A Westminster type model was never on the cards for Wales in 1997. And the Welsh Office team — Ministers and civil servants — didn't have a free hand in designing the model of devolution. Our proposals were subject to wider discussion and agreement in the constitutional committee in Whitehall, chaired by Derry Irvine. Some members of the committee were pretty sceptical about devolution, and we did have trouble with some issues. For example, we weren't allowed to use the term 'Minister' in Wales. We did not get carte blanche to build our own Assembly. We had to broker agreements with other Ministers and other departments.

We did look at other devolved administrations — in Strasbourg, Barcelona, and someone may even have gone to Canada — to get ideas about how they were run. I paid a few visits in Europe as did some of the more junior people involved in devolution but we were mostly interested in practical issues — like how to conduct business bilingually, seating patterns, mechanical voting, the use of modern IT, handling questions and so on.

What do you think will be the role of the Assembly civil servant be in the future? Are the days of a UK Civil Service numbered?

Maybe. Back in 1997, looking 10 years down the track, that's what we probably expected. I did discuss the future of the Civil Service with my opposite number from Scotland and Richard Wilson, the Cabinet Secretary; we could see what was likely to happen in time but we were focussed on managing the transition. I thought it was very important in the short term that the civil service should provide some continuity for a brand new Assembly. But over time the civil service was bound to change.

In fact the localisation of the public service is not peculiar to Wales. It's happening increasingly throughout the civil service as more work gets moved out of London. When I was at the Department for Work and Pensions (DWP) we had people all over the country, and quite a lot of people tended to move around between different bits of the public sector within their locality. That's how the public service is developing anyway, and devolution in Wales and Scotland just gives it a special impetus. What matters is that the change should be managed at a pace which is appropriate given the way the Assembly itself is developing.

When at DWP, did you notice a different attitude to Wales from Whitehall post devolution?

I think there's quite a lot of interest in Wales now –there are some interesting things going on. I don't think it's true that the Welsh are less visible. Prior to devolution the Welsh Office was very thinly staffed and people had to cover so many different fronts, it was hard to make much impact in Whitehall—the Scots were much more aggressive and had louder voices. I always thought the realistic ambition for Wales was to do interesting things, not to try to be a big voice in every UK policy area.

Devolution was a great opportunity. It is now possible to devise policies for Wales across a broad front –and to treat it as a single place, with its own special needs, and not just part of a larger whole. That is what gives Wales the opportunity to do interesting things.

Devolution was a watershed moment –but the changes it unleashed may go on unfolding for some time to come. And people matter. The Welsh model of devolution may not be perfect but there's enough there for people with energy and of vision to do something useful and interesting. That's what matters: we're not in a competition for who's got the best constitution.

Sir Jon's Tale

What were the main change management issues?

I didn't see devolution as a management of change issue initially, I saw it as a policy implementation issue because we didn't know what Welsh devolution was about. We obtained all the relevant Labour Party material on devolution and there wasn't very much there. But we had to take this material and from it try to build a sufficiently robust policy that was true to the key strands in the manifesto and other published documents. The first six to twelve months were spent devising what the constitution reform should look like and then implementing it by getting two Bills through Parliament and a successful referendum. So it was only after a year that it became a change management issue for the Welsh Office itself. It was business as usual all the time this policy was happening. It was like the big bang: it was a spark in 1997 and by May 1999 that spark had embraced the whole Welsh Office, but in the early years we were busy getting the planets in place. It was a case of designing the Assembly constitution and then the implementation was very much the traditional policy implementation, of getting the legislation prepared, through Parliament, all the subordinate legislation, in this case also the work required to develop the Standing Orders. Until you knew what the nature of the organisation was that was to be created, you couldn't determine the impact on the working arrangements and working lives here. The implications for the civil service were end-loaded over the two-year period because we had to define what it was.

What was the involvement of the civil service in designing the structure of the organisation?

The single corporate body was a given — it was in the manifesto — we couldn't tear it up. We had to seek to define what it meant: it was quite clear that the manifesto intended the Assembly to combine an executive and a legislature, very much on a local authority model essentially. The person who was in charge of this will have the definitive answer but my recollection is that we could not depart from the Manifesto and that said that there would be a single Assembly exercising those functions, so we had to find a way of making that work.

When I took on the job, I pulled together three or four handpicked people who shared my room in CP2, including Martin Evans and Hugh Rawlings, and through the election period we set to work drafting a White Paper. This was for two reasons essentially: to help us to think through how it could be made to work — a means of applying our thinking; and because we wanted to demonstrate to the incoming Labour administration that they had civil servants here on whom they could rely. We knew that our draft wouldn't see the light of day, it was just a means to an end, but we used that intensive four weeks to flesh out the bones and it was a chance to say to Ron Davies when he arrived: 'This is what we think you want and it's for you to test it and tell us if we've got it wrong'.

Obviously, when Ron arrived the whole process for developing thinking changed, and we had a programme board, chaired by him, which met every Monday and he drove the work programme. This was a pretty intensive period, the election was on 6 May, and the White Paper was published in the third week of July, having gone through Cabinet Committee, the Legislation Committee and Cabinet and been printed. We didn't have a great deal of time to do this and we certainly weren't able to do the sort of detailed constitutional research which ideally we might have wanted to do. These were ideas which were being developed, tested and challenged in real time.

As far as how we got to Cabinet Government—again I'm sure Hugh's recollection is better than mine—essentially we had a work-shop at the University and Hugh produced a wiring diagram to show how authority would be suffused through the Assembly as it had been devised, and essentially it meant that the authority would go to the Committees and then find its way back up to the Ministers. That seemed illogical to everyone and the politicians were therefore fairly open to propositions put at the meeting that it couldn't be made to work that way. There was nothing manipulative about that. The basic commission was to produce an Assembly that would oper-ate through some sort of committee system. I was always very clear that when you have a committee system, power will always migrate to the political leadership. It was just a question of how it would migrate. Clearly you couldn't have a family friendly Assembly that didn't meet in the school holidays but nevertheless is taking deci-sions in committee. The business of political life in Wales doesn't respect school holidays so we were always going to have an arrange-ment that led to the delegation of responsibilities to Ministers. Once the politicians saw the illogicality of delegation via the Committees they were happy to have delegation to the First Minister [Secretary] and then to the Ministers.

In preparing the civil service for devolution, what were the landmark decisions?

With hindsight, we under-engineered the people aspect—though with good reasons. Until the completion of the work of NAAG, in around October 1998, we didn't have a detailed working model of how it was thought that the Assembly would work, so we couldn't put into place the business systems, etc. With hindsight, the NAAG model was not acceptable to the members anyway, which was a complication further down the line—but it was in the light of that that it became clear what the role of the committees would be, what the relationships should be between civil servants serving primarily the Government and the civil servants who were exclusively serving the Members, and all the protocols that we would need to put in place for that. All that, as I recall, was worked out in the six months immediately preceding the elections, alongside the work led by Bryan Mitchell on physically creating the environment within which the Assembly was going to operate.

The key players were: Martin Evans, who headed the Devolution Unit and who at any one time had most of the total picture in his head (I was still running economic affairs through all this); Bryan Mitchell, who felt there needed to be much stronger leadership in physically creating the Assembly, so he project managed that task from about October 1998—he came to Rachel and me and said: 'There's a vacuum here and I'll fill it for you'; and Hugh Rawlings, who understood more clearly than any of us the constitutional implications of what was being proposed.

How would you describe the culture of the Welsh Office and the Assembly?

The Welsh Office did have the freedom to do some things very differently but it didn't have the capacity to do everything very differently. It could only focus on two or three big issues at any one time in order to differentiate itself from Whitehall, and the price of that was that we had to fairly slavishly follow Whitehall on everything else that was flushing through. So, compared with this organisation, it was more passive than we are and much less in control of its own destiny, and that clearly fed in to the behaviours of the civil servants that served it.

The Assembly is still in a period of transition. This is an organisation that has changed a lot in six years but still has a long way to go. You change organisations from within, not exclusively from the top. I need as many of my staff as possible to be involved with the organisation, not just passively doing what they are told to do, so that it's a much more creative, dynamic organisation than the Welsh Office ever was; and we have some evidence of that. The other thing is that when you are cut-off from Whitehall, no longer some symbiotic part of UK Government, you have to take total responsibility for everything you do, which is why, as Permanent Secretary, I place enormous importance on governance issues. The National Assembly for Wales is the most important public sector institution in Wales by far and therefore it must be the best, but we are not yet the best in a number of ways. That is unacceptable, so there is a huge dynamic which is requiring us to improve the way we do everything. I have to be a very good employer: I am delighted we have just been awarded the gold corporate health standard and I'm increasingly looking for external accreditation so that I can demonstrate that this is an organisation which is increasingly amongst the best. Three parts of the organisation recently got bronze awards in the latest Welsh quality awards, for example.

Although some Welsh Office departments commendably achieved British and European quality management accreditation, because we were part of the UK Government, responsibility for such things rested ultimately with the UK Government. They would tell us what to do, like create executive agencies, and we would do it but not necessarily take proper ownership. But now we have to take responsibility for ourselves in a properly politically abrasive environment. The elected Members do not want us to be off the pace on the issues that are important to them, like sustainability and equality of opportunity. And the public will be critical if they feel the Assembly is not performing as well as it should. I feel these proper pressures very intensely and they drive me and the way I perform my role, and therefore I use them to enthuse, motivate and incentivise my Executive Board. This is an organisation on the move, which has changed significantly over the last five years, but in some respects all that's really happened is that it's helped me to identify where my legacy was well off the pace. I haven't been able to address all aspects of that legacy yet and that's been the challenge of the last six years.

In my judgement there is much less of a dependency on Whitehall than there was. Therefore in many areas there is a growing confidence and we certainly approach the relationship much more as an equal, as opposed to a dependent part. I am sure that there are some areas where there is still a feeling of dependency, at least on the Whitehall side—I'm not sufficiently close to the mosaic of interactions—but as a generalisation my perception is that we have got much more competence in terms of our relationships. But there are some Whitehall departments and officials who see us as the small relation, somewhere between being a serious central Government Department and a minor local authority, and quite often nearer the local authority end of that continuum. Some of my senior Whitehall colleagues ask: 'Who would want to work for the National Assembly?' This is not an evidence based view but I think Whitehall has changed too since Labour came to power. The focus of the Whitehall departments is very much on meeting the No. 10 delivery agenda, and this means that the Assembly just doesn't appear on their radar screens, and if we ever do appear it's just a bit of a nuisance. I think the dynamic of the situation is that devolution is forcing us apart from Whitehall: personally I think that's a good thing, I don't think it's a threatening thing. The more we can develop a proper relationship with Whitehall that doesn't imply dependency, the better.

What differences do you see between 'the Park' and 'the Bay'?

The APS is developing along a Parliamentary model and in the Park we have reinforced our role as the civil service serving Ministers. One of the best things that ever happened was when Rhodri Morgan said: 'We're not going to be called Secretaries any more', as terminology is very important. When we know they are Ministers we can establish the right sort of relationship and social distance from these people. I haven't worked in Parliament but my impression is that the Parliamentary conventions are very different. In Westminster, Parliament is the employer, whereas here it is a more complex model because we are all civil servants and the terms of employment and the process for appointing civil servants are very different. So the APS is naturally evolving away from a civil service culture to a Parliamentary culture, so a very different relationship with Members than we would have with Ministers. That is my impression.

How would you describe the role of the civil servant within the Assembly? Is there a greater managerialism? Is there a sense of Ministers and Group Directors being 'company chairmen' and 'chief executives'?

I would like to see the portfolio Ministers establish their own policy boards, which they should chair, and with their officials they should be driving forward their policy agenda as Ministers. Heads of Department should have management boards to complement the policy boards. They should take overall responsibility for the organisation and management issues but the Ministers should have a strong controlling role in relation to their departments. I think this would be healthy. I am looking to match that more with the First Minister's role and my role being one of ensuring that we can take a strategic view across these energised policy departments.

At the management level, one of the big problems I have is in imbedding corporacy. The first loyalty of my policy department heads is to their Ministers, and if it is perceived to be other than that then everyone is in trouble. That is the reality of working here. But I need strong corporacy for two reasons: one, to help me drive the organisational culture that we need and, two, to ensure that we can operate at the policy level in a sufficiently unified and joined-up way. So my Executive Board, in its two main manifestations, is designed to enable me to drive those two elements. At the weekly business meetings we take stock of the big policy issues and activities that cut across all of us, such as Freedom of Information, and at the monthly meetings we cover the management issues that have to be developed to enable us to improve as a corporate organisation.

If the jobs have changed, are the people winning the jobs different?

I have been consciously trying to develop a 'new breed'. That is why this week *(April 2005)* I have made all Department Heads sub-accounting officers. I think having personal responsibility for your budget of hundreds — and sometimes thousands — of millions of pounds changes and affects behaviour. It will therefore ensure that they look at the wider governance and management issues associated with their roles, as opposed to just focusing on their Minister, which is fundamentally important but should not happen to the exclusion of all other responsibilities.

This wasn't possible a few years ago — have things changed?

I didn't come in with a blueprint — and thank goodness I didn't as the blueprint for how we thought the Assembly would work was torn up in six months anyway and the Members wanted the place to work as a Parliament. I have always regarded myself as a transformational incrementalist: every six months I take stock. I use my summer holidays for thinking, reading and reflection and my Christmas holidays for thinking and reflection, and after every holiday I produce a note for my Executive Board on what I think are the next big challenges and issues. Given the nature of the organisation and the sort of person I am, that's the only way I can do it. There has been so much change internally and externally. I can only take six-month shots at assessing what is or isn't working, because it's not delivering or because things have been happening externally. Everything that is happening with Merlin and ICT is influenced largely by me wanting to catch up with the outside world. It is a huge agenda. I haven't the capacity to internalise it all the time. There is just too much going on. So I do it in six-month bites.

What will the role of the Assembly civil servant be in the future?

Until recently I had the Executive Board ambition statement but that is quite a passive statement of what our behaviours should be, what I couldn't give was the vision that it had to be applied to. Now we have been given that vision and there are four big things on our agenda at the moment:

- split the Assembly by May 2007;

- deliver the *Making the Connections* agenda, which is all about transforming the Assembly's part of the Welsh Public Service;
- deliver our own internal transformation, a series of inter-related change projects, including the location strategy, the mergers, IT changes;
- deliver the Welsh Assembly Government's main public commitments.

Now I have to ensure that we develop the capacity to perform all those things effectively. The biggest issue over the last six years has been developing the capacity of the organisation. In 1999 we had a significantly underdeveloped organisation and I have been developing its human capacity and its business systems capacity, and there is still a long way to go on that.

And the development of the Welsh Public Service?

I have always been an advocate of the Welsh Public Service and in some respects I could be regarded as the architect of some of the present ideas on this. I get very irritated when I hear people using the term 'civil servant' as a term of abuse. I don't differentiate civil servants from any other public servants in Wales; we are here to serve the public to the best of our abilities. I think the direction of travel in Wales is to produce a strengthened, enhanced public service. I see this as an evolutionary process, and the fact that some are civil servants isn't incompatible with that, but I strongly hope that we can use the Public Service Management Wales process to reduce the barriers between parts of the Welsh public sector, to make it much easier for people to move between different parts of their delivery chain. It gives them a much more enhanced and strengthened set of career options and at the same time we will end up with a cadre of Welsh public servants better equipped to deliver better public services to Wales.

Will this lead to the loss of the traditional 'Mandarin'?

The 'mandarin' language doesn't help. I'm seeking to develop public servants with the ability, commitment and loyalty to serve Wales to the best of their ability, as required by Members, Ministers and stakeholders and the public. The critical thing for me is that, as public officials, we retain the civil service values of impartiality and integrity. We cannot serve politicians if our integrity is in doubt. If half the sixty elected members thought that some or all of those serving the Assembly Government were part of the Labour party, we could not serve another administration. So we must be seen to have retained our impartiality, political integrity, the requirement to give advice without fear or favour (which can be challenging at times).

With hindsight, what changes have worked well and what changes have worked 'less well'?

The first years were very difficult in terms of certain political relationships, because different people had different perceptions of their roles and responsibilities, and no-one really knew how the organisation was going to work and different Members and different officials, with the best of intentions, were seeking to help it develop in the way they thought it was required to develop. So when the system came under pressure, some quite difficult situations arose. We had a few of those in the first two to three years and I would much rather that we hadn't, but with hindsight I probably couldn't have avoided them. We were dealing with the real world. There were some very difficult occasions but in my judgement these emerged from the process, not because of any wilful behaviour or actions, certainly on the part of the officials concerned.

Was there any inbuilt antipathy between members and certain civil servants because of previous roles or experiences?

I don't know the specifics. However I was surprised and unprepared for the extent of the antagonism and antipathy that existed between some Members and the civil service. I think some Members arrived with a very strong view of the civil service and wanted to address and confront what they saw as deficiencies of the civil service. One Member said — and I respect him for saying it, I'm not critical of him: 'You civil servants are just a free masonry, a self-appointed oligarchy, when we leave you are still here'. I can see that some, or most, Members may have had difficulty coming to terms with that and wanted to take the opportunity to challenge what they saw as a system that had been foisted on them. This included new and long-standing politicians.

What about the training and development of staff?

The staff were underdeveloped. We only had two years and we had to cut corners and didn't do enough to prepare the staff. I could justify it by saying that until we knew how it was going to work and what the Members wanted, we couldn't put into place training modules to train people, but I don't think we devoted enough time in the early months to supporting staff. We were all under enormous pressure at the time and we didn't really know what to expect ourselves. It was a huge learning process for all of us.

On my management and organisation development agenda, I am two years behind where I would like to be, because it has been a learning experience for me too. I know where we are going now, but in terms of developing an organisation which has the culture needed to serve the organisation as it is now, which is seen to be getting up there with the best public sector bodies in Wales, I am two years behind. I personally was very under-prepared for this job. My background was in delivering big political initiatives, and I had to learn how to transform an organisation in circumstances of great uncertainty and without any precedents to guide me. So I'm a bit frustrated!

C — THE MIDDLE AND JUNIOR CIVIL SERVANTS' TALE

Introduction

As we have pointed out in chapter two, different groups within an organisation perceive matters very differently: it is the essence of the pluralist nature of organisations. Within organisations even managers of similar status, who often sit together around numerous meeting tables, have different perspectives. Therefore, it is little wonder that people from different levels of management, or even from outside the managerial hierarchy, view and understand things very differently.

The concern in this section is to describe the response of the junior and middle ranking civil servants. Within the civil service, those at Head of Division level -the old grade 5 — and above are referred to as the 'senior civil service', or the SCS. In chapter two we pointed out the significance of middle management in managing change, and equally junior staff play a key role for it is they who sustain the organisation, who keep the business going. The purpose of this chapter is to consider the responses and views of this group of staff to devolution. In approaching this issue, we had already discovered two pertinent things about the way in which staff had been prepared for the advent of devolution from our interviews with the former permanent secretary, Rachel Lomax, the current Permanent Secretary, Sir Jon Shortridge, and their senior colleagues. These were:

the junior and middle ranking civil servants had been inadequately prepared in terms of training and the wider aspects of development; as a result of political imperatives, and arguably over-reliance on the productivity benefits of information technology, there was a substantially insufficient number of staff available to introduce devolution. Consequently, the workload of all staff increased significantly.

In some senses this 'story' or perhaps more accurately 'set of stories' explores these arguments.

Two issues are immediately obvious. First, we have already pointed out that the number of civil servants in Wales has grown considerably since devolution. For all Ron Davies' political desire to hold the civil service at no more then 100 additional civil servants, the numbers have increased by nearly 100 percent, though that owes something to mergers. Second, it then follows that a great number of new people have joined the service and many of these will be from outside the service, innocent of the ways of the old Welsh Office. This almost inevitably affects their attitude to devolution and its consequent changes, impacting on the organisational culture, as we outlined in chapter 5. Five quotes taken from the one-to-one interviews with middle managers illustrate this. These quotes — three from longstanding Welsh Office personnel, one from a newcomer to the Assembly and one from a civil servant transferred to the Assembly from elsewhere — demonstrate the wide range of views pertaining to the culture of the Welsh Office and the Assembly, predominantly in its early days.

> The Welsh Office considered itself nimble compared with Whitehall because Whitehall would commit the Welsh Office to things without telling us and we had to react imaginatively. The Welsh Office was regarded as a buffer between Wales and the worst excesses of Whitehall and to some extent this was true: we used to hone-in on any Welsh aspects of policy as an excuse to do things differently. Under devolution we don't have to worry about this anymore. There is no feeling that we lack legitimacy any more, no more paranoia about Whitehall — it's an irritation, but not a nagging fear. It still does things to embarrass us but that feels alright because they are a different organisation. Whitehall is almost irrelevant to what we do. We are now unashamedly native.

> When I came here, shortly after devolution, it was like stepping back fifteen years in time. It was quite a shock. The prevailing culture was Whitehall circa 1986 whereas in Whitehall at that time there were agencies focused on running as a business, delegated budgets, an emphasis on the customer, an emphasis on project management. But it wasn't obvious in Cardiff. But by

2005 the organisation as a whole is far more like Whitehall. In some senses the Assembly has moved a long way because they recognised the need for change, that things couldn't continue as they were. We've improved corporate governance, have a greater customer focus, and work smarter. But there's a resistance to this from some people who've been in the Welsh Office a long time. I sometimes think that there's a lack of maturity between the politicians and the SCS on how to develop their relationship and in the early days there was a fear in senior officials to say 'no' when they found that Ministers were asking for things that couldn't be delivered. Most people see Jon Shortridge as one of the better Perm. Secs.

I think devolution gave us a wonderful opportunity to make a unique contribution to Wales. But, at the time, the Welsh Office was very inflexible, inward looking, not on the whole in touch with the reality of providing public services, and largely going through the motions of consultation. The people were lovely, a friendly atmosphere with colleagues who were loyal and quite supportive. They had many skills, some people don't recognise until they work here, but it's a pity those skills were not harnessed to delivery. By 2005 parts of the office had changed beyond all recognition and other parts have probably not changed. Where there is change they are outward looking, cognisant that it's about implementing policy and that takes different skills and knowledge. Those who haven't changed are not entire groups or divisions but pockets (who are not exposed to external stakeholders) throughout the place. It's especially noticeable in internal policy places and they have no realisation that we are their internal customers. There is also still a tendency for people to say why they can't do things, rather than helping us to do things. There shouldn't be any battles with internal colleagues — it's very time consuming.

The Welsh Office was like some imperial bureaucracy: very inward looking, old fashioned, 'grade-ist', but calmer and less agitated. It was rather happier then, although not innovative but the machine still turned round and round. People had become institutionalised to that model. The Ministers were in London and officials spent very little time with ministers and then it would be grade 3s and 5s who would meet with ministers, and grade 7s and below did not have contact. Now there's a lot more politicians on our doorstep and the whole place is much more politically active. There's been a great increase in the demands and expectations on the organisation, which is still comparatively pretty small. There's also a degree of nervousness and excitement existing ... like rabbits in the headlights.

In the early days the Welsh Office culture was very much like the old civil service and it had more in common with Whitehall than with Wales and Welsh people. It lacked flexibility and the freedom to use your own initiative. Since 1999 it has been a far better place to work with more travel and involvement with the people of Wales, it's more engaging and more open, and there are more ethnic and disabled people.

The experience of civil servants, including how long they had spent in the service, clearly mattered.

Evidence

The Attitude Surveys suggest that, while a number of significant issues exist, civil servants appear to view positively the devolution experience. Our evidence is based on four annual attitude surveys, the focus group and follow-up one-to-one interviews with focus group participants. In general, responses were high and around 96% of the attitude survey respondents were junior civil servants. The detailed reporting from the surveys is contained in Appendix 2.

Typically, all the surveys indicated a considerable degree of satisfaction across the range of issues. Thus the results of the MORI 2001 survey revealed that 'overall satisfaction' and 'satisfaction' on almost all of the topics covered was exceptionally good with more than eight in ten staff stating that they were proud to work for the organisation. However, there were a number of areas within the Assembly that performed better than others. These included a sense that other colleagues were hard working and committed to quality and that the service was well managed, with civil servants aware of what was expected. Further they felt that they were dealt with in a fair and equitable manner. The areas which showed lower levels of satisfaction, than other areas, were: pay, balancing work/life commitments, communication and having the opportunity to do what they are best at every day. As the survey concluded: 'Overall, the results of this survey show high satisfaction with many of the important aspects of working life; however the Assembly still needs to build on these positive results and improve in the areas where results could be higher.'

Generally, staff are aware of the Assembly's objectives and believe that they make an important contribution to them.' More than four in five staff overall (82%) are proud to work for the organisation—something that the Assembly itself should be proud of. Almost all staff feel that the people they work with are committed to doing good quality work and over half of staff feel this strongly. On the whole, staff feel their opinions count and that the Assembly has a describable identity. The Assembly performs very well indeed in terms of having clearly identifiable objectives and employees do feel able to assist in achieving them. They are trusted by their managers to do their work and there is a strong belief that they are working as part of a group of talented, committed staff. Employees feel that their opinions count and the proportion who believe this is increasing over time. In addition staff believe that they offer a high standard of service to their customers and the public. Finally the majority of staff feel that they are treated with fairness and respect.

In sum the 2002 Survey indicated that staff appear to be very satisfied with most aspects of their job, and have a good understanding of what they are expected to achieve, and how their work contributes to the organisation's objectives. Staff feel that they make an important contribution to the organisation's objectives and line management was perceived favourably with staff believing that their manager gives them autonomy to do their job effectively, gives recognition for doing a good job and communicates effectively

These views are repeated in the remaining surveys. In 2003, the highest favourable scores were for the following issues:

The way we do business (68%), feelings about perceptions of individuals' job (62%), including understanding how an individual's work contributes to the objectives of their division (87%): feelings about the National Assembly for Wales (60%), the sense of offering a high standard of service to customers and to the public (86%), what they are expected to achieve at work (83%), the overall sense of commitment from work colleagues (82%) and finally being treated with respect and fairness (82%)

The overall results for the Assembly 2004 Staff Survey have either generally shown improvements or remained in line with the 2003 survey results. When benchmarked to other central government organisations, the Assembly is largely in line or above the benchmark norm. Again similar key strengths were found. These include:

- Clarity about how work contributes to the objectives of the division and the organisation.

- Teamwork and receiving adequate support and information from colleagues.

- Performance planning and review forms being agreed and training and development plans with line managers.

- Being treated with fairness and respect by line managers, and generally within the Assembly.

- Line managers consulting employees on issues affecting them and their work and empowering them to do their job effectively.

- Feeling recognised and acknowledged by line management when a job has been done well.

- High awareness of the policies and practices in place for dealing with customers.

- Providing a high quality of customer service and demonstrating a commitment to equality in policies and services.

- Intention to stay working for the Assembly for the next 12 months.

However, there are clear matters of concern appearing in all the surveys. Thus a (relatively) low proportion of employees feel able to get their work done within working hours and a significant minority are not able to balance work and home commitments. Almost a third do not think there is a good future for them at the Assembly and fewer than half feel their earnings are fair. Employees are less inclined to feel that they have the opportunity to do what they are best at every day. The methods of progression and advancement within the Assembly do not appear to be perceived favourably by staff. And the majority of staff either do not know or do not believe that the Assembly is committed to simplifying the way it does business. Interestingly, from a change management perspective, only a quarter of staff feel senior management in the Assembly set a good example in making the Assembly a success.

Views on the National Assembly for Wales are interesting. While 69% of staff are clear as to how their work contributes to the success of the Assembly a lower percentage of staff indicated that they understand the Executive Board's vision. It is interesting to note that staff working for the Assembly are more likely to indicate that they are proud to work for the Assembly and that on the whole they are satisfied to be working for the Assembly, in comparison with other central government organisations.

Although less than half of all respondents (47%) feel that the Assembly is committed to making the organisation a family friendly place to work, 59% of staff believe that they are able to achieve a balance between their work and life outside

Another key change management area, communication, seems to present difficulties. A significant minority do not feel that it is easy to get the help and advice they need from other parts of the Assembly and only ... around half of staff believe that they can easily communicate their views to senior managers. The 2003 Survey indicated concern about communication in the National Assembly for Wales expressed by 47% of respondents. Equally, and despite positive comments about job satisfaction, concerns were expressed in the same survey about management and their ability to manage people and their job. Thus concerns were expressed about management in the National Assembly for Wales by 59% of respondents and only 11% felt that the Assembly ensures that people are in the right job to enable people to work effectively, and 22% only declared themselves satisfied with the opportunities they have for career development within the Assembly.

The 2004 Survey indicated broadly similar worries. Key areas for improvement identified were:

- Ease of communicating views upwards to senior management.
- Engaging staff when organisational change is being undertaken.
- Opportunities for career development and secondments outside the Assembly.
- Developing good leadership at all levels in the organisation.
- Perceptions towards senior management setting a good example in the work place.
- The Assembly valuing the diversity of its employees.

These views were articulated by some individuals both in the focus group and in the one-to-one interviews.

There was concern that not enough was done to tackle staff who express unacceptable/offensive views, not enough was done to mainstream diversity, at present staff are encouraged to join 'Staff Support Networks' which, whilst supportive of individuals, appear to alienate the diversity of those members of staff from the mainstream. Further there was a sense that not enough was done to support part-time workers; more needed to be done to encourage applications for employment from ethnic minority groups; the further work suggested above would require even more cultural change for the organisation to value and learn from the diversity of its staff, though it was also pointed out to us that the terms and conditions in the civil service are much better than most employers in Wales.

In general views of senior management were positive, though there were a number of ambiguous signals. On the whole, questions relating to leadership and management elicited lower satisfaction ratings than questions on other aspects of life within the Assembly. The proportions of staff who are satisfied are still relatively high. While the vast majority of staff feel that they are trusted to do their job, lower proportions feel consulted, recognised for good work, have someone to talk to regarding career progress/development or are effectively led.

The Executive Board, as a corporate body, was not seen to be very visible, with only the Permanent Secretary and an individual's own director being visible to most staff; though that perhaps may be expected. There was a perception that Heads of Division were far too busy to devote time to demonstrating strong leadership although one wonders why staff in say agriculture might want access to some-one leading education or health. Some members of the focus group also reported that relations between some Heads of Division and Ministers resembled 'game playing' but we found no evidence of this. Constant reference was made, also in the focus group, to the need to change the culture of the office, and there was some reluc-tance to accept the wholehearted commitment of senior leaders to this matter. Dialogue was seen as a positive move to create a link with the Executive Board but there was a feeling that it was not delivering demonstrable change but only stock answers to questions or concerns raised. We report these comments as typical of what many focus group members reported to us but, at the same time, we have to conclude that they do not represent the wider picture we witnessed and also the comments from the majority of staff con-tained in the attitude surveys.

We have identified the middle managers as a key group in change management. Views on leadership emerged from the focus group and the follow-up interviews. Two interesting quotes illustrate the views of focus group participants:

> The relationships aren't as formal and the senior civil service is much more approachable than they used to be, including the Per-manent Secretary. Previously, you wouldn't come into contact with anyone at a senior level. There is a contrast between Jon Shortridge and Rachel Lomax. She really shook up the senior managers in this place, you could see her influence, and she pushed the button on IT which has had a major impact on the

way we work. Jon Shortridge knows the place exceptionally well and is more intellectual and reserved, he's better at the soft, hidden skills and is more approachable.

The current Permanent Secretary shows leadership and has done a lot of things but the Executive Board does not select leaders and the organisation is not training leaders. Rachel Lomax's leadership style was very modern: no one in the organisation could fail to know what her leadership style was — she had people by the balls. These days grade 7s are seriously cheesed off with the workload and grade 5s are much more visible and feeling the heat.

In the Welsh Office it wasn't wildly formal; you were on first name terms with your line manager and perhaps the next grade above that. The culture of the Assembly is more informal. It assumes you use first names: the most junior staff could call the Permanent Secretary Jon — I think he might be a little alarmed but he wouldn't worry unduly. One minister has told me to use first names when we meet alone and the bulk of Ministers are called by their first name by their senior officials. An example of the informality of Assembly Ministers came when we were based down the Bay and my Minister answered my colleague's phone — the person on the other end got a shock but they recognised who they were speaking to.

We wanted to find out what middle management thought were some of the differences between Cathays Park and Crickhowell House. These quotes are representative of what many had to say:

In the Bay, the politicians talk to you and there is a stronger Welsh language element: there is a different purpose. In the Park there is definitely a lot of variation between divisions.

There is a 'them and us' culture: the workers are in Cathays Park and the elite are in Cardiff Bay. In Crickhowell House they are building up a huge big army of people but we get less here. Also, there's an inner sanctum here in Cathays Park—it's for those who are in with the top people.

The Park is different. They work differently, walk around with their heads down, not recognising passers-by. The people who applied to come down to the Bay wanted to come. Everything you do here is public—committee papers, all our work—it says a lot for the civil servant—we are very adaptable.

The view of a 'them' and 'us' is common at various levels of the organisation and the separation of the Assembly Parliamentary Service from the Welsh Assembly Government is recognising what has been de facto for some time.

Relationship Between Civil Servants and AMs

The evidence suggests some concerns about the service managing its relationship with politicians. Some middle managers had concerns that they would cease to be neutral. One quote taken from a civil servant working in the Bay illustrates this:

> In the Welsh Office the majority of civil servants didn't see Ministers but now they are walking around. In the old civil service you were faceless and politically colourless, but today it's completely different. Here in the Bay, we also have a physical closeness to the media, the media research staff, plus the AMs, and the other officials. We share all the facilities, except the car park, and before the smoking room arrived we all congregated on the back terrace; it became quite a club, a genuine feeling that we were all part of the same team which permeated throughout the building. Nevertheless we have retained our political impartiality, serving all AMs, and this is recognised.
>
> Another big difference is that Assembly Ministers are very well networked, they have their own expectations, and in many cases have direct experience of their portfolios. Jane Davidson was a teacher and Brian Gibbons is a GP — so they know what they are talking about. It used to be dangerous to let Ministers out on their own but now it's more dangerous for officials to be out on their own. It's been suggested that everyone in Wales either knows an AM or knows someone who knows an AM. Those who do a lot of talks outside work have to be careful not to say anything contrary to Welsh Assembly Government policy in case something gets fed back. In the old days you didn't worry.

This fear that the civil service might become politicised was most often connected to their views on the development of the Welsh public servant concept. This was seen as posing a potential threat to the traditional impartiality of the civil service. Some quotes illustrate this.

> The proposed Welsh Public Servant would include local government and NHS management. Local Government officials are more politically active, so I'd be concerned that some of their habits would take root in the Assembly. We could end-up with top management clear-outs or suspicion of top management.
>
> One of the main selling points on devolution was the maintenance of the links with the Home Civil Service. I'm just interested in doing a good job — irrespective of who is in power.
>
> I don't think the civil service has changed enough to satisfy the politicians and my fear is that the civil service will be politicised and that a Welsh public servant will be created.
>
> I am concerned about the very different relationship between local government officials and their members — councillors may

walk in to an office and berate an official. The impartiality of the civil service is key to the system working, but under increased pressure to deliver something there is a danger of getting tied in to the Minister. Some political advisers are good, some less so – they get more involved in the system than they used to.

The fundamental role has not and must not change. If it changes it is doomed – the Assembly relies on an impartial, adaptable civil service. There is no pressure from AMs to change; AMs have got used to the idea of the civil service. The Welsh Public Servant concept is an awful idea – the civil service is crucial and valuable.

But more positively an interviewee stated that:

The Welsh Public Servant is an excellent idea. We need to get away from old Whitehall style of civil service. It is being phased-out through recruitment anyway.

Welsh Language and other Significant Issues

A number of interviewees welcomed the development and use of the Welsh language:

There is far greater room for the Welsh language and its use in day-to-day business which is a wonderful thing.

The Welsh language is expected more – it is getting to where Welsh speakers will have an advantage, which is a shame because a lot of talent could be lost because they don't apply for jobs because of a requirement to speak welsh. Welsh is spoken more in regional offices, so in 10-15 years this could be limiting. If you don't speak Welsh and emails and filed documents are in Welsh, you are excluded and at a disadvantage because you can't look at previous work.

But, as the literature review implied, there are tensions between middle and senior management, not least during periods of change. The following quote from interviewees demonstrate this.

We need an independent eye, to take into account the relationships between the Bay and the Park. When we started here at the Bay, we had very close relationships with policy divisions – policy helped steer progress in the committees but this does not happen anymore.

In the future there must be room for everyone – real diversity. Some of the civil service dinosaurs will feel uncomfortable; they are unwilling to embrace change. They exist everywhere and especially the higher up you go, except for Jon Shortridge who is a remarkable character and very welcoming. The senior civil servants don't recognise they're dinosaurs. They are arrogant and think they've got skills that are irreplaceable.

> There are very few people here with a vision. We need consul-
> tants to take a good hard look at us to help us understand what it
> is that AMs need as individual members and as members of com-
> mittees.

Again the point about middle managers bearing the brunt of keeping the business alive is borne out by the sense from some middle
managers that their workload has greatly increased. Keeping the
show going while introducing change is a common theme. Not surprisingly complaints about the increase in workload were at the top
of most people's agenda.

> Where I worked at the time we went from one or two Parliamen-
> tary Questions a month (over which we agonised about our
> responses), to 10 Assembly Questions per week. It was a bloody
> time. Suddenly we were expected to have a 'made in Wales' solu-
> tion to everything and still be able to match everything that was
> announced by Whitehall. We needed a lot more staff.
> In the past an important role of Heads of Division was to keep
> an eye on how their responsibilities fitted-in with everything else
> but now they have zero time to find out what is happening else-
> where. Some feel guilt that they don't know what's going on any-
> more so working hours increase.
> The creation of the Assembly was fire fighting most of the way.
> There was inadequate planning for the Assembly and no sense of
> what was needed to support it. The workload was not antici-
> pated. We are attempting too many things at the same time:
> mergers, Making Connections, the relocation strategy—all at
> once. It always seems to be the same. Do we have too many heads
> of groups and not enough people doing the work?
> We couldn't have been prepared for this because we couldn't
> predict it.
> The senior civil servants were positive about devolution but
> they didn't understand the implications for civil service num-
> bers. And it feels as if they still don't understand: our evidence to
> the Richard Commission said we could move to primary legisla-
> tion powers with a minimal effect on staffing. They just didn't
> think about the huge impact on staff and no-one ever asked us
> about the implications for staff. We felt: 'no-one's listening to us'.
> If you say you can't do something you're seen as negative. I'm in
> favour of devolution but you've got to be realistic.

The other major topic to be raised consistently concerned the
implications of the changes and its impact on the nature of employment as a civil servant:

> There's a decline in the number of 'gifted amateurs' about the
> place. People are tending to stay longer in their posts now, but
> this is partly because of the relocation strategy, as many people

have not wanted to move to a new division until they knew for certain who was being moved to mid or north Wales. We've been trying to address the 'gifted amateurs' issue for 20 years.

The changes were managed badly. The TOTO ('top of the office') didn't think it through enough and I think they were trying to hide the cost of devolution. There is still a cultural lack of change even now — it is too old fashioned — and there are not enough grade 3s and grade 5s talking to ministers. Some processes were handled well, for example the Standing Orders Commission and NAAG, but other things were a catastrophe and this has contributed to the angst and difficulties.

Under Better Government there was a lot of cynicism for Welsh Office change programmes, however the Executive Board had to do it. It would be wrong to have a cynical perspective, but it was mishandled: you didn't get enough of a feeling from the Executive Board that they were behind it. The Permanent Secretary put himself about a lot but the others below, in particular grade 5s, didn't. I respect the effort put in but with 3,000 people it was not enough.

They tried their best to train people and a number of things they got right. The spoof committee meetings were very close to the actuality of how committees work now. A lot of emphasis was given to presentation skills as the civil service, traditionally, were more 'sitting behind desks'.

Conclusion

Drawing conclusions from the various pieces of information presented to us is a difficult challenge. There is evidence to support the views of the middle managers that not enough was done to prepare them for the changes brought about by devolution, that they were overworked and understaffed, and that their senior management continue to struggle with the leadership challenges inherent in a dramatically different organisation from the more staid one in which they were brought up. The cynicism identified by many studies about middle mangers and change is, as we have indicated, often a reflection that they have not properly been brought into the process early enough and provided with adequate resources. There appears to be elements of that here.

However, it is also true that many staff — at both junior and middle level — feel a strong sense of satisfaction with the new Assembly and its management.

Our conclusion overall is that:

- Whilst staff were under-prepared for devolution there were clearly mitigating circumstances — such as no-one being able to describe accurately the full and unprecedented impact of devolution;

- It is also clear, for a variety of reasons — some political and some managerial — that there were insufficient staff to meet the challenge of devolution;

- However, any manager, whether in a private or public sector organisation, reading the attitude surveys, especially those for 2001 and 2002, could not fail to be impressed by the achievements in such a short space of time and some of the percentage response rates in the staff surveys should be displayed boldly in Assembly meeting rooms;

- The survey results in the latter years of our research do not appear to have maintained the momentum that they promised in the earlier years, and the reasons for this and the issues raised by the responses suggest that some of the management initiatives may have plateaued in those years. However, we are aware that the most recent survey is considered to contain the best results as yet;

- Middle managers were a resource which was not used as well as they might have been; and finally

- The worst excesses of the criticism of what management did are unfounded in our view but the issues raised by many staff, such as issues of leadership, on-going training, and the need for continual adaptation, have some merit.

D—THE MERGED BODIES' TALE

Much is being made, and rightly so, of the proposed merger of the WDA (Welsh Development Agency), ELWa (Education and Learning Wales) and the WTB (Wales Tourist Board), amongst others, into the Welsh Assembly Government. According to those in favour of the merger the assimilation has much to commend it as it is seen to be strengthening the role of the Assembly; those opposed to the merger see it as a retrograde step and even, in the view of those with the strongest objections, see the merger as an undemocratic measure, driven by political considerations.

These mergers amplify the point made throughout this book concerning the continuous nature of change in the development of the Assembly and the experiences of the previously merged bodies — organisations such as Tai Cymru, Health Promotion Wales, the Welsh Health Common Services Authority (even though their were in effect abolished and their displaced staff taken into the Welsh

Office), and the creation of the Care Standards Inspectorate for Wales and its location in the Assembly — provide a rich source for organisational learning. All of these organisations were and remain, to a greater or lesser extent, a part of the devolution story and the commitment to a *bonfire of the quangos.*

The following text is written as if spoken by one person, a person from one organisation, but the single voice used reflects the views of a number of people from different organisations and does not mean that each of the organisations quoted would agree with each of the points made. The points are representative of general views and that is why, in a handful of instances, one view may appear to be somewhat contradicted in another paragraph. This approach was adopted in order to ensure anonymity of the interviewees: we recognise that identifying views with particular bodies has benefits but a combination of ethics and pragmatism persuaded us down the road we chose. Some of those interviewed remain as employees of the Assembly and some have moved on to new and bigger challenges. The vast majority of comments refer to a period of time early in the development of the Assembly and much has changed since then, reflecting the Assembly's on-going change management programme led by the Permanent Secretary. However, no matter how much things have moved on the lessons remain highly pertinent for the mergers being considered at present.

The following views are expressed under a number of headings that reflect different aspects of the merger or take over experience.

First Impressions

I think the first impression I had of the Assembly was of an organisation that itself was changing — it wasn't a static organisation — and, in some ways, it might have been easier for us to join it if it had been static, but it was an organisation that itself was going through significant changes. It was beginning to cope with what devolution really meant. Our staff, when they joined the Assembly, brought with them their own different impressions of their own organisation and also various mindsets about what the civil service in Wales was going to be like. So there was this inter-relationship between an evolving culture in the Assembly and a variety of different impressions about what that culture was going to be. And it really did vary in the minds of those joining: from those who had an image of the bowler-hatted mandarin, detached and not understanding what was happening on the ground; to other people who had worked quite closely with Assembly officials and so they had a much more realistic view about the job and about civil servants. There really was a very wide disparity in terms of what staff thought about the people they were going to work with and also about the type of organisation they were about to join.

The crucial difference I found was that the people in the Assembly focused, or concentrated, on what I can only call 'delivering policy issues'. That was their bread and butter and was the main thing driving the colleagues that I went to work with, and that commitment to policy has its own cycle and its own processes. I learnt that the outsider's impression of a long drawn out process, in which people were able to sit back and maturely reflect on matters and allow policy to gradually evolve, did not fit with what I saw my civil service colleagues doing: rushing around, trying to get Assembly Questions (AQs) sorted out and then there was the next debate on such and such a subject (which had to be done by tomorrow afternoon) to worry about. So the impression that existed amongst quite a lot of my staff, of what civil servants were doing, was not actually what we found when we joined. It did actually seem a pretty proactive and hectic place which was not the impression that was prevalent outside the Assembly amongst of my colleagues.

My people also had a variety of feelings, about the civil servants, that ranged from: these are people who know a bit about what we are doing, to a perception, amongst quite a number of staff, that these civil servants didn't understand the business we were talking about. There was also a feeling that we were joining an organisation that had never managed services themselves and therefore couldn't know what the business was about. These were quite strong feelings amongst my staff. The civil servants did not have experience of managing services and delivering things and therefore they didn't understand some of the dynamics that were important, even essential, to us.

I think there were two separate strands that inter-relate in all of that. I think there were feelings amongst staff that this was not a merger it was absorption, or a take-over; that they were being shoehorned into the way in which the civil service worked in Wales. But that has to be interpreted against the background of my staff having a variety of stereotypes, often wrong stereotypes, about what the civil service really was.

Being Inducted into the Assembly and Coming to Terms with the New Feelings of Accountability

I can remember going to a lunch — you have to go through this induction with all these people — and I can remember very clearly that the Permanent Secretary and his senior team welcomed our senior team at the lunch. The Perm. Sec., as I learnt to call him, and his team highlighted the importance of the probity process and the fact that you had to be sure of your facts; 'There was no margin for error when you're dealing with senior politicians!' they told us. And I can remember that when they left the room, and we were left alone, our people were white, if not grey, with fear. It was like 'Aaaahhhhhh' you know: we were now no longer 'top dogs'; we used to be the big top team of an organisation, but now we had become part of a much bigger organisation; smaller fish in a bigger pond; and because of the importance placed on conducting yourself properly, within protocols and processes, we were now part of an organisation that was much more heavily regulated.

The Challenge of Being a Senior Civil Servant

The cultural difference between my old organisation and the Assembly was almost immediate and particularly for me because I felt that as a senior civil servant I was much more conspicuous, paradoxically much more so, than I had been before as a senior public service manager. That was really interesting and unnerving.

My responsibilities for making sure that the new organisation fitted in, performed well and met the requirements was very much a personal responsibility and what I found is that my personal responsibility, and my personal profile within this part of the organisation, was huge and demanding. Quite literally, one of the roles of a senior civil servant is to be absolutely on top of your work, absolutely on top of it, and you have to know everything about the subject areas that you are responsible for, because even more *senior* civil servants than you, and Ministers, come to you and it's you they expect to be able to answer their questions. As a senior manager, outside the civil service, I could always play for time. My job as a senior person was to be charismatic, to provide the leadership, but not necessarily to know everything about what was happening. So that was a big difference.

I've never been in the armed services, but I always think it must have been a bit like what I found in the Assembly; it's the chain of command. It's very clear in the civil service and so being a senior civil servant brings expectations: you're in charge of whatever, your brigade, and the buck stops there. The Permanent Secretary may 'phone and say: 'What are you doing with such and such?' You can't say: 'Oh, I'll just have to go and find out.' That is not the way the civil service operates, and I suspect that these systems are very similar to the way that the armed services have operated. It's very much like that.

People used to say it was very hierarchical and that's because Grade 5 civil servants seem to be the block, the real impermeable line, between those that make the decisions and those who do the work. I actually do see the civil service as hierarchical in some ways: once you hit the senior civil service it's really different and you're seen to be sort of a 'toff'. I actually found that the team I worked with had much more individual responsibility than in any other organisation I have ever worked with before. Isn't that interesting? They had many more demands placed upon them, than I had experienced before, but there was still this class thing.

If you are senior civil service you are officer class. But then it's all very hierarchical and so if you're a Grade 5, you have to behave the way of a Grade 3; and I believe a Grade 3 has to behave the way of a grade 2. So you know your status and your position and there is a way to behave and a way to communicate, although this was beginning to get softer during that time.

A New Sense of Authority and Presence

Before joining the Assembly our organisation operated for several years by marketing our work. In many ways, we were members of an interim marketplace in Wales in the mid-90s and as soon as we were put in this marketplace we had to earn our money and sell our products and services. But when you enter the civil service you get an *authority* and a *presence* that it was impossible to get outside and so it became rather more about delivering projects and services, that the public services outside the Assembly were expected to 'buy' and to do as we said.

By *presence* I mean that you tend to automatically assume more importance because you're a part of the Government machine and therefore you're seen to be an important cog in the machine of decision-making influence. And so people deal with you differently and it was dramatic, I believe in our case, that one day we had to persuade people to take us for what we did, and selling our wares, whereas all of a sudden we were in the Assembly and actually had very close contact with Ministers and senior politicians. We were helping to make the policy and therefore people knew that, sooner or later, they would be required to do what we were saying they should do. The *authority* is that, as part of the policymaking machine, civil servants are responsible for implementing policy and so you are put into a position of telling people what to do, or making it very clear what the Government's requirements are. That's a very different position.

Understanding the New Emphasis on Process, Probity and Protocol

The civil service is still a large bureaucracy and there is a certain way of doing things that you have to follow. So people going into the Assembly have to learn quickly how to access 'the process': mastering the process will either make you or break you in the civil service, and it is the political machine that often dictates the process. So what I found was that when I answered to a Board, before coming into the civil service, I had a lot of influence on that Board and I had a lot of freedom in the way I operated. Of course there were protocols and regulations but within those there was a lot of freedom. When I went into the Assembly I discovered that first of all civil servants are quite definitely there to protect the system, there's no doubt about that; secondly, because the demands of Ministers and politicians are huge – and they are out of your control – you respond to their needs and their needs actually dominate over your needs. So most civil servants will say to you: briefings, jackets, speeches – they're all tight deadlines. You are judged on your performance for those things and therefore a lot of civil servants days and weeks are spent 'feeding that beast'.

But I think that if you underestimate the force of the process and the force of the civil service protocols, you are going to have a problem and that's what any Agency joining the Assembly needs to think about; because the old ways of the civil service are still very much alive and well.

Perhaps *Code of Conduct* would be a better phrase than the word *protocol*. There is a code of conduct and it tells you the way you must behave: you have a very particular purpose being a civil servant – a senior civil servant – and you need to be aware of that and conduct yourself in that way. So, in the old times, that would have meant a very formal relationship, and one which was very 'stiff' sometimes, but these days a different role is required of the new breed of civil servant and it needs to be less formal—but still very politically aware.

I think some people would find the civil service very claustropho-bic and overpowering and if they really enjoyed flexibility and free-dom, and worked to find ways of getting it, then they wouldn't last long in the Assembly. There are civil servants, and I think I am one of these, who enjoy what they are there to do and believe in what they are there to do. But you have to get to know the process and get to know the limits of your flexibility.

In the civil service this emphasis on process has to be the lifeblood of the organisation and the process drives the machine, and until the process is changed the machine doesn't change. In the Assembly, the people are sucked into it and you can happily spend your day writ-ing briefings, jackets and speeches and not doing anything about your subject or subjects.

So there's a dilemma to be faced there. The important thing, from my point of view, was that I couldn't escape the process because I was personally responsible for the quality of every single Briefing Submission that went through to the Minister, and there were a lot of them. The more submissions, the tougher the times, the more the process bites, the more the presumed sensational appetite for infor-mation, to cover for assurances made, to ensure that these are being done and being done properly. All of this generates a machine that always has priority.

Dealing with Ministers

After a short while in the Assembly I was getting regularly involved with meetings with Ministers, and in the meetings there would be other career civil servants. Some of the career civil servants had problems as they found these new bigger politicians very difficult to deal with and it created a sort of 'force field'. So, people like me, who had no history of behaviour in the civil service with Ministers, behaved like I would have done in my old organisation.

So, in my mind, the Minister was my Chairman, and I was happy with that as I would tend to be a bit more relaxed and I wouldn't feel that I had a problem. Whereas I feel that the career civil servants, who had come up with a different experience, were finding that the *Yes Minister* approach was no good with these types of politicians, who themselves had been working as Councillors in County Coun-cils, or whatever, and had a different relationship with their chief executives and officials. You could almost tell who was able to deal with that and who wasn't. So the 'energy' in the traditional civil service could be rather different from the 'energy' needed by officials in the future; they need to be more pragmatic in some ways.

Generalists and Specialists

And it was a very contradictory environment. As far as my job was concerned, because I was an expert with knowledge that very few had I had a lot of freedom, because the traditional civil servant does recognise and respect professional expertise. The majority of the old school civil servants would be generalists, and they ran the systems and processes and would pick up the subject as they went along. With me, and with the big change in the Assembly's techniques, you needed to know your subject and so you had to become a very smooth operator as far as the subject and the systems and processes were concerned, whereas, in the past, you would have a team of professionals who would advise and generalists who would know the process.

Dealing with the Cardiff Centricity

I think the views staff held about the Assembly as an organisation varied very significantly in different parts of Wales. There was quite a strong feeling from people in other parts of Wales that the Assembly was a Cardiff-centric body; the vast majority of its civil service officials worked in what was called CP2 (the main office block in Cathays Park). So there was an immediate perception that the Cardiff civil service would not understand north and west Walians because of geography; and in that sense my staff were reflecting, I suspect, a variety of social attitudes held by the communities that they lived in.

When dispersed organisations join the Assembly there is a need for an immediate flexibility in terms of delivering services such as personnel, finance, and IT. Otherwise, you become aware that you are working in a system that is pretty much Cardiff focused. I remember I had a number of discussions with people about the need for training programmes, for example, to be run outside Cardiff. What I found was that the response was very individualistic: one person would say: 'Of course, I understand that, and I will do it'. Another person would say: 'Oh no, we run these in Cardiff' and I would say: 'I'm not sending 8 people from wherever to a course in CP2'.

Then there was the issue of where we advertised jobs. We had battles over things like Assembly adverts saying: 'these posts are mainly located in Cardiff' under which would be a series of posts in another part of Wales. There were also other cultural indicators, and they seem small issues, but from my staff's point of view they were 'straws in the wind'. The one I remember was staff, based many miles away from Cardiff, saying they fully intended to apply for a place in the gym in CP2, because they wanted to make the point that if that service was available in Cardiff then why wasn't it available across Wales. Access to the play scheme, in those days, was not an all-Wales facility; it was something located only in Cardiff.

They were seen to be things that showed people did not understand what it meant to be an all-Wales organisation. There were other indicators, like the Intranet page would trumpet the latest meals available in the staff restaurant in CP2 and how Friday was going to be curry day or fresh fish day or whatever and I would get letters from staff asking when I was going to deliver this fresh fish to them. I think they reinforced those feelings that they were not actually part of this tribe. I remember one person writing to a very senior official of the Assembly, saying that she hoped that he would instruct his staff to stop referring to everything outside Cardiff as 'out-stations' — and there was action taken in respect of that.

Developing a Different Culture and Managing the Integration of Two Groups of People

I think what has happened, since those early days, is that a specific culture has begun to emerge rather than us being shoehorned into a piece of the civil service culture. Or, I suppose, the other way around, we couldn't have carried on with our old culture, untouched by the rigours of the civil service culture. I think a different animal has emerged out of that process that was neither the stereotype of the civil service culture nor the culture that we brought with us. Something different has actually emerged out of the process rather than in the end there being a take-over by any one part. Some of that I think has been influenced by the fact that the civil service itself has been changing, in particular there was a recognition that it needed to be more heterogeneous than the traditional model that probably existed in the old Welsh Office: an organisation that was there fundamentally to deliver policy. The old objective to serve Ministers was different and when bodies like us started to arrive, whose job was a service delivery function, the culture had to change.

Before joining the Assembly, there I was running a small machine that I was on top of and then it was very much a question of moving into the civil service hierarchy and feeling yourself a part of a bigger family. One of the things I had to do was to manage the integration of a bunch of people who had never regarded themselves as civil servants: '*How can we compete with them?*' was the general feeling.

If you joined the Welsh Office, as a typical civil servant, you saw yourself having a career in the civil service, but my people saw themselves as having a career in their specialism, not necessarily with us as they were people who typically worked in different parts of the sector but always in their field of expertise. So I had a bunch of these experts to integrate with the relevant division of the Welsh Office/Assembly and the people in the Welsh Office/Assembly division, although committed to their work, didn't see themselves as having a career in this discipline — they saw themselves as civil servants who could work anywhere. It was a question of bringing these two different groups together, of mixing the people.

It went remarkably well and in no time at all our people were actually thinking of themselves as National Assembly people. Certainly, we very quickly got the sense of being part of the Assembly and I think it helped greatly that there was such a huge feeling of change and newness in the air that my people could actually feel, rather than feeling they were joining a Welsh Office institution that had been there for ever and was just going to digest them. They could feel that they were in on the ground floor of building the new National Assembly — that was tremendous.

But the biggest challenge really was how staff viewed themselves in terms of what it was they felt themselves part of: one had a group of people that felt themselves to be part of a specialist world, embracing many possible employers, and the other group tended to see themselves as, more or less, career civil servants. The change in moving from a small organisation to a very much bigger one was not too much of a shock because the new department was not that much bigger in scale than the old one had been. So, even though there was a vastly bigger empire, when it came to the people you were talking with, day in and day out, you realised that two out of three of them were actually your immediate former colleagues and you very quickly got to know the others. So that bit of it was good. What began to worry me was that when the department had been up and running for some months one part of it, a part that had always been a bit of a cat that walked by itself, wasn't growing its network of contacts with other parts of the Assembly. I felt they needed to have more of an input into wider policy areas generally and to learn more from other departments generally. So, I devised a plan to split up the department to force it to develop new associations across the Assembly.

It was a bit of disintegration in order to force new bonds to grow and it is interesting that the people did form more linkages, cross-linkages, with other people. It was a change in working location for people and there is nothing more demanding than changing your desk and boss. It was also a change in technology in that the vast majority of the new people had never used e-mail, or other forms of technological communication. For some of them a computer, in the corner and shared between eight people, had been a convenient resting place for their coffee cups. This was very much characteristic of how the services were generally seen at that point in time and they had to move to a position where technology underpinned a lot of what happened. It was also a change interpreted in terms of moving from being relatively isolated units to attempting to create an all-Wales organisation with all the issues of corporateness that went with that.

Becoming Assimilated into the Civil Service and the Civil Service as an Employer

Probably the most significant thing anybody said to me was: 'you're a real trusted pair of hands now, you've virtually assimilated us'. They meant that I was now process driven and that, you know, in terms of being 'a safe pair of hands', that I handled the process well, and that I knew the process inside out and that therefore I was recognised as being almost a career civil servant, which is an interesting comment.

The civil service is the best employer I've ever had. There is lots and lots of training, there was little supervision of me personally, so long as I delivered through the process. I had a lot of freedom within those boundaries, a huge amount of freedom, and a lot of authority and people really listened to you. So if you're a senior civil servant, and if you know your subject and you keep in touch with you customers out there, then it's a great job because you're always popular. Sometimes people out there don't agree with you, but they're not always brave enough to tell you. One of the things I tell my friends in the civil service now is that they must not lose the 'grass roots' feeling and knowledge, because the civil service makes assumptions about how things are; and I discovered that I started to make assumptions about how things were, because I thought I knew, but in some areas I didn't anymore. Being assimilated carries that danger. I knew that if I was seen to be a safe pair of hands I could live out my career in the civil service – as long as I ran the process and performed according to expectations.

There's often a feeling of frustration amongst some civil servants that people in the civil service know what you do and care what you do, but they don't really care about you. So I've never worked in such contradictions. *Modernising Government* was introduced to change things but it was reminiscent of the early days in my former organisation, where the theory's fine but the practice doesn't always match it. They try to persuade people that their views matter, but they could only understand them from a very senior manager's point of view. The thing that causes irritation is when, as a senior civil servant, I am/was totally impotent in areas where I'd been trained previously, and that was in personnel management and real control over budgets and real accountability. In the early days, things were all relatively cosmetic and I had no control over how people should work: I was responsible for a big department and had people issues every day, but I was not allowed to control any solutions. Fortunately, things have and are changing.

How Things Changed with the Arrival of the Assembly

At the start of the Welsh Assembly Government people had a new identity so, quite rightly, the Permanent Secretary and his team wanted to focus on that and use that as an opportunity to change the organisation in some way. The importance was to create a happy team, a team of identity, a skilled team, and a team that was genuinely enthused. But I think this is very difficult to achieve as it doesn't mean to say the troops are automatically going to be happy. When I went into the civil service many typical organisational issues had to be dealt with: like the deception of the hierarchy; the lack of recognition of what was going on; a degree of heavy handedness; the un-approachability and the lack of purpose in some senior civil servants; not a great deal of respect for people at sub-divisional heads (some were thought to be bandits). The Permanent Secretary was determined to deal with these issues and ensure that divisional heads became real managers and a driving force for change. The senior management had a real job on their hands and I have never worked in an organisation before that tried so hard; in a sense it tried too hard. Some people, perhaps many were the cynics, felt it became almost a ritual, there was too much of it, too much expectation for people to get involved in it, and it sort of compounded people's views that those who needed to understand actually didn't understand how the place worked and didn't understand the pressures on people. And so, instead of being a valuable asset, for some people training became an impediment and they became (even more?) cynical about it. They felt the organisation was doing this because they wanted to be seen to be doing it. That was unfair, but that's what some people felt and it demonstrates how difficult it is to bring about fundamental or deep-rooted change.

Greater Attention to Managing the People Issues

It's quite easy to say that more attention should have been paid to the people issues, because the real change was not about a change of law and a change of buildings, it was about enabling people to begin to think differently about how they should work. But, for a lot of the first year, you couldn't really begin the change process until you actually began to change how things operated. I think there is another lesson I learnt: you can do a lot of advance thinking but until the organisation exists change doesn't start to happen, and I have seen that in relation to other major reorganisation as well. The headed notepaper changed, and so on, but it was not until we moved into those new positions, and began to own the problem, that the change actually began to happen. So, it wouldn't have been a good idea to have 18 months as a shadow team, or 18 months as a shadow organisation, because until it's real you don't feel it. I remember vividly going into the office on the day we started and wondering what it would be like. And it actually felt very different on a personal level. It felt differently because the previous week I was a senior executive in a large organisation and the following week I was now part of something much bigger and accountable, but it was different. I don't think you can actually begin those processes of change until you really understand what has to be done and then you have got to allow those organisations time and space to go through those changes. I think we have been going through change for more than a couple of years.

E—THE TALE FROM THE BAY

Introduction

As with all of these Tales the story is told from the perspective of the storyteller. Recording the views of people from 'the Bay' may demonstrate many of the real differences that exist between Assembly staff in Crickhowell House and Cathays Park on various issues but they also show the common ground they share, and the way they have collaborated for the benefit of the Assembly and the people of Wales. The extent of that collaboration is shown throughout other parts of this book.

The development of a distinctive parliamentary body in Wales is one of the least explored and perhaps one of the more fascinating stories of devolution. If there was a rather sketchy template for a government in Wales, there was absolutely no template or blueprint for a parliamentary body for reasons described in earlier chapters.

This Tale examines the emergence of the legislative branch of the National Assembly, the newly named and increasingly assertive Assembly Parliamentary Service (APS), the former Office of the Presiding Officer (OPO). In the words of the Presiding Officer, Lord Dafydd Elis-Thomas,

> I'm determined that the new Government of Wales Act will provide for the equivalent of the House of Commons Commission to run the Assembly and the equivalent of a Parliamentary Service to meet the needs of it.

APS provides a full range of parliamentary services including: procedural and legal advice in support of Plenary and Committee proceedings; research and information services for Members; communications and ICT; bilingual support services including translation, interpretation and the Record of Assembly Proceedings; public information and education about the Assembly. APS functions to serve the 60 Members of the National Assembly for Wales, operating under the guidance of the Presiding Officer, in accordance with the Civil Service Code and without regard to the political affiliations of those Members.

This overarching purpose, constrained at times by what became seen as the incongruence of its corporate design, remains exactly the same today as in 1999. But there is one important addition. The mission statement now includes reference to its operating under the direction of the House Committee as well as under the guidance of the Presiding Officer. Following the Assembly's resolution to promote a clearer separation between the services provided to all Members and those provided to the Welsh Assembly Government (WAG), the House Committee was reconstituted under a new Standing Order in December 2002. At the same time, it was given delegated responsibility by the Assembly to provide services and facilities to Members generally. The Presiding Officer told us that 'it has been a temporary arrangement and what we've seen here is the growing of a democratic body'.

Therein lies the story of change. It is the story of a Welsh parliamentary service forging a strong and distinct parliamentary identity, culminating in the opening of a new Assembly Chamber in 2006 — *Y Senedd*. This Tale focuses on some of the organisational changes it has faced, the civil servants who work in it, and the challenges it is about to face in the light of the Government of Wales Bill, published in December 2005, which sets out, amongst a raft of proposals, to formally separate the executive from the legislature.

A Parliament by Any Other Name

Few organisations can have undergone as many changes of name within such a short space of time as this one. The Assembly Parliamentary Service (APS), renamed in April 2004, has emerged from its previous incarnation, the Presiding Office, formally the Office of the Presiding Officer. Both of the previous names were deemed to be confusing to the public and not descriptive of the full range of services provided by the staff.

As Rawlings (2005:71) commented, 'The early years of the National Assembly for Wales are best remembered for the rapid emergence of a virtual parliament'. This 'virtual parliament' is now facing the final split from the body corporate, a process which has been a (relatively) long time in the making.

The joining of executive and legislature into a single entity was seen by some as unsustainable from the start, as we show in our previous chapter. Many of the tensions, particularly of the first year of operation, arose from the single corporate body model. Further tensions came from Assembly Members, many of whom were politically inexperienced and bent on testing the extent of their powers. As Osmond (2000:39) has observed, significant forces, not least emanating from the Presiding Officer himself, sought to prise the executive and the legislature apart:

> One of my mantras in the situation of disagreement with officials—my bottom line—always is 'if it doesn't happen in West-

minster, in my experience, it should not happen here'. So what I've applied from the start is the test of a Parliamentary body to this place and that was what was endorsed, by my understanding, by the resolution of the Assembly to seek maximum separation under the Act. That of course has now gone on to public discussion, public statements from the First Minister and others. So it has been a temporary arrangement and what we've seen here is the growing of a democratic body. It is clear to me that you cannot have a constitution that doesn't have separation of powers between the executive and legislature, and the Government of Wales Act doesn't have that but it does have certain Parliamentary-type mechanisms, such as the delegation of functions from the Assembly to the Ministers.

There has barely been a procedure or policy left untouched in the short history of APS. Organisational change, political turmoil, internal reviews and external reports on its workings have come thick and fast.

There have also been a long series of incremental changes and we have chosen three changes, from many, to illustrate efforts to move from the virtual to a real parliament. The first example is the current use of the term 'Minister' that had become widely accepted in relation to 'Assembly Secretaries' as they were originally called, and this change was subsequently clarified in Standing Orders. The second example is the approval by the House Committee of a new logo, that most obvious of cultural signifiers, to represent the Assembly as a whole rather than that signifying the Welsh Assembly Government. This was in keeping with the practice of other legislative bodies in the UK. The overall Assembly now has two logos, one for the Assembly Government, the other the symbol of the National Assembly for Wales, the corporate identity for Assembly Members and APS (although, interestingly, neither of these logos applies to the Permanent Secretary's post). And the third example is the administrative separation of core services, most recently, the translation service, which had been located entirely within APS, and which now finds itself divided between APS and the Assembly Government in order to ensure separate accountability. HR and many finance functions had already been separated. Full administrative separation, initiated and fully supported by the Permanent Secretary, is to be achieved by 2006, in preparation for the abolition of the Assembly's corporate body status as set out in the Government of Wales Bill.

The determination to ensure separation is seen in the Presiding Officer's comments to us:

What was got off the ground was this inherently internally contradictory body. So whenever there have been common services for the Bay and Park, I have been involved in the struggle that continues, even to this day, for the allocation of resources. For example over ICT — a big issue at the moment — between the Park and the Bay: the needs of Government and the needs of Members. I think there hasn't been sufficient recognition from the staff that what goes on here is not some addendum, not some additional bit of activity, it is the Members that legitimate what the officials do, not the other way about.

Throughout, the Presiding Officer has been unequivocal in his calls for a parliamentary body in Wales and has consistently championed the rights of the Assembly against, what he considered to be, pressures exerted by the executive. In the light of this, he has sought to assert the independence of the Presiding Office together with the independence of advice given to backbench AMs. David Lambert, for example, was appointed as his legal advisor days after the Alun Michael resignation in February 2000, a political event which the Presiding Officer characterised as the first day of devolution.

A Bay official commented that the Presiding Officer,

> …was once referred to as the Marxist of Merionnydd. The Welsh Office was an anathema to him. It was no lover of the Welsh language, of North-West Wales or of the socialist agenda — all important things to him — and he was brushed off by people who now find themselves sitting across the same table.

A Strange Group of Civil Servants

In December 2000, the Presiding Officer announced the appointment of Paul Silk as Clerk to the Assembly as successor to John Lloyd, who retired in March 2001. Paul Silk, appointed following an open competition had over 25 years experience as a Clerk in the House of Commons, most recently as Clerk to the Foreign Affairs Select Committee. He was also a former Clerk of the Welsh Grand Committee; was Clerk in charge of the Government of Wales Bill and contributed to drafting the first Standing Orders of the National Assembly.

This appointment panel was chaired by the First Civil Service Commissioner, with the Permanent Secretary as a panel member, and although usual procedures were followed the appointment of a 'parliamentary' individual was interpreted by many as a symbolic move away from the traditional Welsh Office civil service and as a reinforcement of the emerging two bodies. Yet, both civil service officials and parliamentary officials are bound by the very same values and principles of impartiality, integrity and probity, excellence in service delivery and continuous improvement, commitment to facilitating the democratic process; openness, fairness and good communications. It was simply a case of the best person getting the job.

In paying tribute to John Lloyd in plenary, Rod Richards, AM, spoke of John Lloyd as exemplifying 'all that is best in the British Civil Service'. And it was these qualities, plus an experience of Parliamentary procedures, that made the appointment of Paul Silk seem a natural one.

As the Presiding Officer told us:

> And it is Paul, with quiet but very, very determined ways of internal management, respected throughout the Commonwealth as a Parliamentary Clerk, who has transformed the culture of this place, by putting out messages very clearly. There are others here...people at Grade 6 and 7, who see themselves as servants of the Assembly. Whatever they may have done before and whatever they may seek to do again, that does not affect the quality of what they do around this table, and that's the thing I value the most. They have decided to throw their lot in with this bunch of politicians because they realise that's the only way it will work – if they have servants that they know they can trust.

Paul Silk described the significant differences in culture between Westminster and Cardiff:

> One tends to compare it with previous employment – this is very different from the House of Commons. To give an analogy, working at the House of Commons was like being in the engine room of an aircraft carrier in the southern oceans in calm weather – here it is more like being on the bridge of a mine sweeper in the North Sea in winter – much more exciting in some ways, much rougher, and more challenging. That partly reflects where I sat in the other organisation but also that the House of Commons had been operating for 600 years and people knew what they were doing. The Assembly is a result of a big change and is an organisation that is changing rapidly and will continue to change.

In January 2003, Dianne Bevan, a qualified Solicitor who previously worked as a local government lawyer and senior manager, became Deputy Clerk to the Assembly. Although she had been appointed via a panel chaired by a Civil Service Commissioner many interpreted this appointment as another example of a non-traditional civil servant reinforcing the emerging parliamentary culture of the Bay. It reinforced the feeling that, in the words of one senior Bay official, many working in APS considered themselves to be 'temporary civil servants'.

Temporary they may feel, but the Clerk to the Assembly and all APS staff are civil servants (until the formal separation) and, as such, are subject to a series of statutory accountabilities in their ultimate responsibility to the Permanent Secretary.

As we have indicated in chapter three, one of the continuities in both the Welsh and Scottish devolution settlements was that civil servants remained part of the unified Home Civil Service, whilst Northern Ireland had long had its own civil service. Early Assembly documentation makes no mention of establishing a separate civil service in Wales: rather it demonstrates a clear intention that civil servants should remain part of the Home Civil Service. Maintaining a Home Civil Service which included Scottish and Welsh officials was one of the checks and balances of the devolution settlement, 'designed to prevent any drift towards conflict and isolation' (Parry 2002) and, according to another analyst, Welsh civil servants favoured remaining within the Home Civil Service as a protection against the vagaries of elected politicians who might seek to influence appointments and promotions (Laffin, 2002: 33). Conversely, it has been argued that the main reason for retaining the Home Civil Service was to assuage a nervous civil service hierarchy in London (Cole et al 2003). The Civil Service Code, which sets out the constitutional framework within which all civil servants work, was thereby strongly retained and provided a basis of stability following devolution.

Whilst Lord Elis-Thomas admired the way in which numbers of trained and long-standing civil servants managed to transform themselves into officials of Parliament, he had doubts about the understandable conflict that civil servants would face in serving both executive and legislature. There were clearly tensions. Laffin and Thomas (2001), in their examination of political-official relations in the National Assembly over the first year and a half of its existence, found tensions between the roles of those 'generalist' and 'specialist' civil servants and the ambiguities of working for a single corporate body. This ambiguity of role is also echoed in the research of Cole et al (2003) who examined the Welsh civil service after devolution. The research found 'a good deal of ambiguity' in that all civil servants were employed by and accountable to the single corporate body of the National Assembly for Wales.

Lord Elis-Thomas was unequivocal on this subject:

> I am very clear that officials of Parliament should not be civil ser-
> vants. There have been instances, for example when, early on, I
> was informed in no uncertain terms that it was not appropriate
> for an interpreter, who was a civil servant, to provide interpreta-
> tion to a party group meeting. There have been lots of issues of
> that kind where a view has been taken … The body corporate is
> only a description of a body which is not a Crown Body: this
> place was called a body corporate because they couldn't call it a
> Parliament, so all those difficulties have arisen in the way it has
> been administered. So my view, quite frankly, is that the culture
> of the Assembly hasn't developed as much as it should have
> done.

As senior civil servants pointed out to us frequently, it is important
to note that civil servants are servants of the Assembly and, as such,
are not paid to help and support individual political parties. As the
law stands, politicians receive public funds to assist them and
should not in addition receive the support of civil servants for political purposes.

His criticism of the system, rather than necessarily the individuals
administering the system ('It's not personal, it's institutional' he told
us), continued:

> I had serious doubts about the possibility of civil servants being
> able to function as parliamentary officials: those doubts have
> been proved right and we are now in the middle of a difficult sep-
> aration. The Assembly agreed in principle to seek the maximum
> separation within the Act. Therefore my view is very much col-
> oured by my own experience of struggling to establish a Parlia-
> mentary body within the constraints of the Act, within this
> notion of the body corporate which was interpreted, in my view,
> from the beginning as a way of ensuring that the Assembly
> became some kind of advisory body to the Welsh Office rather
> than a Parliamentary structure.

A deeply held view but not one supported widely through our
research. Most of the civil servants we spoke to explained that as the
Assembly was not established as a Parliament attempts to turn it into
one inevitably created problems for them as there came a point
beyond which certain activities would become unlawful.

Such are the differences between the two locations that some
interviewees believed that certain Cathays Park civil servants were
reluctant to change, or indeed were even making a conscious effort
to put the brakes on further change. The Presiding Officer remarked
that:

The way that legislation has been treated until very recently here
you would think that the making of legislation was some added
chore, not part of democratic scrutiny. There is a cultural issue
there, which goes back to my prejudiced view that what was
being created was 'business as usual' as much as possible, in
other words that the old Welsh Office should continue to function despite the fact that it now had to be accountable to an
elected members.

There are lots of issues of that kind which point me in the direction of a view that it is the least possible change then and my
understanding is that there are people seriously canvassing at
the highest level in the civil service still who believe it should be
the least possible change now. In other words, that the Government of Wales (Amendment) Bill should not be as far reaching as
I believe the overwhelming majority of Members here think it
should be — that is that it should be modelled on Scotland.

This view exemplifies the on-going challenges inherent in introducing fundamental change and the fact that change, as we have
argued previously, in an on-going process. Civil servants take the
view that it is the Members and Business Committee that control the
legislative process in the Assembly and that none of the legislation
has been challenged. They also point out that the Government of
Wales Bill has very largely been shaped by Assembly Government
civil servants and gives everything that was wanted short of primary
legislation, which is not yet politically deliverable. As we say, it
exemplifies the change management challenges.

Working within the confines of the corporate legal structure has
meant that APS officials also have had to work hard to secure the
confidence of Members and the understanding of other Assembly
staff in its ability to operate effectively. One of the watch words of
the Assembly is 'agility' and one of the ways in which parliamentary
officials have been able to respond to what Members have wanted
has been a willingness to think in what a senior official has termed a
'slightly heterodox way'. The admirable result, thanks to the efforts
of APS and WAG staff, has been a *de facto* division of the two sides of
the Assembly without any breach of the law. If the *Government of
Wales Act* is seen as a straightjacket, parliamentary officials have
worked hard to find any loose fitting points to enable Members to
move around within it. Many of the staff in APS would concur with
the view expressed by one senior Bay official that there is certainly a
recognition amongst staff in APS that 'Members are our own-
ers — we are the AMs' instruments':

We are a very strange group of civil servants — the only group in the country not (directly) responsible to Ministers. I am very conscious at meetings that I often have to say, 'this doesn't work for the APS'. I don't think any of my colleagues have groaned openly at that but I wonder if they have groaned inwardly, whether they think we are something of an irritant. We have a different set of accountabilities and a different philosophy in how we approach our Members — it is very important that we work for sixty Members and they come from five parties. My colleagues in the Welsh Assembly Government are there to serve a government of just one party. When the government changes they serve the new party, so in that sense they are impartial, but we need to be impartial in a very different way.

View from the Bay

The view from the Bay is good, literally — beautiful even. Located amongst the new buildings and apartment blocks of Cardiff Bay, a visitor to APS can look out the windows onto the Bay waterway, the new Assembly Chamber and the showpiece performance arts venue of the Wales Millennium Centre. The APS building itself, whilst architecturally uninspiring, seems light, airy and busy when compared to the much older and mainly windowless Cathays Park. The Welsh language permeates Crickhowell House: it is spoken in the corridors, in the dining room, in committee and plenary. It was put to us, by a senior Bay official, that:

> There's a lightness about the way people work in the Bay — partly the physical environment and partly because they are younger, and fewer have a long civil service background.

Many would disagree with that view but almost all of the interviewees concurred on one point. They may have expressed consternation about defining the nature of organisational culture, but most were able to identify striking differences in culture between the Bay and the Park. The Bay comprises a population made up of more new staff, younger people from a variety of non-civil servant backgrounds and, put crudely, less 'grey suits'. One particularly illuminating anecdote described how a new member of staff was asked, at induction training, if they had worked at the Welsh Office to which came the reply, 'Goodness, no, I didn't work in the Welsh Office, I used to protest outside it!'

APS is clearly an organisation which is youthful both by virtue of its staff profile and its history, but it is also constantly shifting. There may well be lightness to the way people work, but there are also some negative effects in the shape of uncertainty, change and insecurity.

When asked what adjectives describe APS, a senior official responded with the following:

> Cautious, complemented by a bit of risk taking — caution turning up at the edge. There are good reasons for caution — propriety, accountability to the public — but there is also recognition that avoidance of risk is not necessarily the goal. An organisation which is not yet entirely open to its own staff but again recognises that it has to be more open. More politically aware because there are now more politicians. An organisation in change, we are seeing some of the negative effects — uncertainty and insecurity, though some of that is due to external issues, such as pensions, but an organisation that realises it is changing. There's an element of turmoil and excitement. On the Welsh Assembly Government side there's the merger with the ASPBs, and on ours the separation from the Welsh Assembly Government. Quite a dynamic organisation.
>
> A hard trick to balance — being cautious and dynamic — and sometimes you see the strained interaction between some individuals that result from that.

Youth, risk taking and freshness come at a price and many interviewees in parts of Cathays Park argued that these characteristics equated to inexperience and naivety and to the fact that the Bay staff did not have major services to run (these views are elaborated upon in an earlier chapter).

If officials working in Cathays Park are criticised for little experience of policy making, then it is true to say that officials in the Bay had even less experience of parliamentary procedures. The short timescale to deliver devolution resulted in a clear imperative to get the institution up and running and much of the focus was given to the corporate support needed for the new Assembly Members, with additional demands coming from relations with Europe, foreign delegations and committees. It became clear very early on that more staff with new and different skills would be needed, with officials working in APS doing a very different job to those working in the Assembly Government in Cathays Park. It was to be the case that APS would experience difficulties in recruiting and retaining new staff and that high vacancy and turnover levels were the norm for some time. In April 2002, out of an expected complement of staff of 306, only 224 posts were filled. The situation had improved, but with the specialist nature of much of the work it is likely that recruitment and retention will continue to be one of the most significant resource challenges for APS. And expectations of all staff were and remain high—elected members were to be supported by experienced officials with high professional standards, bound by the Civil Service Code.

Conclusion

APS staff see their future as promising. At such time as the proposals set out in the Government of Wales Bill become law, there will be changes to the Assembly's structure, legislative powers and electoral arrangements, involving legal separation (supported by all political parties), a move to framework powers, a greater scrutiny role for committees and more.

There are many interesting and familiar sounding questions surrounding these changes, some of which echo the research questions we have sought answers to in this book.

- How will the organisation manage the change to become a leading parliamentary body?

- Will APS have learnt any change management lessons in taking forward the challenges of the separation agenda it is about to face?

- How will parliamentary officials cope with the new roles, new ways of working and the loss of civil service status?

- How will staffing issues be managed and will staff be prepared for the changes?

The House Committee will have a key role to play in steering through the necessary changes, assisted by the soon to be ex-civil servants of APS. APS will face greater openness, higher visibility, closer media scrutiny. It is devolution, perhaps in microcosm, and all over again. A final question remains:

- When the crutch of Cathays Park is finally removed, will APS walk tall?

Postscript

You elect sixty Members and bring them together in something grandly called the National Assembly for Wales and those members are going to think they are there to run the country, or at least argue about how the country is going to be run: I think its called Parliamentary democracy—there's a lot of it about! But it was never here before. As we move into the Government of Wales Amendment Bill, I'm hoping people feel that they can let it go more. After all, it is the Welsh electorate which will decide if the people here are good or not. It's a different dynamic to what you have in a territorial department, whose main area of operation was to do things in the interstices of UK Government policy. Now we have a multi-party democracy and Members will want to have their say on things. There is a lack of understanding that politicians will be politicians — and if you don't like politicians being politicians, you shouldn't be a public official [The Presiding Officer].

Chapter 8

The Future of the Civil Service in Wales

Introduction

Fundamental changes to the Welsh civil service and other public services will be seen by many political scientists as part of a wider strategy to transform the UK public sector. As Newman (2002) has identified:

> The character of New Labour's social policy agenda means that a modernised public sector is critical to the government's capacity to achieve its goals. The public sector becomes the agent through which the new policy agenda can be delivered rather than the main target of the reform programme itself ...
>
> But a distinctive feature of New Labour's approach has been the explicit focus on partnership as a way of governing. This focus is evident both in the strength of the partnership rhetoric and in the government's approach to the delivery of public policy ...
>
> Labour emphasised the need both for better horizontal integration (partnership working between public sector organisations, voluntary sector bodies and private sector companies) and stronger vertical integration (between central, local and community tiers of government, and between those involved in the shaping of policy and those affected by its delivery). This emphasis reflects concerns about the hierarchical, 'silo' relationships built into the UK system of government and calls for a more 'holistic' approach to governance.

In many other European countries, along with New Zealand, Canada, Australia and the USA, reforms to the public services are occurring and, whilst there are many distinctive differences, the reforms also contain surprising similarities. Some common features driving the reforms include:

- Leadership enhancement and an improvement in the quality of management

- Sharper focus on services, customers and/or clients and delivery and as a result much emphasis on performance measurement and enhancement;

- Improved collaboration and networking across the different parts of the respective public sectors with support of inter-organisational development — in short the rise of governance (see Kjaer 2004, Rhodes 1997);

- An intention, through each of these measures to improve the situation of, and services for, the population served by the public sectors.

In essence this list reflects New Public Management, albeit one that has developed from its initial articulation into what is now termed Modernisation (see for example Ingraham and Lynn 2004, Massey and Pyper 2005, Pollitt 2003). We don't, of course, imply that these changes are implemented in the same way or have the same priority in different countries. But they are certainly reflected in reform initiatives in the UK.

The developments described in a number of chapters in the book have to be seen in conjunction with the above. The impetus for developing public management in the National Assembly will reflect devolution and its progress as well as these broader trends.

This chapter examines a number of changes that will impact on civil servants and other public servants in Wales. These three sections reflect both trends described above. Part A considers the development of the Welsh public servant concept; Part B reviews the role of the Public Sector Management Wales (PSMW) — the former public sector management initiative (PSMI); and Part C examines further changes to the role of the civil servant.

A: The Development of the Welsh Public Servant Concept

You suspect something might be thought to be a very good idea when various people claim that they are, in some way, partly responsible for the development of the idea in the first place, as many did when we interviewed them or examined their documents.

The Welsh Assembly Government's *Putting Wales First: A Partnership for the People of Wales*, in October 2001, announced:

> We will review the existing structures and workings of Assembly officials to ensure they are in tune with the reality of political

devolution. We seek to move towards an increasingly independent and Welsh-based civil service—investigating ways of introducing an Assembly 'fast-track' programme to attract and retain high quality staff.

This commitment was echoed in First Minister Rhodri Morgan's 2002 Swansea speech (referred to as his 'clear red water' speech):

> A great deal has been achieved, I think, in turning the machine of the former Welsh Office from an engine of administration into one which analyses and develops policy choices. Looking ahead, however, I think we have to find ways of building on this still further. We need to invent a new form of public service in Wales, in which individuals are able to move far more easily than now between one form of organisation and another ...
>
> ... As well as tapping into the accumulated knowledge and research capacity of academics in social policy and other disciplines, I want us actively to explore the ways in which you as individuals and as institutions can be part of the new, permeable public service we need to create in Wales.

Plaid Cymru, in their evidence to the Richard Commission, made clear their views:

> An integrated public service would include public servants working for local authorities and other public bodies, including the health service and ASPBs, as well as the Assembly's own civil servants. This would make possible the creation of career paths for public servants within Wales, broader experience of government at all levels, and strengthen mutual understanding between those levels. It would entail the establishment of a National Public Service College.

When we interviewed Mike German, the leader of the Liberal Democrats, he claimed, with pride, that:

> The Welsh Public Servant was one of our ideas—it was in our manifesto in 1999 and we got it put into the partnership.

He showed us documentary evidence to substantiate his claim and pointed to the Welsh Liberal Democrats' evidence to the Richard Commission:

> An independent Welsh civil service should support the Welsh Government ... we support a fully independent and impartial Welsh civil service with clear lines of accountability and responsibility to Wales, with a greater capacity for specific Welsh policy-making.

A Cabinet Minister informed us:

> I would claim some credit for this. Going back five or six years
> ago, it struck me that Whitehall was full of Scots. I discussed this
> with the Permanent Secretary and he said it was a real problem;
> he couldn't get his staff to go on secondment. So I thought: 'How
> can we turn to our advantage this unwillingness to leave? Why
> not have a situation where people can work for us on second-
> ment or officials go to work in the public and voluntary sector?' I
> said: 'What you should be doing is help develop that cadre of
> senior Welsh public servants'. It's taken a while but with the
> Making the Connections agenda, and particularly the ASPB
> mergers, it gives us critical mass.

And the Permanent Secretary told us:

> I have always been an advocate of the Welsh Public Service and
> in some respects I could be regarded as the architect of some of
> the ideas impinging on this. I get very irritated when I hear peo-
> ple using the term 'civil servant' as a term of abuse. I don't differ-
> entiate civil servants from any other public servants in Wales; we
> are here to serve the public to the best of our abilities.

No doubt, all of them played a part in the creation of a wider and
emerging form of public servant in Wales.

Widespread Support for the Concept

We asked Rhodri Morgan to explain the thinking behind his Welsh
public servant concept. He told us:

> I think there are two things involved. You need the fire power
> and you need the critical mass to give the promotional opportu-
> nities, not exactly as in Whitehall but not dissimilar to that in
> Scotland. When you join a department as a public servant, you
> join as somebody who wants to serve Wales In the public service
> and you have a particular expertise and interest in fulfilling
> yourself in economic development, transport, education, envi-
> ronment, agriculture, or whatever it might be. Now that doesn't
> mean you can't ever apply for a job elsewhere but you should be
> expecting to specialise in the same way as if you join the DTI
> because you're interested in trade and industry and you may
> well stay the whole of your career in trade and industry. We have
> never ever done this in Wales but, in future, if you join Economic
> Development and Transport, for example, you can (… have a job
> in a range of those activities). We've never been able to do that in
> Wales before so it was essential that the mergers of the quangos
> took place to give the critical mass. Policy ideas can be generated
> much more easily if you have critical mass, and the quality of the

ideas will improve with the length of time that you've sat on the same egg to hatch this particular egg, as it were.

Our interviews with senior civil servants (attributable, non-attributable, 'on' and 'off-the record' interviews) found widespread support for the concept of the Welsh public servant and the further development of the Welsh public service. This was clear and genuine support and the words of two such civil servants capture that commitment:

> I think it is essential in Wales, I think it is not a useful thing that we might do, I think it is essential in Wales, because I think it is better for us to see, to think about there being a public service that people will have a variety of experiences rather than remaining in your particular silo. Like a lot of people in my position in local government ... I don't think I understood how the Assembly system operated, and what you needed to do to make the system operate, until I joined it. Similarly I would suspect therefore that people whose life has been based in the civil service will not understand the local government world, or they will understand it as I understood the civil service: theoretically but not actually understanding what it is like. I think that experience is important.
>
> The idea of dropping the civil servant is a good idea: call ourselves 'officials' instead. I think we've made more strides towards that than we realise: we have a lot more meetings in partnership with Chief Executives Local Authorities or ASPBs. It's easy to forget what a citadel the Welsh Office was, we tossed press notices or glossy brochures over the wall. We have learned to trust each other and share ideas. That is much more important than having formal processes. The fact that we hold these bodies to account is just a question of roles and responsibilities.

Support Tempered by Realism

Despite the widespread senior civil servant support there are some concerns, expressed by a minority, over 'how much of it is really doable in practical terms remains to be seen'. As one perceptive person explained:

> I'm a great fan of Welsh public service. However, it's easy to be a fan at the highest level of generality, at the maximum level of rhetoric. You know 'pulling together for Wales with local government, with other government departments in Wales and so on'. You can make a great mood music around public service in Wales (and that) is very good. However, there are some people who deploy the term public service principally because they want to use words, any other words, than civil service. Because

there is this really dark stereotyping of the civil service which, frankly, if you swapped the term civil service for something gender or race-related you'd be before the courts in an instant. I think that the service is ultimately despised and people either despise it or they're utterly dependent on it and you never know quite which.

I think: 'What does public service mean in practice?' Well it certainly means, in the mergers context, that if the new organisations emerge as nothing more than what people see as the worst features of the civil service (you know: risk averse, process orientated, detached, uninterested in delivery, academic), if it's marked by all of that then we won't have achieved, we won't have taken an opportunity that's there for the taking. And the number of people who are really, genuinely interested in secondments, for reasons that are related to Wales and its future as well as their own interests, is pretty small and actually the numbers of people who are capable of — and this is arrogance I suppose, so forgive me — the number of people who can do senior jobs in the Assembly Government is also very limited in Wales. And as Wales, as a political culture and the constitutional governance of Wales, departs from that in England so the barriers to moving into Wales at senior level will be, I think, greater than they are currently on the whole. So you might find somebody in business or industry looking to take the new EDT job, somebody of real weight who has considerable business experience, but will he or she want this job given the political character of the role, given the constraints, the inhibitions, given that you won't necessarily add lustre to your reputation by taking it on. You know the numbers of people who will rush to Wales and the Assembly Government and who are capable of doing these senior jobs I think is overestimated. So although I am a definite supporter in terms of joint development, joint training, building constituencies' networks of support across employment boundaries in the public service, and although I think lots more can be done by way of secondment, attachment, in all sorts of directions, in Wales, outside of Wales, internationally and that it should be much more vigorous, I think it right to be cautious about expecting overmuch over the next decade.

Those comments were made by a senior civil servant who is, undoubtedly, a committed supporter of the Assembly, of the development of the public service in Wales and of the delivery of better public services to the people of Wales. However, the comments about the practicalities of turning aspiration into achievement need to be considered dispassionately.

Outright Concern

Support for the concept is not universal and one senior politician, disagreeing with his/her Party's line, expressed the concerns of many:

> I have an issue with the Welsh Public Servant because, in my view, there are quite different responsibilities that follow from the all-Wales, all-UK or pan-European perspective. I would expect government officials to be able to see the broadest possible picture in terms of their management of public resources, as opposed to the organisation of local government and the local health boards.

Despite the widespread support amongst senior civil servants for the development of the concept the support that came from more junior civil servants was more circumspect. There were a number who expressed their concern that the Welsh public servant might compromise their position and even lead to the politicisation of the civil service in Wales:

> The fundamental role has not, should not, must not change. If it changes it is doomed – (the Assembly) relies on an impartial, adaptable civil service. There is no pressure from AMs to change – AMs have got used to the idea of the civil service. The Welsh Public Servant is an awful idea – the civil service is crucial and valuable.

Others had concerns that were concerned with the everyday practicalities of life in the Assembly and the dread that it might resemble a local authority:

> I am concerned about the very different relationship between local government officials and their members: councillors may walk in and berate an official. The impartiality of the civil service is key to the system working, but under increased pressure to deliver something there is a danger of getting tied in to the Minister.

Another voiced the opinion that:

> We think the Welsh public servant is part of a political agenda: part of an independent Wales. While cutting us off from Whitehall has much to recommend it – and it's happening anyway – I would be concerned that it could become too incestuous.

B: Public Sector Management Wales (PSMW) —
The Former Public Sector Management Initiative (PSMI)

The principal vehicle by which the Welsh public servant is to become a reality, rather than remaining an aspiration, was through the introduction of what became known as Public Sector Management Wales (PSMW) the more advanced form of the Public Sector Management Initiative (PSMI). The importance attached to this initiative was and remains considerable, and cannot be over- emphasised, and this high level commitment and the appointment of a senior Assembly civil servant to direct the programme illustrates the significance attached to it.

The Permanent Secretary informed the Richard Commission:

> I am currently giving leadership to what is being described as our 'public service management initiative'. This will seek to build on the fact that the Assembly is very largely drawing upon a Welsh labour market. If successful it will involve the establishment of common leadership and management training for staff working in all parts of the public sector in Wales — the Assembly civil service, the National Health Service, Local Authorities, Sponsored Bodies, and other Civil Service Departments. This should mean that over time Wales will develop its own cadre of public servants with experience in and understanding of different parts of the public sector in Wales. They should also have an established network of contacts in different parts of the Welsh public sector. This, coupled with the policy on open recruitment, should mean that there will increasingly be a common set of values and experiences amongst staff in the Welsh public sector.

This major commitment was accompanied by a series of internal Assembly arrangements to ensure that these bold assertions would be realised. In July 2003, a progress report declared that PSMI was intended to create a stronger Welsh public service, and thus a significant improvement in the provision of public services in Wales by:

- providing high quality shared training and development opportunities for people across all parts of the public sector in Wales, to build their own capacity and that of their organisations;

- largely through this, building a better understanding amongst Welsh public servants about how policies and services work, what they are there to achieve and how they can be delivered more effectively.

The PSMI project recognised that as the Welsh public sector was undergoing major change with the establishment of the National

Assembly for Wales, a consequent restructuring of several ASPBs, NHS reorganisation and the establishment of LHBs and new governance arrangements in local government. If these structural changes were to be successful in supporting the implementation of Assembly policies then they would require increasingly collaboration and partnership working. They would also require a major enhancement in the leadership and management skills of senior managers.

So the main focus of PSMI became to develop and deliver high quality training and development activities, geared specifically to the needs of Wales, while retaining a broader outlook to avoid the dangers of parochialism and to build on a wide base of best practice. Working together in this way, it was hoped, should also facilitate greater movement between the various sectors, broadening career opportunities and increasing mutual understanding. The anticipated outcomes would be to improve individual and organisational capacity and, thereby, the delivery and effectiveness of policy and services for the people of Wales.

As stated, the significance and importance placed upon PSMI was considerable.

By November 2003, those charged with the successful delivery of the programme had garnered various evidence to identify a number of areas of cross-cutting work to be the focus of activity. These included:

- Optimising service delivery, drawing on a wide evidence base
- Incentivising service improvement and innovation, particularly in cross cutting areas
- Engaging the public/consumer in service development and improvement
- Performance management and accountability, particularly on cross cutting issues

To translate those aspirations into practice a programme of activities was identified. The programme was expected to relate to the needs of individuals and their organisations, and, particularly, the relationships between organisations. A broad capability framework would help underpin the development of individuals, together with two general competencies: self-awareness and adaptability. The initial focus, in terms of staff to be developed, was likely to be on chief executives and their senior teams, key middle managers and fast track recruits with potential.

Rather boldly an annex to the paper identified a set of anticipated benefits directly arising from PSMI activities and these included:

- Improved capacity of individuals and their organisations (arising directly from the design and implementation of individual activities)

- Improved mutual understanding and therefore improved co-operation in areas of joint working, through development activity focused on those areas

- Improved capacity to support the broader improvement agendas, through development activity focused on those areas and sharing of best practice and experience

There were also wider benefits envisaged aimed at building capacity and at an organisational level these would show themselves in:

- Improved Partnership, Networking and Interchange

- Better understanding of each other's priorities, challenges and capacities resulting in more effective joint planning and action

- Interchange of ideas, policy development and implementation, including better alignment of local and national priorities and associated objectives

- Identification and exchange of best practice and ways to embed it so as to encourage continuous improvement in service delivery and quality

- Enhanced reputation of the Welsh Public Service as progressive and innovative organisations and exemplar employers

- Better learning and development opportunities at an individual and organisational level to allow people to contribute their full potential

- Improved career opportunities including greater mobility between sectors

- Improved service quality and delivery

Also, in late 2003, the University of Warwick was commissioned to identify the support for PSMI in Wales and the key activities needed to bring the commitment to fruition. The report, published in March 2004 and launched at a Cardiff hotel to an audience of senior people from across the public sector (including one of the authors of this book), was greeted with overwhelming support. Its conclusions and recommendations for PSMI were that:

- PSMI needs to be focused on the achievement of clearly stated goals and outcomes, and a clearly articulated theory of change.

- PSMI should be a 'catalyst for greater connectivity' in the Welsh public service, cultivating the capacity to work across and between boundaries.

- PSMI should build on the best of the leadership and management development programmes for the specific services, and complement these with the additional knowledge and capabilities needed to lead and manage inter-organisational partnerships and networks.

- PSMI should aim to harness the best programmes and initiatives from elsewhere in the UK, and adapt them to the Welsh context.

- PSMI should target 4 key leadership and management cadres for capacity building and development:
  - New entrants into the Welsh public service
  - Middle managers
  - Top management teams — develop a rapid programme of leadership master- classes and leadership networks
  - Political leadership teams — build on the IDeA's model of a Leadership Academy for local councillors

- PSMI should design and launch a programme with short, medium and long-term objectives and activities.
  - Short Term: Quick visible wins can be achieved through a series Leadership Masterclasses for political leaders and top management teams
  - Medium Term : the design and development of a Middle Management Development Programme for Wales could lead to launch of a national programme in April 2005
  - Longer Term: Investment now in the design and development of co-ordinated fast track graduate entry programme into the Welsh public service could lead to the launch of a pilot programme in April 2005

- Welsh Public Leadership College: PSMI could be treated as a relatively small-scale pilot to test the feasibility of a longer term and larger scale development of a Welsh Public Leadership College

- Substantial core funding is necessary from Government to kick start the initiative, and to act as a magnet for the additional funding to be raised from subscribing members. A budget of around £1m per year for 3 to 5 years gives an approximate order of magnitude, with government expected to contribute

40%-50% of this total, with the rest coming from subscribing partners and fees from courses.

- Academic Advisory Committee: We recommend the setting up of an Academic Advisory Committee for PSMI, to be chaired by a senior Welsh Vice Chancellor.

- A Moment of Opportunity: Our research suggests that you have a moment of opportunity to create in Wales something innovative and potentially of world-class.

The level of commitment from those present meant that the PSMI Director had a substantial mandate to introduce the proposals and ensure that PSMI played its full part in the transformation of the Welsh public sector.

In April 2004, the commitment was turned into an enabling document known as *SECURING TOMORROW'S LEADERS FOR PUBLIC SERVICES IN WALES* with the intention of stimulating discussion about the role of PSMI in ensuring a pool of high quality individuals to succeed those currently holding posts as chief executives and at board level in public sector organisations in Wales.

In May 2004, a strategy was launched: *PUBLIC SECTOR MANAGEMENT WALES – learning for public service excellence. A five-year strategy (2004–2009) for improving public services in Wales by developing the capacity of public servants.*

Once more, and given the overwhelming mandate for PSMW, the document asserted in its Measures of Success:

> PSMI will not itself transform public services. It is a catalyst for change and we will – through evaluation – identify the role PSMI has played in achieving any improvements. PSMI will champion the development of a series of baseline indicators across the public services that will help determine the extent to which public services are improving. And we will map existing data to see what conclusions can be drawn about public services and managerial and leadership capacity across the public service.

To accompany the strategy an Overarching Competency Framework was identified for senior public servants:

- Motivates, Empowers & Develops
- Inspiring, Promoting and Facilitating Change
- Providing Purpose and Vision
- Impact and Integrity

- Influencing and Negotiating
- Building Teamwork and Partnership
- Focus on Customers and Delivery
- Learning and Self Awareness

July 2004 saw the launch of the PSMI curriculum development and, at the time of writing, following the departure of the original Director to another organisation outside the civil service and Wales, a new Director has taken over the reins.

When we spoke to senior civil servants, in mid-2005, there was a certain ambivalence concerning the direction of PSMW. The following comments may represent a minority but should be of concern to the proponents of PSMW as they were made by two such proponents:

> PSMW is proving too slow to achieve transformation change. I can't see enough evidence of what has been achieved: it's not working for me yet, although I have tried genuinely to engage. It needs more fizz, oomph. We need to see key people getting involved and getting on.
>
> PSMW hasn't delivered anything as yet. There's a lot of support for it. It is the right way to go. I believe passionately in delivering public services on Wales but whether PSMW is the best way to do it, well the jury is still out.

C: The Civil Servants' Continuing Changing Role

Without a doubt it is the development of the Welsh public servant concept, and its delivery through PSMW, that will have the greatest impact on the future role of the civil servant. Since the arrival of the Assembly the civil servants have undergone substantial change, as First Minister Rhodri Morgan recognised:

> There's been a lot of restructuring since then, mostly related to trying to get the Ministers into the right jobs and then the consequences of that on the administrative set-up. Probably there has been quite a lot of discomforting, or discombobulation, of senior civil servants as they not only have to live with working for a different Minister ... but also in a different structure or department, getting used to things and maybe thinking that this is either a bit of a demotion, or it may be a bit of a windfall promotion. There have been an awful lot of changes and we all accept that.

However, change will impact on the civil servant in many other ways also. In our discussions with civil servants and politicians

seven factors likely to impact and bring about change were mentioned on many occasions.

1. Links with the Home Civil Service

Inevitably, the arrival of the Assembly, with different policies and
practices from Whitehall, plus the commitments inherent in the
development of the concept of the Welsh public servant have led to a
different relationship between the Assembly civil servant and the
Home Civil Service and this point revisits some of the issues discussed in chapter three above. A critical question concerns the extent
of that difference and whether it is preferable and/or necessary to
diminish, if not sever, the links between Assembly civil servants and
the Home Civil Service.

What struck us as unusual was the fact that it was the senior civil
servants we interviewed who appeared to be more in favour of a
fundamentally changed relationship than the senior politicians we
interviewed. The following four quotes are typical of what many
civil servants told us:

> I'd say probably most of the senior team in the Executive Board
> are sceptical about the added value at this stage of us being part
> of the Home Civil Service. We can see the attractions of it but if
> we're serious about developing a Welsh public service ... then
> the Home Civil Service link strikes me as a bit of an obstacle to
> that. It also seems slightly anomalous for the Head of the Civil
> Service in the Assembly Government (to have) some sort of line
> link with the Head of the Home Civil Service in Whitehall. I'd put
> a fair bit of money on it, that within perhaps not 5 years but not
> long after that that we would have a Welsh public service in
> Wales. It isn't that the world isn't changing in Whitehall signifi-
> cantly but it's not on the same drumbeat as in Wales. I personally
> don't feel a member of the Home Civil Service any more. We get
> regular communications from Whitehall, but I'd be the first to
> admit that I don't give them as much attention as I should. I give
> much more attention to the work that we're doing here on HR
> strategies and senior management strategies that we're develop-
> ing here than I do to actually finding out what's happening in
> Whitehall. That doesn't mean we shouldn't be benchmarking
> what we do. I think it's useful to have Whitehall benchmarks.
>
> I do think that it would be a step forward if we could actually
> get a formal pronouncement that the Assembly Civil Service was
> no longer a part of the national civil service. (Then) it would be
> easier to establish the concept of a Welsh Public Service if the
> major part of the Welsh Public Service were not very highly visi-
> bly labelled as being part of something else. People who work for

Cardiff City Council or Swansea City Council are not labelled as being part of a national local government service; they are part of a public service that is within Wales. I think we could take a step, a symbolic step that would actually recognise the reality of things. Not to put too fine a point on it, you know, the Cabinet Secretary, the Head of the UK Civil Service, is simply too bloody far away to have any real impact in my view on what day-to-day relationships are like between the Assembly Cabinets and senior civil servants.

I actually don't have an image of the Home Civil Service. It doesn't have any meaning for me. I don't feel part of a Home Civil Service, I feel part of a Welsh public sector and when I read stuff about Whitehall in the newspaper, I don't tend to think of myself as part of that world. That's probably a very different feeling from someone who would have been brought up in that and might have spent some time in a Whitehall department. That's certainly completely outside the image I have got.

The mandarins will be a rarer species. There are huge implications for a unified civil service across the UK; I'm not worried about that—I can't see that surviving long term. Sir Richard Wilson said after devolution that the civil service was 'part of the glue holding the UK together'—you wouldn't give the UK much chance if that were true, but actually I don't think it is true. I instinctively feel that the Welsh Public Servant is the correct way forward. The Assembly should have staff with expertise of the sectors: a cadre of people who understand more about Wales from different perspectives.

But, when we raised this point of links with the Home Civil Service with the First Minister we received a different, and somewhat surprising, perspective. This quote is taken from his wider deliberation on the purpose and functioning of the Welsh public servant:

But this does not exclude the fact that you have to consider where your very top civil servants are going to come from. You would need a completely different attitude towards the broadening of the mind and experience and expertise of the people you think are going to become your top public service managers, from age of 40 through to 60-odd, and you have to have a specialist sort of staff college. You can go to the Civil Service College, you can go to a lot of different places. Wherever it might be doesn't matter really. It's the purpose of it and the structure, how you perceive and plan in advance if this is the structure that you've got in mind. But you have to have a senior staff college facility somehow, either in-house, out-of-house, shared with others, or on your own. By bringing the quangos in-house it enables you to have more numbers to play with to justify the investment in developing a system to train your top management.

The leader of one of the opposition parties made a similar point to the First Minister:

> One problem we suffer from in Wales is critical mass: that we need to ensure that we attract the very highest calibre of candidate into the civil service and retain them. One fear I have is that we cannot offer the same career structure now that we are semi-detached from Whitehall: I think it's more difficult to make the transition to other branches of the civil service. Although to a degree it will be less of a problem when the quangos come in-house, I think it will still be difficult to recruit and retain high-flyers, which I think may be to the detriment of Welsh political and public life. There are dangers in weakening the links with Whitehall.

Discussions with staff from the Wales Office brought to the forefront another dimension of the links with Whitehall. Whilst Wales Office staff thought the notion of Assembly civil servants seeing themselves as part of a Welsh Public Service was sensible they did not see why that also required them to cut themselves off from the Home Civil Service. The Wales Office staff believed that to be regrettable and that it made for 'bad business'.

When we asked them to clarify the term 'bad business' they told us that, in their view, Assembly civil servants acted as if they no longer knew how to deal with Whitehall effectively and there was a feeling, in Whitehall, that Assembly Ministers were also suspicious of Assembly civil servants dealing directly with Whitehall civil servants. They explained that the way 'business' was done in Whitehall meant engaging in discussions with a wide range of people, over many months, to ensure that policies were formulated sensitively to one's needs. In the view of some Wales Office staff the Assembly no longer engaged in that process and when the Assembly developed a policy it consulted within Wales but did not consult meaningfully within Whitehall. Typically, an Assembly Minister would write to a Whitehall Minister saying 'this is what the Assembly wants to do' — it may concern legislation — and there would often be a lack of effective communication between the two. As a result of this relationship, the Assembly did not always get the results they wanted; the Assembly needed to become more of a part of policy development in Westminster. Assembly civil servants, to some extent, had forgotten how to deal with Whitehall and they should realise that they would not get what they wanted by merely saying: 'We're a democratically elected organisation, this is what we want, so you have to give it to us'. According to the Wales Office the Assembly civil servants would get better results by patient negotiation. It seemed that many civil servants, who were in the Welsh Office before devolution, no longer played the 'game', and if they didn't play the game by the established rules then they wouldn't get what they wanted.

2. The Need to Become Effective Managers and a Greater Focus on Delivery

Two messages we heard on many occasions concerned the very nature of being a civil servant and the realisation, unfortunately a slowly dawning realisation with some, that the civil service needed to become more managerial — that is skilled in management techniques and possessing a managerial outlook on life — and that they needed to concentrate on the delivery of more effective public services rather than the promulgation of more policies.

The following quote from a Cabinet Minister is typical of this view:

> If I have a criticism of the civil service, it is that what we as politicians regard as talent — intelligence, creativity, lateral thinking and the ability to deliver — is not valued as much as intellectualism and the ability to express yourself on paper. Management skills are not rewarded or recognised as much.

One senior civil servant, in a rather exasperated tone explained:

> We've got to learn how to be proper managers. Colleagues in senior positions in the Assembly are very good thinkers, very good at being creative, energetic at generating policy, but we're much, much less good at operationalising it and I think we have to learn how to work in partnership with colleagues outside to help us do that operationalising. Inside, we've got to learn how to be better managers, to be more effective managers. We're good at creating, we're much less good at doing, and I don't think we can carry on being like that anymore. I think we really do have to change and ... between us we need to get the right set of skills and the right way of working so that we can make things actually happen. There are actually lots and lots of excellent examples about the place but what we don't do is we don't share, we don't look at each other's practice, we don't celebrate it and we need to develop for that a much more appreciative kind of approach and get out of our silos and share a bit more.

3. Dealing with a Greater Public Prominence

The words of two senior civil servants exemplify the point perfectly:

Public profile was quite a shock for a number of us. Also we've had a much more public profile with the Assembly Committees and I think it's good that we're not just shadowy mandarins in the background, but it's tricky in that you can't be your own spokesman. We've had to get used to being quoted in the newspaper.

It's rather a perverse consequence of devolution: transferring all this power from the Welsh Office to the elected body has actually resulted in the civil servants coming out from behind the screen in a much more public way. I used to joke that the most important decision any civil servant had taken was to ask 'What colour tie shall I wear on TV today?' All of a sudden we started appearing weekly, fortnightly in committees on television.

4. *Specialism v Generalism: A Broadening of Expertise*

Anyone versed in the traditions of the civil service will appreciate that the differentiation between senior staff was between the generalist — the 'gifted amateur' — and the specialist, such as architects, doctors or lawyers. These days that differentiation is far less clear as two factors take effect: the first is the immense growth in the number of civil servants who consider themselves to be specialists and the fact that as the traditional generalists spend more and more time in one department they, in turn, are becoming specialists in their area of operation.

As one Cabinet Minister explained thoughtfully:

In the next 10 years you'll find a narrowing of experience but a broadening of expertise. There is a vertical broadening of expertise rather than a horizontal broadening. This is a natural process.

A senior civil servant echoed the Minister's point:

I think it is going to sharpen the debate about specialism and generalism. There is a much greater expectation about the Assembly delivering for the people of Wales. With that goes an increasing expectation of expertise: you are not central to what is happening unless you can hold your head up in some fairly combative discussions with the world out there and that does require a degree of expertise in your field. So I think there is going to be a much greater and significant pressure towards expertise and I think I have seen one type of civil servant probably not moving round as much as they traditionally used to move around. There are some downsides: since I have become part of the civil service, I have appreciated more the value of people whose expertise is policy development than probably I would have seen from outside. And it is easy to caricature them: they don't actually know about the subject they are talking about; they have only been there for two years; they are in charge of health today, agriculture yesterday and economic development tomorrow. I think there are dangers of throwing out some of the expertise in how to develop policy and I think it would be regrettable if all that disappeared in a rush towards expertise and I think there is a debate about how you get a proper balance between those two issues.

5. Developing a Greater Risk Appetite

Anyone attending a Treasury sponsored course or conference will know that there is a drive to make the public sector less risk averse — they talk of developing a risk appetite. Similarly, anyone with experience of the public sector will appreciate that a risk appetite bordering on the anorexic might represent judicious practice. However, the notion of reducing risk aversion is having an impact on thinking in Wales, as a senior civil servant explained:

I hope we will become less risk averse but that's tricky in a very small, pressurised, political atmosphere. It easy to say that the civil service needs to take risks but you know you'll have a pretty hard time in the press and in front of your committee if something you undertake does go wrong. There needs to be a bit of give-and-take with the media and the political side: there's a difference between having a greater appetite for risk and eliminating risk altogether; sometimes things will go wrong, you'll have bad luck, but there's no room for bad luck in government accounting.

6. Nature of Civil Service Appointments

One Opposition senior figure, clearly in iconoclastic mood, recounted that one of the most frightening aspects facing a Minister was a very senior civil servant saying: 'You can ask us to undertake a task but you can't tell me who should do it'. Our indignant interviewee continued:

I can't think of any other job where the head of an organisation can't say 'I'd like so-and-so to do this job' or appoint their own staff internally. I think it needs to be clear that politicians who have a policy agenda should be at least able to say: 'This is a job for so-and-so'.

When we asked whether s/he had any concerns about the potential politicisation of the civil servants delivering services s/he responded:

Of course I have concerns but I think there needs to be a more open way of selection, perhaps involving more interviewers than a single politician. The process for appointing boards of quangos involves Opposition and Government parties, and external assessors. If that's good enough for them why not have this system for the senior civil servants? I mean the very senior civil servants.

But iconoclasm is obviously not the sole prerogative of politicians and one senior civil servant explained his view:

If, politicians do have a role in the appointment of senior employees, through at least a sounding out process, where politicians feel that they've played some sort of broad role in shaping the posts that's bound to make the Cabinet and the senior civil service more collegiate. It would still be a civil service, still not politicised, but just a greater level of comfort on the body politic side that you've got a range of people with fresh, up-to-date skills who've got no baggage from the old regime.

Interestingly, it was pointed out to us by other senior civil servants that, to a very significant extent, this indeed is what happens currently.

7. Age Profile and Turnover

Anyone aware of the membership of the Executive Board, over the past two or three years, will be only too aware of the similar age profile of its members, the substantial numbers (in proportionate terms) of those who have left and the number who are preparing for imminent retirement. Some of those who have left did so, at retirement or before retirement age, in a disaffected state for many reasons. It is quite clear that workforce planning played little part in the appointment of these people many years ago and the substantial turnover of the most senior civil servants can either be seen as an opportunity or a threat. Two members of the Board, one who may leave soon and one with many years to serve, were asked if the turnover will be an opportunity or a threat. Their comments are interesting:

It's got to be an opportunity. Every organisation needs to move on and we haven't got the right age or skill balance in the team at the moment and certainly within 3 or 4 years there's going to be quite a different complexion upon the senior team here, and I think it might actually help to increase the level of trust that there is between the body politic and the civil service. Although it's unfair, and largely untrue, we're still seen as part of the old guard. I think we will find the best of the existing team coming through stronger and there's the really talented people waiting to come through, together with a good smattering of the very best of people from other walks of life in Wales and beyond; provided we can deal with the terms and conditions issue.

It's both isn't it? I suppose I'm a sort of optimist and a person who likes change. We've been through a huge amount of change and yet, somehow, we haven't lost; we're not floundering around with the loss of institutional memory. And as long as you've got a significant degree of change going on as you move forward I don't see that in itself as a problem. Things that concern me more, I suppose, would be: are we doing enough by way of developing those people who are the next lot who will step into those particularly senior shoes? And then again there's a big jump between Grade 7 and heading up a division – probably the biggest single jump – and a lot of people are going to be in that situation, so it would be nice to stagger that process over a period and I think people will need some help with that and some will struggle to start with. There's a huge amount of talent around this organisation. We've taken in some extraordinary people, you know, in some quite junior grades in cases.

As we showed earlier, the extent to which senior civil servant appointments have been opened up to external competition has had a major impact on this issue.

Conclusion:
The Evidence from the De Facto Welsh Public Service

Whether by means of the development of the Welsh public sector, and its PSMW creation, or through the impact of the other factors it is evident that change will remain a constant factor (to quote the change management cliché).

In April 2003, one of us facilitated a meeting of senior people who had experience of working in three or more public sector settings. The delegates represented experience of public service in the former Welsh Office and the Assembly, local government in Wales and England, universities in Wales and England, overseas government, the Training and Enterprise Councils (TECs), the Welsh Local Government Association, the NHS, S4C, the Audit Commission, nationalised industry, housing associations, the Prince's Trust, the National Rivers Authority, and even some private sector companies.

In the light of the commitment to develop the Welsh public service the delegates at the meeting were asked to consider the process of moving from one part of the public sector to another, identify the distinct characteristics of those parts of the public sector in which they had experience, and then to identify notable points based on their own experience. Their unprompted responses were fascinating and are germane to the change management challenges currently facing the Assembly (Prosser 2003):

First, whilst there were obvious benefits in achieving a greater collaboration between the various public sectors, it was realised that there were times when a properly managed creative tension resulted in better outcomes. Collaboration should be used to remove the defensive stances that were sometimes adopted and true partnership should be on the basis of a partnership of equals. However, it was realised that even this ideal state could be difficult when one part of the public sector is expected to hold another part to account (the argument of principals and agents).

Second, one delegate had experience of working for an overseas organisation that provided the full range of public services. He made the point that having a single organisation did not guarantee collaborative working. There remained a temptation to remain in professional and organisational silos and the real challenge lay in changing values, attitudes and behaviours.

Third, any scheme to bring together the various parts of the public sectors should be aware of the dangers of reinventing the role of the generalist—a Welsh public sector manager who gave the impression that s/he could work effectively in any part of the public service. Evidence suggested that there was much benefit in continuing the move towards the employment of professional staff in specific areas and generalists in those areas where they were best suited (which itself needed further clarification).

Fourth, in any system where a large number of experts are grouped together, it is less likely that they will recognise the existence of relevant expertise outside of their bailiwick. If this in turn leads to a monopolistic process of policy making, then that can be intellectually, politically and socially unhealthy.

Fifth, issues of corporate governance and public accountability, especially where these are accompanied by a heightened media interest, can be seen to be a factor that encourages people to remain in areas where they possess a depth of understanding and support that will carry them through potential times of trial. Raising one's head above the parapet is seen to be a hazardous occupation at times.

Chapter 9
Conclusion

The title of our book contains the words *Making It Happen*. Note that there is no question mark, no sense of hesitation or ambivalence – it did happen: devolution has been introduced to Wales. A National Assembly has been created and is functioning, and the civil service has changed to accommodate that reality. Policy is made across a number of areas and is delivered. We can of course discuss how well or badly this happens, but it happens. Devolution has arrived and it is against this substantial achievement (civil service and political) that we make these concluding observations.

But what is this thing that did happen? Remembering the oft-repeated slogans of the need for 'continuity and change' and that devolution would be 'a process and not an event', the first point to be made is that the notion of devolution has grown and developed – and continues to grow and develop – as it plays out in real time. The dynamic nature of change – as we observed in chapter two – needs to be stressed. Whatever everyone thought they had secured – and there were different views – it altered and shifted. The reality of politics and administration intruded and with that there developed critical reflections on the model of devolution in Wales. The result is that the model of a single planned clearly defined change is – once again – inadequate to describe the reality of what actually happened and the nature of the management challenges that were confronted.

It is therefore not surprising that unanticipated consequences abound: the increase in the size of the civil service, the high rates of turnover amongst senior civil servants, the departure of the one Permanent Secretary and the arrival of the new one, the outcome of election results, the various mergers and, perhaps most of all, the dramatic demise of Ron Davies. All were not anticipated, though perhaps some of them should have been in some guise. 'Events, dear boy, events' to quote Harold Macmillan again and these 'events' certainly came—for the process is a series of events—and impacted on the nature of devolution and changed significantly what had to be managed.

One of the events is the nature of personalities in the process. Case studies of this sort are interesting for social scientists as they demonstrate the interactions of structure and agency. We are hostile to the argument that it is all about people, but there is no doubt that at crucial times particular individuals made a significant difference. John Smith's short period as Labour Leader made devolution an acceptable policy and even when he was no longer there, his legacy meant that Labour, despite the considerable scepticism of many in the party including some in senior positions, could not alter it. Ron Davies's role is another that is particularly significant. His knowledge of what was acceptable in the Labour Party and his excellent relations with other key players, including senior politicians in other Parties and civil servants, was significant. It is also clear that his departure came when most key decisions had been taken. Rachel Lomax and then Jon Shortridge, and their small teams, played crucial roles in translating policy into practice and deserve fulsome praise. And their relationships with political players were significant in making this contribution.

Thus personalities matter. But they are embedded within contexts and structures. Our research indicates that the very senior members of the civil service were and are highly regarded within the service. And it is also clear that both Permanent Secretaries, Rachel Lomax and Jon Shortridge, are and were sensitive to people management issues. Yet it is also clear that communication with both middle and junior staff was seen by some to be inadequate, though latterly improving. It might be argued that this demonstrated that the senior civil service focused on policy issues as compared with management issues. That the civil service made a significant contribution to developing the devolution policy is without doubt: it is much less clear that the resultant managerial implications were fully considered although many were not susceptible to full consideration in advance of introduction. And a consequence of this is demonstrated in our chapter on middle managers, and those who displayed a cynicism about the process which may be interpreted as reflective of their sense of not being involved and of not being properly prepared.

The experience of middle ranking civil servants is fascinating. There is evidence that middle managers in most organisations are hostile to major change, usually for good reasons. They are the group who are expected to keep 'business as usual' going and they often feel that changes are imposed on them, while they are undertaking this. For them the understandable excitement of senior managers involved in major changes is frequently at their expense. In turn their cynicism is equally understandable though we must remember that, as the attitude surveys reveal, that this reaction was limited to some middle managers.

As we have demonstrated there is clear evidence that the civil service learned and developed through the devolution process. We were much impressed by talk of a new culture which emphasised this learning mode. However two points are worth making. Yet again there is evidence that structures can defeat or at least inhibit learning. There is evidence that the legendary silos of bureaucratic organisations come into play when for example new changes are taking place. People would rather seek new solutions than go outside the silo—old cultures win out—as it does among some middle ranking civil servants uncomfortable with the new relationship between civil servants and politicians.

Second, while there is evidence of new cultures, not all of the manifestations of this are evidently good. In our view it was inevitable that cultures would develop around the Bay and Cathays Park. The tensions between these two institutions are inevitable and should not be overstated, but they exist.

Both these points about culture raise the issue of the extent to which cultural change occurs, as it were, naturally as a result of inevitable other changes, the extent to which it is deliberately created and the extent to which this cultural change in turn influences other developments. Thus it is clear that devolution has been embedded in Wales and, while the recommendations of the Richard Commission apparently will not be implemented in full, the White Paper and the Government of Wales Bill makes clear that more changes will take place and will enhance devolution. It is also clear that the old Welsh Office has gone forever and it has been replaced by something new, warts and all. This something is more inclusive, more policy-oriented and more Welsh than before. In a sense devolution was about achieving this and to that degree can be said to have succeeded. In turn that will create a new challenge, namely managing the tension between the National Assembly civil servants remaining part of the Home Civil Service and their relationship in a potential Welsh Public

Service. Will the pull of being part of the old civil service conflict with the push of the new Welsh polity?

In conclusion we turn again to our initial point—namely devolution has happened. Despite the speed with which it was introduced, despite the frequently repeated arguments that there was no policy making capacity in the Welsh Office (though we have made clear that we think there were policy making capabilities if not adequate capacity), despite various stumbles along the way, the stories and myths we were told all reflect the fact that there has been a shift in British politics and policy making and that distinct policy developments occur in Wales and are implemented. That perhaps is the ultimate tribute to the civil service.

Appendix 1

Research Methodology

Aims and Objectives

Combining empirical research and literature review, the aim of the study is to examine how the civil service managed the change from the Welsh Office to the National Assembly for Wales. Chapter two indicates the themes and issues we explored. These included the political context, the changing structure of the civil service, the changing culture, the nature of people management, as well as various perspectives on the future of the civil service in Wales. As chapter two indicates we were confronted with the dynamic nature of devolution and its implementation.

The objectives of the study were:

- To analyse the change management processes adopted in the move from Welsh Office to National Assembly for Wales.

- To analyse the change management processes adopted during the first and second terms of the National Assembly for Wales.

- To analyse the context within which devolution took place.

- To examine the impact of existing and emergent organisational structures on managing change.

- To identify key management issues associated with the advent and consolidation of devolution.

- To examine managerial mechanisms utilised in managing the devolution change.

- To examine understandings and impact of leadership within the emergent and consolidated National Assembly for Wales.

- To identify strengths and weaknesses of management of change approaches and lessons to be learned both for the National Assembly, other devolved governments and newly devolved organisations.

- To provide opportunities for organisation development and learning.

Methods

Our study is located within a qualitative research framework. A particular feature for us is valuing storytelling. To quote Gabriel (2000)

> Organisations do possess a living folklore, though this is not equally dense or equally vibrant in all of them. This folklore, its vitality, breadth, and character, can give us valuable insights into the nature of organisations, the power relations within them, and the experiences of their members (p. 22).

As we undertook the research, and particularly the early scoping study where we were not armed with tape recorders, the number of anecdotes we were told overwhelmed us. It seemed that everyone we spoke to, regardless of their position in the organisation, had a story to tell that, for them, encapsulated the introduction of devolution to Wales. Most of them told how the civil service had triumphed against the tight deadlines set in 1997–99 to make devolution a reality, of the long hours, the victorious battles and the enormous relief when they finally made the thing happen. They also told us stories about politicians and their approaches to issues (we've tended not to use these stories as we are telling the civil service story, even though the vast majority of stories were to the credit of politicians), we engaged in good-natured and usually 'off-the-record' gossip over various cups of tea and coffee, and together we built an impressive gallery of devolution tales.

We welcomed each and every story especially where it became clear that senior colleagues, sometimes colleagues whose offices were no more than yards apart, had very different takes on the same incident and some believed the organisational equivalent of an urban myth when a nearby colleague would deny categorically that any such event took place. The classic example of this is what took place on referendum night and the view of more than one civil servant that the ordering of the announcement of the results had been arranged to heighten the drama: in other words, the Carmarthenshire result had been held back to make for a dramatic climax to the night's events. Not only did the person organising the referendum vehemently deny this but also we were contacted by a much more junior civil servant, via a colleague of his who knew one of us, to tell us that he had taken the eventful call that night and he could swear that every result was given in the order they were received. The fascinating point is the existence and utility of such stories.

As Gabriel argues:

> ... storytelling in organisations ... opens valuable windows into the emotional, political, and symbolic lives of organisations, offering researchers a powerful instrument for carrying out research. By collecting stories in different organisations, by listening and comparing different accounts, by investigating how narratives are constructed around specific events, by examining which events in an organisation's history generate stories and which ones fail to do so, we gain access to deeper organisational realities, closely linked to their members' experiences. In this way, stories enable us to examine organisational politics, culture, and change in uniquely illuminating ways, revealing how wider organisational issues are viewed, commented upon, and worked upon by their members (p. 2).

Support for the importance of stories comes from narrativist accounts of self. For example, Alistair Macintyre (1984) argues that human action in general can be seen as enacted narratives. 'We all live out narratives in our lives' (Macintyre 1984, p. 212). Listening to these stories then gives powerful insights into the sense-making of individuals. Our approach therefore reflects the interpretative approaches which have arisen in popularity as a mode of understanding in politics and other social sciences (see for example the debate in *The British Journal of Politics and International Relations* 6, 2, 2004).

We sought to integrate these stories into our book. As we conducted the interviews and heard more and more stories to place alongside our organisational theories and diagnostic approaches it struck us—indeed it was even suggested to us by a senior civil servant—that an intriguing approach would be for us to take a Canterbury Tales approach to the book so that we would be able to tell everyone's story and allow the readers to make up their own minds. Such an approach appealed to us greatly and is in concord with our belief that storytelling is a legitimate academic device in organisation analysis. Again to quote Gabriel (2000):

> There are times, however, when stories crystallise around particular interpretations. Different versions may diverge in numerous details but seem to agree on the story's core symbolism. This symbolism seems very powerful, the stories being treated as part of the heritage of an organisation or of a group. When researchers encounter such stories, they may sense that what is being related is no mere trifle of organisational life, but something deeply sig-

nificant. It is offered to them on the basis of trust and respect, the way that a valuable artefact might have been. Questioning or doubting such stories is not easy and may lead to the exclusion or ostracism of the researcher and the breakdown of the research relationship (pp. 42–43).

However we have decided not to take a Tales approach in each and every chapter as this would encourage unnecessary repetition of points made previously and hinder, if not break up, the development of themes that should be pursued in an orderly manner. Therefore, the book has thematic chapters examining certain dimensions of change, in addition to the Tales approach where we allow the story to be told through the eyes of someone else or even through the eyes of a group of people.

As such, while mindful of the relevant literature, we utilised an iterative approach, allowing key themes to emerge through a multi-method approach. The key elements of this approach were documentary analysis, semi-structured interviews, attitude surveys and a focus group.

Literature Review

A descriptive literature review was undertaken on organisational change and on the impact of devolution upon the civil service in particular. The literature was synthesised and analysed to produce a theoretical framework within which the findings of the study are located.

Documentary Analysis

We gained unprecedented access to hundreds of National Assembly registered files and documents, the most illuminating coming from the pre-devolution period of 1997–1999. The National Assembly's Records and Information Management Division provided invaluable guidance and assistance in helping us navigate our way through the files most relevant to the aims of the project — change management, organisational structures and development, management and leadership. Documentation not clearly related to these areas was excluded. The analysis then focused predominantly on high level processes and sought to generate convergent themes.

In accessing unpublished documents, we undertook that no individual staff would be identified, nor would be identifiable in any subsequent publications. The only exception to this may be those working at the most senior levels within the organisation and a small number of individuals who played a central role in the managerial and organisational processes of the change from Welsh Office to National Assembly. Consent has been sought from these individuals.

Semi-structured and Informal Interviews

A total of forty-eight semi-structured interviews were conducted with the National Assembly's senior civil servants, civil servants across different grades, with Assembly Government Ministers and with Assembly Members. Interviews were also conducted with the key players in the devolution story, the former Secretary of State for Wales Rt Hon Ron Davies and the Permanent Secretary at the Welsh Office from 1996-1999, Rachel Lomax. Participation in interviews was voluntary and consensual.

Anonymity and confidentiality was guaranteed, unless specific consent was given to individual identification. All requests for interview were met with positive responses and only two politicians refused to be interviewed.

In addition to the formal interviews, a series of informal interviews and conversations were carried out with a number of senior officials. These were very helpful in enabling us to scope the key areas in preparation for the more formal interviews.

Interview questions were then generated through the informal scoping interviews, literature and documentary analysis. The key questions we asked were:

- Outline your work history within the Assembly and describe your current role.

- How would you describe the culture of the Assembly? How has this changed since you started working in the Assembly/Welsh Office and if so, how and in what ways?

- How would you describe the role of the civil servant within the Assembly? How has it changed and if so how and in what ways?

- What will the role of the Assembly civil servant be in the future and what implications will this have for the way in which the Assembly is organised and managed?

- There have been a lot of changes to the organisations since devolution. In terms of how these changes have been managed, what do you think has worked well and what has worked less well? What could have been done differently?

Focus Group

An open invitation was extended to all employees via the Assembly's intranet news pages requesting participation in a focus group meeting. We received a good response and began a dialogue with the volunteers, the purpose of which was to guide the study, to help identify areas of examination and to discuss findings. While, the group did reflect a range of different grades from Executive Officer to Grade 5 level, most of the respondents were grade seven.

The focus group was voluntary, consensual and conducted confidentially and anonymously. The participants were self-selecting and therefore we do not claim to have captured a stratified or representative sample of the organisation as a whole. All participants came with a mixture of experience gained from different divisions within the organisation and many had started their careers in the Welsh Office.

Of particular interest to us were three key questions:

- How were the staff and the organisation prepared for the changes which were brought about by devolution?

- How has the culture of the organisation changed as a result of devolution?

- How do you think the role of the civil servant has changed as a result of devolution?

To indicate more precisely our approach we include details of the process we adopted.

The week before the Focus Group we sent out an e-mail setting out, in very general terms, what will happen and how important this event is for us. The agenda was as follows:

1215–1230: The four of us welcome (warm and friendly welcome to colleagues rather than clients) the people as they arrive and invite them to take some food and sit at a table.

1230:   Introduce the four of us; possible 'ice-breaker' (they introduce themselves); purpose of Focus Group and its importance; what we've done so far (in general terms).

1240:   The methodology
            The findings to date

1255:   Introduce groups to the two/three questions:

1300:   Group work

1330:   Group feedback and discussion — facilitated.

1400:   Thanks and end (prompt).

Notes:

1   The 1240 and 1255 presentation made with OHP support.

2   Each group will have access to flip chart

3   Room lay out will be cabaret style

4   The 3 or 4 of us will circulate during group work

5   The atmosphere will be 'colleague to colleague' rather than academic/consultant to civil servant'.

The focus group participants were asked to discuss three questions in groups and their responses, recorded below in the point form contained on their flip charts, are self-explanatory and illustrate their concern over the way in which they had been prepared for devolution.

Question 1: How were the staff and the organisation prepared for the changes which were brought about by devolution?

Lack of clarity about roles and structures.

Element of fear — unexpected nature of change.

Poor communication.

Project Board didn't include all the key stakeholders.

Lack of Memorandum of Understanding, lack of concordats with 'partners'.

Lack of training.

'Educating Whitehall' — we needed to make them understand. Keeping us in the loop.

Not prepared for the increase in workload.

In Office of Presiding Officer (OPO) there was good training and preparation for new demands/customers.

In denial of likely impacts.

Major IT change had not been completed.

Office of SOS not prepared for it.

WAG staff were not clear about the role of OPO.

Lack of clarity about functions to be transferred.

Lack of understanding of the legal implications of devolution — e.g. delegation of power/ultra vires.

N.B. Many of these have not necessarily been resolved.

Question 2: How has the culture of the organisation changed as a result of devolution?

Perception — WAG has a duty/responsibility to the people of Wales (no longer just a 'mini-Whitehall').

More openness / transparency.

More professional, more business-like, even slicker, smarter approach to business.

Breaking down barriers.

More flexible approach to team working, co-operation and individual's responsibility.

Executive Board making progress in giving clarification, offering feedback — managing cultural change.

Increased workload pressures.

Terms/conditions of service improved.

More valued as an individual but ... concerns

Question 3: How do you think the role of the civil servant has changed as a result of devolution?

Our names in the paper.

More and closer contact with politicians.

Contact at different levels of the organisation.

Closer to public.

More politically aware.

Consequences (of not being in favour).

Longevity of politicians.

Impartiality / loyalty / corporate / Parliamentary.

'Partnership' / scale of change (works in Wales).

Delivery — more focus, less advice.

Media focus.

Workload increased dramatically.

We followed the focus group with One-to One Interviews with participants. Three of us conducted the interviews on the same basis that we had conducted the interviews with the politicians and the senior civil servants, with two exceptions: they were not taped, as we thought that might be less necessary and possibly a little intimidating; they were one-to-one whereas in the other interviewers one of us acted as an additional note-taker and occasional questioner.

The conversations were conducted around two standard questions.

Question 1: How would you describe the culture of the Assembly and has this changed? If it has changed, in which ways has it changed?

Question 2: How would you describe the role of the civil servant within the Assembly? Has this changed? If it has, in what ways has it changed?

Attitude Surveys

Four attitude surveys had been conducted and the results of these were made available to us. We have included details of results in Appendix 2.

Appendix 2

Reports from Staff Attitude Surveys

National Assembly for Wales Staff Survey 2001

The results of the MORI survey revealed that 'overall satisfaction' and 'satisfaction' on almost all of the topics covered was exceptionally good with more than eight in ten staff stating that they were proud to work for the organisation. However, there were a number of areas within the Assembly that performed better than others. The areas which showed lower levels of satisfaction, than other areas, were: pay, balancing work/life commitments, communication and having the opportunity to do what they are best at every day.

Those questions where more than 30% of staff stated that they 'strongly agree' with a statement were:

- Most of the people I work with are committed to doing good quality work (52%)
- I feel my line manager trusts me to do my job (48%)
- I know what I am expected to achieve at work (36%)
- My line manager is an effective leader and a good motivator (32%)

Whilst the questions which elicited the highest level of disagreement were:

- My earnings are fair considering my duties and responsibilities (52% disagree)
- Everyone makes the best use of e-mail to communicate (47% disagree)
- I get my work done within my normal working hours (43% disagree)

- It is easy for staff to communicate their views to senior managers (43% disagree)

As the survey concluded:

> Overall, the results of this survey show high satisfaction with many of the important aspects of working life, however the Assembly still needs to build on these positive results and improve in the areas where results could be higher.

The following extracts from the report highlight the key findings:

Contribution to National Assembly for Wales Performance

Generally, staff show a very high level of satisfaction when asked about their understanding of what they are expected to achieve at work. They are aware of the Assembly's objectives and believe that they make an important contribution to them.'

Assembly Culture

Encouragingly, almost all staff feel that the people they work with are committed to doing good quality work and over half of staff feel this strongly. On the whole, staff feel their opinions count and that the Assembly has a describable identity. However, employees are less inclined to feel that they have the opportunity to do what they are best at every day.

Leadership/Management

On the whole, questions relating to leadership and management elicited lower satisfaction ratings than questions on other aspects of life within the Assembly. The proportions of staff who are satisfied are still relatively high, however, although this may be due in part to the rating system employed. Although the vast majority of staff feel that they are trusted to do their job, lower proportions feel consulted, recognised for good work, have someone to talk to regarding career progress/development or are effectively lead.

Working Life

Disappointingly, a (relatively) low proportion of employees feel able to get their work done within working hours and a significant minority are not able to balance work and home commitments. Almost a third do not think there is a good future for them at the Assembly and fewer than half feel their earnings are fair.

Communication

Communication is one of the areas which shows lower agreement than the other areas. A significant minority do not feel that it is easy to get help and advice they need from other parts of the Assembly and only ... around half of staff believe that staff can easily communicate their views to senior managers.

Pride in Working for the National Assembly for Wales

Arguably, the most important question asked in the survey is that of pride in working for the Assembly. More than four in five staff overall (82%) are proud to work for the organisation – something that the Assembly itself should be proud of.

Conclusion

The Assembly performs very well indeed in terms of having clearly identifiable objectives and employees do feel able to assist in achieving them. They are trusted by their managers to do their work and there is a strong belief that they are working as part of a group of talented, committed staff. Employees feel that their opinions count and the proportion who believe this is increasing over time.

However, there are clear areas which also require focus. Areas that could be focused on in order for the Assembly to improve overall satisfaction amongst its employees include:

- Giving staff the opportunity to do what they are best at every day.
- Staff getting their work done within normal working hours.
- Everyone making the best use of e-mail to communicate.
- Ensuring it is easy for staff to communicate their views to senior managers.
- Staff feeling their earnings are fair considering their duties and responsibilities.
- Ensuring it is easy for staff to find the information they need from the Intranet and Bulletin Board.

National Assembly for Wales:
Employee Opinion Survey 2002

ORC International undertook the 2002-2004 surveys and throughout the report the Assembly results are compared with external benchmark scores calculated from ORC International's Perspectives database. The Perspectives database, during this period, held the survey results from over 150 organisations, representing the views of over 1.1 million employees and so, in the opinion of ORC, 'gives a robust indication of typical levels of satisfaction'. The data held in the Perspectives database could also be broken down into specific sectors and the Assembly was compared against results for Central Government. The following key extracts are taken from the survey:

Key Strengths

- Staff appear to be very satisfied with most aspects of their job, and have a good understanding of what they are expected to achieve, and how their work contributes to the organisation's objectives. There also appears to be good co-operation amongst colleagues.
- Staff feel that they make an important contribution to the organisation's objectives.
- Line management is perceived favourably with staff believing that their manager gives them autonomy to do their job effectively, gives recognition for doing a good job and communicates effectively.
- Staff believe that they offer a high standard of service to their customers and the public.
- The majority of staff feel that they are treated with fairness and respect.

Key Areas for Improvement

- The methods of progression and advancement within the Assembly do not appear to be perceived favourably by staff.
- Less than a third of staff (29%) indicated that they understood the Executive Board's vision.
- The majority of staff either do not know or do not believe that the Assembly is committed to simplifying the way it does business.
- Only a quarter of staff feel senior management in the Assembly set a good example in making the Assembly a successful organisation.
- 10% of staff feel that the Assembly ensures that people are in the right job to enable them to work effectively.

About the National Assembly for Wales

- 69% of staff are clear as to how their work contributes to the success of the Assembly, however only 29% of staff indicated that they understand the Executive Board's vision. Nearly a third of respondents (32%) stated that they did not understand the vision.

- The majority of staff (73%) indicated that they are treated with fairness and respect at work, which is above the benchmarking average of 67%.

- Although less than half of all respondents (47%) feel that the Assembly is committed to making the organisation a family friendly place to work, 59% of staff believe that they are able to achieve a balance between their work and life outside.

It is encouraging to note that staff working for the Assembly are more likely to indicate that they are proud to work for the Assembly and that on the whole they are satisfied to be working for the Assembly, in comparison with other central government organisations.

National Assembly for Wales Staff Attitude Survey 2003

The highest and lowest scoring sections and questions identified in the survey report were (note: the results in this section show the % favourable scores for the best and worst performing three sections and five questions in the survey):

Highest Favourable Scores

Section E:	The way we do business	68%
Section A:	You and Your Job	62%
Section F:	About the National Assembly for Wales	60%

- I understand how my work contributes to the objectives of my division—87%

- I believe I offer a high standard of service to our customers and to the public—86%

- I know what I am expected to achieve at work—83%

- The people I work with co-operate to get the job done—82%

- My line manager treats me equally, with fairness and respect—82%

Lowest Favourable Scores

Section C: Your Training and Development   39%

Section B: Communication in National Assembly for Wales   47%

Section D: Management in the National Assembly for Wales 59%

- The Assembly ensures that people are in the right job to enable us to work effectively — 11%

- I am satisfied with the methods of advancement used within the Assembly — 16%

- Where possible, I am given the opportunity to go on secondment/work experience outside the Assembly — 21%

- I am satisfied with the opportunities I have for career development within the Assembly — 22%

- Senior management in the Assembly set a good example in making this a successful organisation — 27%

National Assembly for Wales: Staff Attitude Survey 2004

Overview

The overall results for the Assembly 2004 Staff Survey have either generally shown improvements or remained in line with the 2003 survey results. When benchmarked to other central government organisations, the Assembly is largely in line or above the benchmark norm.

Key Strengths

- Clarity about how work contributes to the objectives of the division and the organisation.

- Teamwork and receiving adequate support and information from colleagues.

- Performance planning and review forms being agreed and training and development plans with line managers.

- Being treated with fairness and respect by line managers, and generally within the Assembly.

- Line managers consulting employees on issues affecting them and their work and empowering them to do their job effectively.

- Feeling recognised and acknowledged by line management when a job has been done well.

- High awareness of the policies and practices in place for dealing with customers.

- Providing a high quality of customer service and demonstrating a commitment to equality in policies and services.

- Intention to stay working for the Assembly for the next 12 months.

Key Areas for Improvement

- Satisfaction with working environment.

- Ease of communicating views upwards to senior management.

- Engaging staff when organisational change is being undertaken.

- Opportunities for career development and secondments outside the Assembly.

- Developing good leadership at all levels in the organisation.

- Perceptions towards senior management setting a good example in the work place.

- The Assembly valuing the diversity of its employees.

Diversity

Although staff would probably have viewed the question as relating to the full spectrum of diversity—race, gender, sexual orientation, religion, age, part-time working etc—responses were likely to have been influenced by personal experience in only one of these areas. There was concern that not enough was done to tackle staff who express unacceptable/offensive views, not enough was done to mainstream diversity, at present staff are encouraged to join 'Staff Support Networks' which, whilst supportive of individuals, appear to alienate the diversity of those members of staff from the mainstream; not enough was done to support part-time workers; more needed to be done to encourage applications for employment from ethnic minority groups; the further work suggested above would require a cultural change for the organisation to value *and learn from the diversity of its staff.*

Leadership

As with diversity, personal experience with an individual was likely to have influenced response to the questions in the Survey. The Executive Board, as a corporate body, was not seen to very visible, with only the Permanent Secretary and an individual's own director being visible to most staff; there was a perception that Heads of Division were far too busy to devote time to demonstrating strong leadership; there was a feeling that directors would occasionally create additional work for their teams on fruitless tasks because they wanted to delay telling Ministers that the desired outcome is not achievable; there was a perception also that at times of crisis the 'rule book' was discarded, by Heads of Division and above, in favour of an 'end justifies the means' attitude; reference is made constantly to the need to change the culture of the office but there appeared to be little leadership from the top to do so; dialogue was seen as a positive move to create a link with the Executive Board but there was a feeling that it was not delivering demonstrable change but only stock answers to questions or concerns raised.

People, Dates and Events

1) Membership of the National Assembly Advisory Group (NAAG)

2) Membership of the Standing Orders Commission

3) National Assembly for Wales election results

4) Presiding Officer and Deputy Presiding Officer

5) First Secretary/Minister and Cabinet

6) Chairs of the Subject Committees

7) Chairs of the Standing Committees

8) Chairs of the Regional Committees

9) Membership of the Richard Commission

1) Membership of National Assembly Advisory Group (NAAG)

- John Elfed Jones (Chair)
- Nick Bourne
- Ioan Bowen Rees
- Marjorie Dykins
- Ken Hopkins
- Mari James
- Helen Mary Jones
- Howard Marshall
- Eluned Morgan
- Joyce Readfearn

- Viscount St Davids
- Ray Singh
- Ian Spratling

2) Membership of the Standing Orders Commission

- Gareth Wardell (Chair)
- Roger Jarman
- Michael Jones
- Peter Price
- Alwyn Roberts
- Anne Sherlock
- Susan Smith
- Sir Michael Wheeler-Booth

3) National Assembly for Wales Election Results

6 May 1999

Labour	28 seats	(27 constituency seats + 1 electoral region seat)
Plaid Cymru	17 seats	(9 constituency seats + 8 electoral region seat)
Conservative	9 seats	(1 constituency seats + 8 electoral region seat)
Liberal Democrat	6 seats	(3 constituency seats + 3 electoral region seat)

1 May 2003

Labour	30 seats	(30 constituency seats)
Plaid Cymru	12 seats	(5 constituency seats + 7 electoral region seat)
Conservative	11 seats	(1 constituency seats + 10 electoral region seat)
Liberal Democrat	6 seats	(3 constituency seats + 3 electoral region seat)
Independent	1 seat	(1 constituency seat)

On 18 Apr 2005, Peter Law AM left the Labour Party to become an independent Assembly Member.

4) Presiding Officer and Deputy Presiding Officer

At the inaugural plenary meeting of the National Assembly for Wales on 12 May 1999, Lord Elis-Thomas AM (Plaid Cymru) was elected as Presiding Officer and Jane Davidson AM (Labour) was elected Deputy Presiding Officer.

On 19 Oct 2000, Dr John Marek AM MP (Labour) was elected as Deputy Presiding Officer.

Following the second elections to the National Assembly, Lord Elis-Thomas was elected as Presiding Officer and Dr John Marek AM was elected as Deputy Presiding Officer (7 May 2003).

5) Cabinet

Note: Members of the Cabinet were known as 'Secretary' until 16 October 2000, when it was announced that the term 'Minister' had been adopted by the Cabinet 'in order to distinguish clearly between members of the Cabinet and members of the Civil Service where the term 'Secretary' is a common title'.

On 12 May 1999, the Assembly elected the Rt Hon Alun Michael AM MP as First Secretary, and he appointed the Cabinet.

• First Secretary	Rt Hon Alun Michael AM MP (Labour)
• Business Manager	Andrew Davies AM (Labour)
• Secretary for Agriculture and the Rural Economy	Christine Gwyther AM (Labour)
• Secretary for Economic Development	Rt Hon Rhodri Morgan AM MP (Labour)
• Secretary for Environment, Local Government and Planning	Peter Law AM (Labour)
• Secretary for Health and Social Services	Jane Hutt AM (Labour)
• Secretary for Post-16 Education and Training	Tom Middlehurst AM (Labour)
• Secretary for Pre-16 education, Children and Young People	Rosemary Butler AM (Labour)

Following the resignation of the Rt. Hon Alun Michael AM MP on 9 February 2000, the Rt Hon Rhodri Morgan AM MP was elected as First Secretary on 15 February 2000. He announced changes to the Cabinet on 22 February 2000:

• First Secretary and Secretary for Economic Development	Rt Hon Rhodri Morgan AM MP (Labour)
• Business Manager	Andrew Davies AM (Labour)
• Secretary for Agriculture and Rural Development	Christine Gwyther AM (Labour)
• Secretary for Education and Children	Rosemary Butler AM (Labour)
• Secretary for Finance	Edwina Hart AM (Labour)
• Secretary for Environment, Planning and Transport	Sue Essex AM (Labour)
• Secretary for Local Government and Housing	Peter Law AM (Labour)
• Secretary for Health and Social Services	Jane Hutt AM (Labour)
• Secretary for Post 16 Education and Training	Tom Middlehurst AM (Labour)

The appointment of the first Deputy Secretaries was announced by the First Secretary on 23 February 2000:

• Deputy Secretary for Agriculture, Local Government and Environment	Carwyn Jones AM (Labour)
• Deputy Secretary for Education and the Economy	Christine Chapman AM (Labour)
• Deputy Secretary for Health and Social Services	Alun Pugh AM (Labour)

On 23 July 2000, the First Secretary announced that Carwyn Jones AM would replace Christine Gwyther AM as Secretary for Agriculture and Rural Development. On 24 July, Delyth Evans AM (Labour) was appointed as Deputy Secretary for Agriculture, Local Government and Environment in place of Carwyn Jones AM.

A new coalition partnership between Labour and the Liberal Democrats was announced on 5 October 2000. In response, Tom Middlehurst resigned as Secretary for Post-16 Education and Training. The new Partnership Cabinet was announced on 16 October, with the term 'Minister' being adopted to distinguish Cabinet members from senior civil servants:

• First Minister	Rt Hon Rhodri Morgan AM MP (Labour)
• Deputy First Minister and Minister for Economic Development	Michael German AM (Liberal Democrat)
• Business Minister	Andrew Davies AM (Labour)
• Minister for Culture and Sports	Jenny Randerson AM (Liberal Democrat)
• Minister for Education and Lifelong Learning	Jane Davidson AM (Labour)
• Minister for Environment	Sue Essex AM (Labour)
• Minister for Finance and Communities	Edwina Hart AM (Labour)
• Minister for Health and Social Services	Jane Hutt AM (Labour)
• Minister for Rural Affairs	Carwyn Jones AM (Labour)

On 17 October, the First Minister appointed new Deputy Ministers:

• Deputy Minister for Economic Development	Alun Pugh AM (Labour)
• Deputy Minister for Local Government	Peter Black AM (Liberal Democrat)
• Deputy Minister for Health	Brian Gibbons AM (Labour)
• Deputy Minister for Rural Affairs, Culture and Environment	Delyth Evans AM (Labour)
• Deputy Minister for Education and Lifelong Learning	Huw Lewis AM (Labour)

Also on 17 October 2000, the First Minister appointed Christine Chapman AM (Labour) as Chair of the Objective One Monitoring Committee, which was responsible to the European Commission for the implementation of the Objective 1 programme.

Michael German AM stepped down temporarily as Deputy First Minister on 6 July 2001. Rhodri Morgan AM (Labour) took over responsibility for Economic Development, while Jenny Randerson AM (Liberal Democrat) was appointed Acting Deputy First Minister.

Andrew Davies AM (Labour) was appointed Economic Development Minister on 26 Feb 2002.

Michael German AM (Liberal Democrat) was reinstated as Deputy First Minister on 13 June 2002 and, on 17 June 2002, was appointed as the Minister for Rural Affairs and Wales Abroad. Carwyn Jones AM (Labour) was appointed as Minister for Open Government alongside his duties as Business Minister.

Following the second elections to the National Assembly, the Rt Hon Rhodri Morgan AM was re-elected as First Minister on 7 May 2003. He announced his new Cabinet on 9 May:

• Minister for Assembly Business	Karen Sinclair AM (Labour)
• Minister for Culture, Sports and Welsh Language	Alun Pugh AM (Labour)
• Minister for Economic Development	Andrew Davies AM (Labour)
• Minister for Education and Lifelong Learning	Jane Davidson AM (Labour)
• Minister for Environment, Planning and Countryside	Carwyn Jones AM (Labour)
• Minister for Finance, Local Government and Public Services	Sue Essex AM (Labour)
• Minister for Health and Social Care	Jane Hutt AM (Labour)
• Minister for Social Justice and Regeneration	Edwina Hart AM (Labour)

The First Minister appointed his Deputy Ministers on 13 May 2003:

• Deputy Minister for Economic Development and Transport	Brian Gibbons AM (Labour)
• Deputy Minister for Health and Social Care	John Griffiths AM (Labour)
• Deputy Minister for Social Justice	Huw Lewis AM (Labour)

On 10 January 2005, Dr Brian Gibbons AM was appointed as Minister for Health and Social Services and Jane Hutt AM was appointed as Business Manager.

The First Minister announced the appointment of two new Deputy Ministers on 14 January 2005:

| • Deputy Minister for Economic Development and Transport | Tamsin Dunwoody-Kneafsey AM (Labour) |
| • Deputy Minister for Education & Lifelong Learning and Finance, Local Government & Public Services | Christine Chapman AM (Labour) |

Jeff Cuthbert AM (Labour) was appointed chair of the Objective One Monitoring Committee.

6) Chairs of the Subject Committees

The first Panel of Subject Committee Chairs were elected on 19 May:

• Agriculture and Rural Development	Ieuan Wyn Jones AM MP (Plaid Cymru)
• Economic Development	Rt Hon Ron Davies AM MP (Labour)
• Health and Social Services	Kirsty Williams AM (Liberal Democrat)
• Local Government, Environment, Planning, Housing and Transport	Sue Essex AM (Labour)
• Post-16 Education and Lifelong Learning	Cynog Dafis AM MP (Plaid Cymru)
• Pre-16 Education, Schools and Early Learning	William Graham AM (Conservative)

Val Feld AM (Labour) was elected as the Chair with effect from 14 July 1999.

On 14 March 2000, Rhodri Glyn Thomas AM (Plaid Cymru) was elected Chair of the Agriculture and Rural Development Committee.

On 29 March 2000, Richard Edwards AM (Labour) was elected as Chair of the Environment, Planning and Transport Committee and Gwenda Thomas AM (Labour) was elected as Chair of the Local Government and Housing Committee. The Local Government, Environment, Planning, Housing and Transport Committee ceased to exist.

On 9 November 2000, the following Chairs were elected:

• Agriculture and Rural Development	Glyn Davies AM (Conservative)
• Culture	Rhodri Glyn Thomas AM (Plaid Cymru)
• Education and Lifelong Learning	Cynog Dafis AM MP (Plaid Cymru)

The Post-16 Education and Lifelong Learning and Pre-16 Education, Schools and Early Learning Committees ceased to exist.

On 3 May 2001, Christine Gwyther AM (Labour) was elected to replace Val Feld AM (Labour) as Chair of the Economic Development Committee.

On 3 June 2003, following the Assembly elections in May, the following chairs were appointed to the Subject Committees:

• Culture, Welsh Language and Sport	Rosemary Butler AM (Labour)
• Economic Development and Transport	Christine Gwyther AM (Labour)
• Education and Lifelong Learning	Peter Black AM (Liberal Democrat)
• Environment, Planning and Countryside	Alun Ffred Jones AM (Plaid Cymru)
• Health and Social Services	David Melding AM (Conservative)
• Local Government and Public Services	Ann Jones AM (Labour)
• Social Justice and Regeneration	Janice Gregory AM (Labour)

7) Chairs of the Standing Committees

On 23 June 1999, the Assembly passed a Motion to elect the following Committee Chairs in plenary:

• Audit	Janet Davies AM (Plaid Cymru)
• Equality of Opportunity	Jane Hutt AM (Labour)
• European and External Affairs	Rt Hon Alun Michael AM MP (Labour)
• Legislation	Michael German AM (Liberal Democrat)
• Standards of Conduct	Nicholas Bourne AM (Conservative)

David Melding AM (Conservative) was elected as Chair of the Standards Committee on 24 November 1999.

The Rt Hon Rhodri Morgan AM MP (Labour) was elected as Chair of the Committee on European and External Affairs on 29 February 2000.

On 15 March 2000, Edwina Hart AM (Labour) was elected as Chair of the Equal Opportunities Committee.

Mick Bates AM (Liberal Democrat) was elected as Chair of the Legislation Committee on 9 November 2000.

On 19 November 2002, David Melding AM resigned as Chair of the Committee on Standards of Conduct.

Following the Assembly elections in May 2003, the following committee Chairs were appointed on 3 June 2003:

• Audit Committee	Janet Davies AM (Plaid Cymru)
• Equality of Opportunity	Gwenda Thomas AM (Labour)
• European and External Affairs	Sandy Mewies AM (Labour)
• Legislation Committee	Glyn Davies AM (Conservative)
• Standards Committee	Kirsty Williams AM (Liberal Democrat)

8) Chairs of the Regional Committees

Election of Regional Committee Chairs 2 July 1999:

• North Wales Regional Committee	Gareth Jones AM (Plaid Cymru)
• South West Wales Regional Committee	Peter Black AM (Liberal Democrat)

Election of Regional Committee Chairs on 9 July 1999:

• Mid Wales Regional Committee	Glyn Davies AM (Conservative)
• South East Wales Regional Committee	Jenny Randerson AM (Liberal Democrat)

On 6 July 2001, Rhodri Glyn Thomas AM (Plaid Cymru) was elected as Chair of the South West Wales Regional Committee.

Following the 2003 elections, the following Regional Committee Chairs were appointed:

• North Wales Regional Committee	Janet Ryder AM (Labour)
• Mid Wales Regional Committee	Helen Mary Jones AM (Plaid Cymru)
• South West Wales Regional Committee	Tamsin Dunwoody-Kneafsey AM (Labour)
• South East Wales Regional Committee	Michael German AM (Liberal Democrat)

On 22 Feb 2005, the Assembly approved an amendment to change the boundaries of the Regional Committees to be coterminous with the Assembly's electoral regions, which meant the creation of five Regional Committees. On 27 April 2005, members were appointed to the five committees. Chairs of the committees:

• North Wales Regional Committee	Eleanor Burnham AM (Liberal Democrat)
• Mid and West Wales	Christine Gwyther AM (Labour)
• South West Wales	Janet Davies AM (Plaid Cymru)
• South Wales Central	Owen John Thomas AM (Plaid Cymru)
• South East Wales	William Graham AM (Liberal Democrat)

9) Membership of the Richard Commission

- Rt Hon Lord Richard of Ammanford QC (Chair)
- Eira Davies
- Tom Jones
- Dr Laura McAllister
- Peter Price
- Ted Rowlands
- Vivienne Sugar
- Huw Thomas
- Sir Michael Wheeler-Booth KCB
- Paul Valerio

Staff Numbers – Welsh Office, National Assembly for Wales and Wales Office, 1993-2004					
	Welsh Office – National Assembly for Wales[1]				Wales Office
	Permanent	Permanent Headcount		Casual	Permanent & Casual
	Full-time equivalent	Full-time	Part-time	Full-time equivalent	Full-time equivalent
01 April 1993	2,388	2,222	267	159	–
01 April 1994	2,337[2]	unavailable[2]	unavailable[2]	219[2]	–
01 April 1995	2,152	unavailable[3]	unavailable[3]	240	–
01 April 1996	2,074	1,981[3]	258[3]	189	–
01 April 1997	2,122	1,997[3]	293[3]	207	–
01 April 1998	2,050	1,960[3]	236[3]	210	–
01 April 1999	2,206	2,057	236	153	–
01 April 2000	2,570	2,420	230	210	30
01 April 2001	3,090	2,880	320	280	40
01 April 2002	3,370	3,110	400	230	40
01 April 2003	3,550	3,230	500	80	50
01 April 2004	4,290[4]	3,980[4]	460[4]	60[4]	50

Source: Cabinet Office (CROWN COPYRIGHT)
http://www.civilservice.gov.uk/management_of_the_civil_service/statistics/index.asp
[Footnotes on opposite page]

Footnotes to Table

1 The Welsh Office (1993–1999): the National Assembly for Wales (2000–2004). Includes Cadw and industrial and non-industrial staff but, except where stated elsewhere in the footnotes, excludes Estyn (the Office of Her Majesty's Chief Inspector of Education and Training in Wales: successor to the Office of Her Majesty's Chief Inspector of Schools, Wales).

2 1994 data: the Cabinet Office website notes that 'the master file is corrupted and needs to be rebuilt'. These data, from 'Civil Service Statistics 1994 Edition', combine the Welsh Office with the Office of Her Majesty's Chief Inspector of Schools, Wales (OHMCI). For comparison purposes, OHMCI comprised just over 70 full-time equivalent staff in 1993 and 1995. Headcount data at Departmental level is not provided. http://www.civilservice.gov.uk/management_of_the_civil_service/statistics/publications/pdf/annual/css94.pdf

3 Headcount data from 'Civil Service Statistics' 1996-1998, which combine the Welsh Office with OHMCI. OHMCI comprised 60–70 full-time equivalent staff at this time. 'Civil Service Statistics' does not provide headcount data at Departmental level for 1995. http://www.civilservice.gov.uk/management_of_the_civil_service/statistics/civil_service_statistics/index.asp

4 01 April 2004 data are not published for the National Assembly for Wales: these figures refer to 01 October 2003.

References

Allaire, Y and Firsirotu, M., (1984), Theories of Organisation Culture , *Organisation Studies* Vol. 5, No. 3, pp. 193–226.

Alvesson, M., (2002), *Understanding organizational culture*, Sage: London.

Argyis, C. and Schon, D., (1978) *Organizational learning: a theory of action perspective*, Addison Wesley: New York.

Ashburner, L., Ferlie, E., and Fitzgerald, L., (1996) Organizational transformation and top-down change: the case of the NHS, *British Journal of Management*, 7, 1, pp. 1–16.

Bartunek, J., (1984), Changing interpretative schemes and organizational restructuring: the examples of a religious order, *Administrative Science Quarterly*, 29, pp. 355–372.

Balogun, J. (2003), From blaming the middle to harnessing its potential: creating change intermediaries, *British Journal of Management*, 14, 1, pp. 69–83.

Barberis, P (2001), Civil society, virtue and trust: implications for the public service ethos in the age of modernity, *Public Policy and Administration*, 16, 3, pp. 111–126.

Barry Jones, (1997), Welsh politics and changing British and European contexts in J. Bradbury and Mawson, J., (eds), *British regionalism and devolution: the challenges of state reform and European integration*, Jessica Kingsley Publishers/Regional Studies Association: London.

Barry Jones, J. and Osmond, J. (2002), (Eds), *Building a civic culture: institutional change, policy development and political dynamics in the National Assembly for Wales*, Institute of Welsh Affairs: Cardiff.

Bate, P., (1994), *Strategies for cultural change*, Butterworth Heinemann: Oxford.

Bogdanor, V., (1999), *Devolution in the United Kingdom*, Oxford University Press: Oxford

Brunsson, N. and Olsen, J.P., (1993), *The reforming organization*, Routledge: London.

Caldwell, R., (2005), Things fall apart? Discourses on agency and change in organizations, *Human Relations*, 58, 1, pp. 83–114.

Campbell, C. and Wilson, G.K. (1995) *The End of Whitehall: Death of a Paradigm?* Oxford: Blackwell

Christenson, C., (1997), *The innovator's dilemma: when new technologies cause great firms to fail*, Harvard University Press: Boston.

Christenson, C. and Raynor, M.E., (2003), *The Innovator's solution*, Harvard University Press: Boston

Cole, A. with Barry Jones, J. and Storer, A. (2003), Inside the National Assembly for Wales: The Welsh Civil Service under Devolution, *The Political Quarterly*, 74, 2, pp. 223–232.

Collins, D., (1998), *Organizational change*, Routledge: London.

Connolly, M., Connolly U., and James C. 'Leadership in educational change', *British Journal of Management*, 11, 1, 2000, pp. 61–70.

Connolly, M., Jones, N. and Turner, D., (Forthcoming), E–Learning: A fresh look, *Journal of Higher Education Management and Policy*.

Czarniawska, B., (1997), *Narrating the organization: dilemmas of institutional identity*, Sage: London.

Dawson, P. (1994), *Organizational change: a processual approach*, Paul Chapman Publishing: London.

Deal, T. and Kennedy, A., (1988), *Corporate cultures: The rites and rituals of corporate life*, Penguin: London.

Deacon, R.M., (2002), *The governance of Wales: The Welsh Office and the policy process 1964–99*, Welsh Academic press: Cardiff.

Denning S (2005) *The Leader's Guide to Storytelling: Mastering the Art and Disciplines of Business Narrative*, Jossey-Bass, San Francisco.

Department for Education and Skills and the Department of Trade and Industry, (2002), *Managers and leaders: raising our game*, Department for Education and Skills: London.

Dowding, K. (1995) The Civil Service London: Routledge Chapman, R.A. (1997) 'The End of the Civil Service' in P. Barberis (ed.) *The Civil Service in an Era of Change* Aldershot: Dartmouth.

du Gay, P., (2000), *In praise of bureaucracy: Weber, organization, ethics*, Sage: London.

Dunn, J., (2000), *The cunning of unreason: making sense of politics*, Harper and Collins: London.

Ferlie, E., Hartley, J. and Martin, S., (2003), Changing public service organizations: current perspectives and future prospects, *British Journal; of Management*, 14, S1–S14.

Ferlie, E., Pettigrew, A., Ashburner, L. and Fitzgerald, L., (1996), *The New Public Management*, Oxford University Press: Oxford.

Fernandez, S. (2004), Developing and testing an integrative framework of public sector leadership: evidence from the public education arena, *Journal of Public Administration Research and Theory*, 15, 2, pp. 197–217.

Frost, P.J., Moore, L.F., Louis, M.R., Lundberg, C.C. and Martin, J., (1985), *Organizational culture*, Sage: Beverley Hills, CA.

Fry, G.K,. (1997), Civil service systems in comparative perspective, Paper presented at conference Indiana University, USA.

Gabriel, Y. (2000) *Storytelling in Organisations: Facts, Fictions and Fantasies*, Oxford: Oxford University Press.

Garret, B., (2003), *The Fish Rots from the Head: The Crisis in Our Boardrooms*, Profile Business: London.

Geva-May, I., (2002), From theory to practice: Policy analysis, cultural bias and organizational arrangements, *Public Management Review*, 4, 4, pp. 581–591.

Grant, R., (1997), *Hypocrisy and integrity: Machiavelli, Rousseau and the ethics of politics*, The University of Chicago Press: Chicago.

Greenwood, R., Suddaby, R. and Hinings, C.R., (2002), Theorizing change: the role of professional associations in the transformation of institutionalized fields, *Academy of Management Journal*, 45, 1, pp. 58–80.

Grey, C., (2005), *A very short, fairly interesting and reasonably cheap book about studying organizations*, Sage: London.

Grint, K., (1995), *Management, a sociological introduction*, Polity Press: Oxford.

Hinings, C.R., Brown, J.L. and Greenwood, R., (1991), Change in an autonomous professional organization, *Journal of Management Studies*, 28, pp. 375–393.

Hood, C. and Peters, G., (2004), The middle aging of New Public Management: into the age of paradox? *Journal of Public Administration Research and Theory*, 13, 3, pp. 267–282.

House of Lords Select Committee on the Constitution (2002), *Devolution: Inter-institutional relations in the United Kingdom, Report and Appendices*, The Stationary Office: London.

House Committee Annual Reports 2002–03 and 2003–04

Human Relations 2004 Special edition on boundaries in the study of organizations, 57, No. 1,

Ingraham, P.W. and Lynn, L.E. (eds), (2004); *The art of governance*, Georgetown University Press; Washington.

Johnson, G., (1990), Managing strategic change, the role of symbolic action, *British Journal of Management*, 1, 4, pp. 183–200.

Kaufman, H., (1995), *The limits to organizational change*, Transaction Books: New Jersey.

Kjaer, A.M. (2004), *Governance*, Policy: Cambridge.

Kimberley, J.R. and Quinn, R.E., (1984), *Managing organizational transitions*, Irwin: Homewood, Ill.

Kotter, J., (1996), *Leading Change*, Harvard Business School Press: Harvard.

Kunda, G., (1992), *Engineering culture: Control and commitment in a High-Tech Corporation*, Temple University Press: Philadelphia.

Labour Party General Election Manifesto 1997: 'New Labour because Britain deserves better'}

Laffin, M. (2002) *The Engine Room* in Jones, B. and Osmond, J. (eds). *Building a Civic Culture*, Cardiff: Institute of Welsh Affairs.

Laffin, and Thomas, A., (2000), Designing the National Assembly for Wales, *Parliamentary Affairs*, 53, 3, pp.557–576.

Leavy, B. and Wilson, D., (1994), *Strategy and leadership*, Routledge: London.

Lipsky, M, (1980), *Street level bureaucracy: dilemmas of the individual in public services*, Sage: New York.

Loughlin, J and Sykes, S. (2004) *Devolution and Policy-making in Wales: restructuring the System and Reinforcing Identity* ESRC Research Programme on *Devolution and Constitutional Change*

Lukes, S. (2005), *Power: a radical view*, Second Edition, Palgrave: London.

Lynn, L.E., (2001), Globalisation and administrative reform: What is happening in theory? *Public Management Review*, 3, 2, pp. 191–208.

Mahler, J., (1997), Influences of organizational culture on learning in public agencies, *Journal of Public Administration Research and Theory*, 7, 4, pp. 519–540.

Massey, A. and Pyper, P., (2005), *Public Management and Modernisation in Britain*, Palgrave: London.

McAllister, L., (1999), The road to Cardiff Bay: the process of establishing the National Assembly for Wales, *Parliamentary Affairs*, 52, 4, pp. 634–648.

Metcalfe, L and Richards, S., (1987), *Improving Public Management* Sage: London.

Metcalfe, L. and Richards, S., (1984), The impact of the efficiency strategy: political clout or cultural change? *Public Administration*, 62, 4, pp. 439–454.

Meyer, J.B. and Rowan, B. (1979), Institutionalised organizations: formal structure as myth and ceremony, *American Journal of Sociology*, 83, pp. 340–363.

Meyerson, D. and Martin, J., (1987), Cultural change: an integration of three different views, *Journal of Management*, 24, pp. 623–647.

Milner, E. and Joyce, P., (2005), *Lessons in leadership: Meeting the challenges of public services management*, Routledge: London.

Morgan, G., (1986), *Images of Organisations* Sage: London.

Moore, M., (1995), *Creating public value*, Harvard University Press: Harvard.

Munir, K.A., (2005), The social construction of events: a study of institutional change in the photographic field, *Organization Studies*, 26, 1, pp. 93–112.

Newman J., (2002) The New Public Management, Modernisation and Institutional Change in McLaughlin K et al (eds.) *New Public Management*, Routledge, London.

Newman, J. (1996), *Shaping organizational cultures in local government*, Pitman: London.

Ormerod, P., (2005), *Why most things fail: Evolution, extinction and economics*, Faber and Faber: London.

Osborne, S.P. and Brown, K. (2005), *Managing change and innovation in public sector organizations*, Routledge: London.

Osmond, J. (2000) *A Constitutional Convention by Other Means*, in Hazell, R. (ed.) The State and the Nations: The First Year of Devolution in the United Kingdom, Exeter: Imprint Academic

Osmond, J., (2005) 'Providence and Promise' in *Welsh Politics comes of age*, J Osmond (ed), Institute of Welsh Affairs: Cardiff.

Osmond J., (2005), (ed), *Welsh Politics comes of age*, Institute of Welsh Affairs: Cardiff.

Osmond, J, (2000) *A Constitutional Convention by Other Means*, in Hazell, R. (ed.) The State and the Nations: The First Year of Devolution in the United Kingdom, Exeter: Imprint Academic

O'Toole, L. J., Meier, K.J. and Nicholson-Crotty, Managing upward, downward sand outward: networks, hierarchical relationships and performance, *Public Management Review*, 7, 1, 2005.

Page, S., (2005), What's new about New Public Management? Administrative change in the human services, *Public Administration Review*, 65, 6, pp. 713–727.

Page, E. and Jenkins, B., (2005), *Policy bureaucracy: Government with a cast of thousands*, Oxford University Press: Oxford.

Parker, M., (2000), *Organizational culture and identity*, Sage: London.

Parry, R. (May 2002) *Written Memorandum to the House of Lords Select Committee on the Constitution, Devolution: Inter-Institutional Relations in the United Kingdom*, published in HL 147, July 2002

Parry, R. (2004), The Civil Service and Intergovernmental Relations, *Public Policy and Administration*, 19, 2, pp. 50–63.

Peters, T. and Waterman, R., (1982), *In Search of Excellence*, Harper and Row: London.

Pettigrew, A., (1985), *The Awakening Giant: Continuity and change in Imperial Chemical Industries*, Blackwell: Oxford.

Pettigrew, A., (1987), Context and action in the transformation of the form, *Journal of Management Studies*, 24, 6, pp. 649–670.

Pettigrew, A., McKee, L. and Ferlie, E., (1988), *Shaping strategic change: the case of the NHS*, Sage: London.

Pollitt, C., (2003), *The essential public manager*, Open University Press: London.

Pollitt, C., Girre, X., Lonsdale, J., Mul, R., Summa, H., and Waerness, M., (1999), *Performance or compliance? Performance audit and public management in five countries*, Oxford University Press: Oxford.

Prosser S (2003) *Development of a Welsh Public Service*, Institute of Welsh Affairs, Cardiff.

Pye, A., (2005), Leadership and organizing: sensemaking in action, *Leadership*, 1, 1, pp. 31–50.

Quinn, R.E., (1996), *Deep change: discovering the leader within*, Jossey-Bass: San Francisco.

Quinn, R.E., (1988), *Beyond rational management: Mastering the paradoxes and competing demands of high performance*, Jossey_Bass: San Francisco.

Quinn, R..E. and Cameron, K.S., (eds), (1988), *Paradox and transformation; towards a theory of change n organization and management*, Ballinger: Cambridge, MA.

Rawlings, R. (2005) *Law Making in a Virtual Parliament: The Welsh Experience* in Hazell, R and Rawlings, R. (Eds) Devolution, Law Making and Constitution, Exeter: Imprint Academic

Rawlings, R., (2003), *Delineating Wales*, University of Wales Press: Cardiff.

(The Richard Report), www.richardcommission.gov.uk/content/print page.asp?ID=/content/evidence/written/jshortridge/index.asp

Rhodes, R., (1997), Understanding governance: Policy networks, governance, reflexivity and accountability, Open University Press: Buckingham.

Riley, P. (1983), A Structurationist Account of Political Culture, *Administrative Science Quarterly*, 28,3, pp. 414–437.

Shapiro, I., (2003), *The moral foundations of politics*, Yale University press: New Haven.

Shortridge, J. (December 2002) Evidence to the Richard Commission by the Permanent Secretary of the National Assembly for Wales.

Smircich, L., (1983), Concepts of culture and organizational analysis, *Administrative Science Quarterly*, 28, pp. 339–358.

Story, J., (2005), What next for strategic-level leadership research? *Leadership*, 1,1, pp. 89–104.

Sturdy, A. and Grey, C., (2003), Beneath and beyond organizational change management: exploring alternatives, *Organization*, 10, 4, pp. 651–662.

Talbot, C., (2005), *The paradoxical primate*, Imprint Academic: Exeter.

The National Assembly for Wales Annual Report 1999–2000

Thomas, A. and Laffin, M., (2001), The first Welsh constitutional crises: the Alun Michael resignation, *Public Policy and Administration*, 16, 1, pp. 18–31.

Trindale, S., (1996), (Ed), *The State and the nations, The politics of devolution*, IPPR: London.

Walsh, K., Hinnings, B., Greenwood, R. and Ranson, S., (1981), Power and advantage in organizations, *Organisation Studies*, 2, pp. 131–152.

Weeks, J., (2004), *Unpopular culture, The ritual of complaint in a British Bank*, The University of Chicago Press: Chicago.

Weick, K., (1979), *The Social Psychology of Organising*, (Second edition), Addison-Wesley: Reading, MA.

Wilkinson, D., (1997), Whole system development—rethinking public service management, *International Journal of Public Sector Management*, 10, 6/7, pp. 505–534.

Williams, A., Dobson, P. and Walters, M., (1989), *Changing culture*, Institute of Personnel management: London.

Wilson, D., (1992), *A strategy of change: concepts and controversies in the management of change*, Routledge: London.

Yulk, G., (2006), *Leadership in organizations*, (Sixth Edition) Pearson Prentice Hall, New Jersey.

Yulk, G., (1989), Management leadership: a review of theory and research, *Journal of Management*, 15, 2, pp. 251–289.

Wales Office (June 2005) *Better Governance for Wales* Norwich: The Stationery Office

1 Devolution Briefings, The Report of the Richard Commission: An Evaluation *Briefing No*

2 12, June 2004, Findings from the Economic and Research Council's Research Programme on *Devolution and Constitutional Change*

House Committee Annual Reports 2002–3, 2003–4, 2004–5

Index

Index

National Assembly 7, 241
comparison with Welsh system 89,
173, 230
and devolution 36, 39
Ron Davies' view on 159
and Human Resources 95
perceived Scottish domination in
230
relationship with Assembly 84-6,
184, 233, 240, 242
transfer of sovereignty to Cardiff
161, 233
view of Lord Elis-Thomas on 218
and Welsh Cabinet Office 114
and Wales Office 85-6, 107-8
and Welsh Office 172, 183
Wigley, Dafydd 60
Williams, Lord Gareth 38
Wilson, Barbara (Director of Research
and Development Group) 100
Wilson, Sir Richard (Cabinet
Secretary) 88, 179
on devolution 241
WTB *see* Wales Tourist Board

Y Senedd (Assembly Chamber) 216
'Yes for Wales' Campaign 40